Access® 2
Programming

By

EXAMPLE

que

Greg Perry

Access 2 Programming By Example

Copyright ©1994 by Que® Corporation

Library of Congress Catalog No.: 94-65315

ISBN: 1-56529-659-1

97 96 95 94   4 3 2

Interpretation of the printing code: the rightmost double-digit number is the year of the book's printing; the rightmost single-digit number, the number of the book's printing. For example, a printing code of 94-1 shows that the first printing of the book occurred in 1994.

Publisher: *David P. Ewing*

Associate Publisher: *Michael Miller*

Managing Editor: *Michael Cunningham*

Product Marketing Manager: *Ray Robinson*

Publishing Manager
Don Roche, Jr.

Acquisitions Editor
Nancy Stevenson

Product Director
Joyce J. Nielsen

Development and Production Editor
Jill D. Bond

Technical Editor
Philip Sabotin

Book Designer
Amy Peppler-Adams

Indexer
Michael Hughes

Production Team
Gary Adair
Angela Bannan
Kim Cofer
Stephanie Davis
Rich Evers
Brook Farling
Jenny Kucera
Bob LaRoche
Joy Dean Lee
Amy Steed
Becky Tapley
Mike Thomas
Tina Trettin
Elaine Webb
Donna Winter

Composed in *Palatino* and *MCPdigital* by Prentice Hall Computer Publishing.
Screen reproductions in this book were created by means of the program Collage
Plus from Inner Media, Inc., Hollis, NH.

Dedication

For the wonderful Cianetti family: Mario, Maria, Marica, and Fabiana and Maria Elena Camilli. Thanks for making Rome seem like home. Grazie!

About the Author

Greg Perry is a speaker and writer in both the programming and applications sides of computing. He is known for bringing programming topics down to the beginner's level. Perry has been a programmer and trainer for the past 16 years. He received his first degree in computer science and then received a master's degree in corporate finance. Besides writing, he consults and lectures across the country, including at the acclaimed Software Development programming conferences. Perry is the author of 25 other computer books, including *QBasic By Example*, Special Edition, *C By Example*, Special Edition, and *Turbo C++ By Example* (all published by Que Corporation). In addition, he has published articles in several publications such as *Access Advisor*, *Software Development*, *PC World*, and *Data Training*.

Trademark Acknowledgments

Overview

Contents

Contents

Part III Primary Access Basic Language Elements

Contents

Contents

Contents

Contents

Introduction

You already know the fundamentals of Microsoft Access, and you're ready to take your database skills to the next level. You have only two problems: you've never written a program in your life, and you have no idea where to start. This book is for you!

This book teaches the newcomer to programming all about programming in Access Basic. Teaching Access Basic is more difficult than teaching a more traditional programming language such as C, QBasic, or Pascal. Access Basic is just a small part of the Access database system, and the Access Basic commands must work within the framework of the database environment.

The good news for you, however, is that Access Basic is easier to learn than a traditional programming language because Access does so much of the tedious work for you that you normally have to accomplish on your own. Although you'll have to tackle many controlling statements and language specifics, you won't have to know them in the detail that other programming languages require.

Welcome to Access Basic

As you no doubt already realize, Microsoft Access is one of the easiest database management programs on the market for creating ready-to-use database applications. Unlike many other database management systems, Access requires no programming for common database applications, and you can create many advanced database applications that also require no programming.

Nevertheless, there will come a time when you need to do more than Access provides without more help on your part. Despite Microsoft's forethought, which provided Access with some of the most powerful database-creation tools to be found, you will be ready to take Access to the next higher level than the click-and-point interface provides. That's where this book comes into the picture: *Access 2 Programming By Example* teaches you the programming skills that you will need as you build more powerful Access applications.

> **Note:** This book does not assume that you've ever programmed a computer in your life. You need to be familiar only with the common Access objects such as tables, forms, reports, and queries. If you've built one or two complete database systems with Access, you are ready for the concepts in this book.

This book covers all versions of Microsoft Access including Access 2.0. Although the Access Basic capabilities have not changed much from version 1.0 to 2.0, Microsoft made Access even easier to use in the newer version.

Who Should Use This Book

This book teaches at the following three levels: beginning, intermediate, and advanced. Text and numerous examples are aimed at each level. If you are new to programming, this book attempts to put you at ease and gradually builds Access Basic programming skills. If you are an expert at another programming language and need to see how Access Basic differs, this book is for you also.

> **Tip:** If you have ever used Visual Basic, you'll feel at home with Access Basic. The two languages are extremely similar. Microsoft is attempting to combine all its Basic-like languages (QBasic, QuickBasic, Visual Basic, and the Basic that comes with applications such as Word Basic and Access Basic) into a single Visual Basic for Applications (VBA) language. Access Basic and Visual Basic both work with forms and databases in very similar ways.

This Book's Philosophy

This book will teach you Access Basic with a holistic approach; not only will you learn the mechanics of the language, but you will learn tips and warnings and how to use Access Basic for different types of applications.

Whereas many other books build single applications, adding to them a little at a time with each chapter, this book's stand-alone chapters show you complete programs that fully illustrate commands shown in the chapter. You'll find programs for every level of reader, from beginning to advanced.

This book contains more than 100 sample program listings. These programs show you ways that you can use Access Basic for finance, school, business record keeping, math and science, and general-purpose applications. The wide variety of programs will show you that you can use Access Basic to create some extraordinary Windows programs that don't even have to interface with the database to perform a useful job. Experienced programmers can learn what they need by skipping to those programs that demonstrate specific commands.

One of the primary advantages this book offers is its partial dependence on code that you already have on your computer. *Access 2 Programming By Example* does not require lots of typing. Many of the examples use or work in conjunction with the sample databases, which come with Access. You won't have to enter tons of data just to try an Access Basic command because most of these examples work with Access's sample databases, which already contain hundreds of records.

Overview

This book is divided into seven parts. Part I introduces you to the introductory concepts needed for programming and reviews some needed Access concepts. Starting with Part II, the book presents the Access Basic programming language, divided into six logical parts. The final part comprises the appendixes. After mastering the elements of the language, you then can use the book as a handy reference. When you need help with a specific Access Basic programming problem, turn to the appropriate area that describes the part of the language in question to see numerous examples of code.

To give you an idea of the book's layout, here is a description of each part of the book.

Part I: Preparing for Access Basic

This part explains what Access Basic is by giving a brief history of programming and Access Basic and explains how Access Basic compares and differs from other programming languages. You also will review the fundamentals of macros to get used to automating Access. As a result, you'll get used to the idea of writing stored instructions for Access to carry out, as you have to do with Access Basic.

Part II: Getting a Feel for Programming

This part of the book teaches you how to think in terms of the Access Basic programming language instructions. You'll find out how to use the help system from within the Access Basic environment. You'll also see the importance of breaking your problems into small tasks called procedures.

Part III: Primary Access Basic Language Elements

In this part you will learn the rudimentary Access Basic language elements, including variables, math and string operators, and introductory output commands. This material presents the true foundation of Access Basic. The most important reason for using a database such as Access is your data, and this part explores some of the ways to store data from within Access Basic.

Part IV: Adding Control

Access Basic data processing is most powerful due to the looping, comparison, and selection language constructs it offers. This part of the book shows you how to write programs that correctly flow and control computations to produce accurate and readable code.

Part V: The Built-in Routines

Access Basic provides one of the richest set of built-in functions you will find in any programming language. The built-in routines, just as macro actions do for macros, simplify your programming job by providing routines so you don't have to write them yourself. Access Basic includes powerful data-manipulation, numeric, string, date, time, and financial functions.

Part VI: Data Structures

Access Basic offers single-dimensional and multidimensional arrays that hold multiple occurrences of repeating data but do not require a great deal of effort on your part to process. By learning the fundamentals of arrays, you begin to build powerful data areas that can hold many occurrences of table data in your programs.

Part VII: Handling Table I/O

Access Basic would be too limiting if it offered the same disk I/O commands found in other programming languages. Access Basic fully integrates with your database data, and now that you've mastered the elements of the language, you're ready to take Access Basic to its next level: interacting with tables, queries, dynasets, and snapshots.

Appendixes

The appendixes supply support information for the rest of the book. You will find a comprehensive ANSI table, answers to all the Review Questions from the ends of the chapters, and a glossary for the new terms found in the book. In addition, the last appendix gives you insight into your next step into Access and Access Basic by describing more advanced features of Access Basic that you can tap into once you master this book. You'll also find other resources to turn to for more advanced Access Basic programming help.

Conventions Used

The following conventions are used in this book:

- ♦ Command and function names are in `monospace`. In addition to code lines, variable names and any text you would see on-screen are also in `monospace`.

- ♦ Placeholders within code are in *`italic monospace`*.

- ♦ User input is in **bold**.

- ♦ New terms, which can be found in Appendix C, are in *italic*.

- ♦ Shortcut keys in menu options appear in **bold**. On your screen, you see these characters underlined, but they appear in bold here so that you can see them more easily.

Index to the Icons

 Beginner's level indicates an example or exercise appropriate for newcomers to programming and Access Basic.

 Intermediate level indicates a more detailed and thorough example or exercise.

 Advanced level indicates an example or exercise that requires more thought and study than the other two kinds

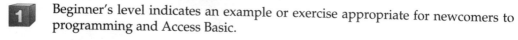
Tip: Tips provide helpful shortcuts or solutions.

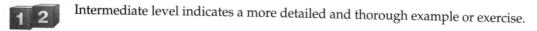
Caution: Cautions provide warnings or describe potential problems to avoid.

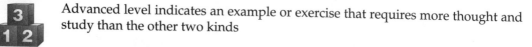
Note: Notes provide extra information about the subject just discussed.

The code continuation character (➡) indicates that a line of program code has been broken for the purpose of fitting on the page. When you're entering programs, however, you should type that text all on one line.

Start Access and Program

After you have turned on your computer and have loaded Access, you're ready to turn the page and begin Chapter 1. Good luck. Your Access Basic future often is rewarding, sometimes challenging, and always fun.

Part I

Preparing for Access Basic

CHAPTER 1

Welcome to Access Basic

As you no doubt already realize, Microsoft Access is one of the most flexible database management programs on the market for creating ready-to-use database applications. Unlike many other database management systems, Access requires no programming for common database applications, and you can create many advanced database applications that also require no programming.

Nevertheless, there will come a time when you need to do more than the interactive Access *graphical user interface (GUI)* provides. Despite Microsoft's forethought that provided Access with some of the most powerful and automatic database-creation tools to be found, you will be ready to take Access to a higher level than the click-and-point interface provides. That's where this book comes into the picture; *Access 2 Programming By Example* teaches you the programming skills that you need as you build more powerful Access applications.

Note: This book does not assume that you have ever programmed a computer in your life. You need to be familiar only with the common Access objects such as tables, forms, reports, and queries. If you have built one or two complete database systems with Access, you're ready for the concepts in this book.

This chapter introduces the following topics:

◆ Programming concepts

◆ Access compared to other languages

◆ Event-driven Access programming

◆ Backing up your work

This chapter whets your programming appetite and prepares for you a positive mood for programming in Access Basic.

Introduction to Programming

Computers cannot think on their own.

A *program* is nothing more than a list of instructions. A program to a computer is like a recipe to a cook. The only difference (and it is a big difference indeed) is that a cook can think but a computer cannot. The computer is a dumb machine. People often get the mistaken idea that computers have minds and can think intuitively on their own. Although this thinking is the kind of stuff that makes exciting movies, it does not make for realistic computing.

Because a computer cannot think, you must instruct the computer on what to do and how to do it. Your programs supply the instructions needed. If computers could think and if they understood English, there would be little need for programming languages. English, as well as any spoken language, requires insight and interpreting skills that are not owned by computers.

At their lowest level, computers really understand only on and off states of electricity. Your computer is nothing more than thousands of on and off electrical switches and those switches are turned on to let electricity flow or they are turned off to stop the flow. These on and off states of electricity (called *binary states*) combine to form thousands of patterns that produce work such as word processing and database management.

Computer scientists often use 1s and 0s to represent the internal on and off states of electricity. If the decision were up to the computer, you would issue instructions in 1s and 0s. If, however, this decision were up to non-computer people, you would speak to computers in English. A middle-ground must be found, and that is where programming languages come in.

Note: You don't have to understand anything about the internals of your computer to be an expert Access Basic programmer. It helps to know all that you can about your computer, just as it helps to know more about your automobile than just how to drive. This background attempts to lead you into understanding why you need to learn programming languages if you want to communicate directly with the computer.

Access Basic is only one of many programming languages. A programming language is English-like in that it uses words and phrases similar to some that you say every day. Unlike a spoken language though, a programming language is very structured and has many rules and patterns so that a nonthinking computer can interpret the language. As Figure 1.1 shows, a programming language helps you talk to computers (through the keyboard) and helps computers understand what you say.

Figure 1.1

A programming language such as Access Basic enables you to give orders to computers.

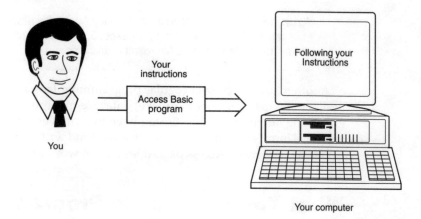

Access Basic and Other Programming Languages

Access Basic is based on the beginner's BASIC language.

The more detailed a programming language is, usually the more difficult it is to learn. The BASIC programming language was created for beginners many years ago. The C programming language, one of the most popular programming languages in use today, often is considered to be too advanced for beginners. Generally, the more advanced a language is, the more it does, but the harder it is to learn the language.

Access Basic seems to break that common pattern of being advanced but difficult. Access Basic is based on the BASIC language of years ago, so Access Basic is fairly easy for beginners to learn. Unlike many beginning programming languages, however, Access Basic is extremely powerful and flexible. Access Basic provides an interactive approach to programming; the elements in Access such as tables, forms, reports, and queries directly interact with Access Basic. You can add an Access Basic program to any of your existing Access database applications if you need your database applications to do more work.

Tip: If you have used Word for Windows WordBasic or Visual Basic, you may have found that Access Basic is very close to both languages. Each of these BASIC-like dialects contains *object-oriented* features (described later in this chapter) that enable your programs to respond to whatever the user wants to do.

Note: Access Basic is almost identical to Microsoft's new *Visual Basic for Applications* (*VBA*) that comes with Excel 5, Microsoft Project, and the VBA that will be added to future Microsoft applications.

Another advantage over regular programming languages is that Access Basic brings to the programmer high-level database manipulation power. With a programming language such as C, you have to write very complicated and tedious low-level input and output routines that read and write data to and from disk files. Unlike a C program, Access Basic does all that work for you.

What You Face while Programming Access

You should automate Access if you find yourself repeating the same keystrokes often or typing the same action in more than one location. Also, as you see throughout this book, the nonprogramming Access user just cannot accomplish some procedural steps. If you need to control the user's input more than allowed in a form or database view, open more than one database at the same time, or repeat the same operation for all records in a table, you need to automate Access through programming.

Access provides three ways to program so that you can automate your tasks. They all involve the Access Basic language to one degree or another. These three methods are as follows:

◆ Macros

◆ Function procedures

◆ Sub procedures

You already may have used macros in your database applications. Access comes with several supplied macro *actions* (commands that go inside macros), and you can write your own as well. *Macros* are database objects that help automate actions you want done at certain times throughout the use of a database.

> **Tip:** This book reviews the fundamentals of macros. Access Basic program-
> mers often integrate Access macros with their Access Basic code. You need
> to be sure that you understand macros before learning the Access Basic
> programming tools, however. If you have worked extensively with macros,
> you can skim the next two chapters, which deal with macros.

The majority of this book concerns itself with the second two programming methods: *function procedures* and *sub procedures*. In function procedures and sub procedures, an understanding of Access Basic is required. Function procedures and sub procedures contain the Access Basic programming statements that execute when certain events happen.

Along the way, this book discusses several built-in functions. By giving you some commonly needed functions, Access Basic saves you from having to write them yourself to accomplish a routine task.

> **Note:** Often, this book refers to function procedures as simply *functions* and
> sub procedures as *subroutines.* The terms *functions* and *subroutines* are
> more commonly used by the programming community, and these terms are
> generic references to their Access Basic function procedure and sub
> procedure counterparts.

OOP's Event-Driven Programming

You use event-
driven techniques
every day.

The Microsoft Windows environment introduced a new facet to programmers' jobs. The graphical user environment of Windows requires that programs respond to the user in an *event-driven* manner.

The term *event-driven* sounds difficult, but in reality it is a concept that people deal with most in real life. Think about a complicated Access data-entry form such as that in Figure 1.2. Access does not require that the user respond to the form's controls and boxes in a top-to-bottom, left-to-right order. Rather, the user is free to click, press, and enter data in any order that he or she wants. On many data-entry forms, the user can even ignore many controls.

All of Access is an event-driven environment that consists of controls, menus, and data-entry boxes which wait around to respond to events determined by the data or by the user. All of Windows is event-driven; at any given time, you might select a menu option, start a program, or switch to a different window.

Before the graphical environments like Windows came along, programs were known as *procedural* (sometimes called *linear*), which meant that the programs led the user through expected and ordered steps, allowing the user the freedom to change course in only a limited manner or not at all.

Figure 1.2

Access data-entry forms do not require that the user enter data in any order.

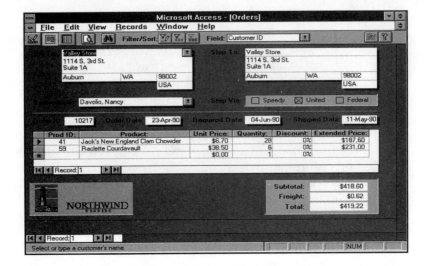

You can think of the Access event-driven environment as being like the controls on your VCR. When you use your VCR, do you touch the buttons in the order they appear? You don't. Instead, you might change the channel, you might set the timer, you might turn off the VCR, you might adjust the tape speed, or you might do whatever you want to do in whatever order you want. The VCR is made in such a way that you can trigger almost any event any time you want.

> **Note:** Sometimes, your Access application must control some of the order, just as your VCR does at times. You have to tell the VCR the channel, date, and time of a program that you want to record before the VCR records anything. In an Access form, the user might be required to choose a printing option (such as the destination of either screen or printer) before the printing can begin.

Access is not pure OOP.

Unlike some programming languages and environments, Access Basic requires you to write many small sections of *code* (code is another word for the program's instructions). That's what function and sub procedures really were designed to be: small sections of code that sit around waiting for an event to occur (such as a user's selection from a form) before doing their job. As much as the application allows, the function and sub procedures must work independently of each other and be able to execute in whatever order the user or data requires.

> **Caution:** Despite what you might hear, don't believe the rumor that Access
> Basic is a pure *object-oriented programming* (*OOP*) language. The event-
> driven facility of Access Basic makes Access Basic's objects respond in a
> manner similar to that of objects in a pure OOP language such as C++.
> However, Access Basic does not support other requirements of OOP such
> as *inheritance* and *polymorphism* (silver-dollar buzzwords from OOP
> languages) that are required to qualify a language for pure OOP.

Forms Bring Everything Together

Much of this book concerns itself with integrating Access Basic functions, modules, and macros with forms. This book discusses some forms design and assumes that you've already designed forms to one degree or another in your previous work with Access. Nevertheless, the book presents some review of form design in the light of integrating your forms with the Access Basic programs that you write.

Philosophy on the Book's Examples

Where possible, *Access 2 Programming By Example* utilizes program examples that come with your copy of Microsoft Access. You will see examples from the North-wind Traders (NWIND.MDB) sample database as well as from the orders (ORDERS.MDB) and solution (SOLUTION.MDB) sample database files that come with copies of Microsoft Access. You are probably familiar with these databases from the tutorials that come with Access. Sadly, Access does not provide many tutorial-style instructions for Access Basic programming, but this book fills that void nicely.

Using the sample databases means that you can begin learning Access Basic right away without first creating a stand-alone database and typing a bunch of code. Some programming books begin creating an application in Chapter 1 and add to it with each chapter. This method would not work well here because sometimes you might want to try a specific Access Basic command taught in the middle of the book, and you would like to execute it to see if that command works similarly in your own application. (People are event-driven!)

Back up the
sample database
for posterity.

By using the sample databases, you already have many of the examples in this book typed in for you. Therefore, you are ready to begin learning Access Basic and can hit the ground running without a lot of typing preamble. There will be several code examples that don't appear in any of the sample database files, so you'll have to type a few in.

At times this book makes suggested modifications to a sample database to teach a particular point. Therefore, you should make a backup of the sample databases now so they remain intact. Depending on how you are most comfortable managing files, you can back up the databases from Windows or from DOS. Refer to the following Windows or DOS section that meets your needs the best to back up the files.

> **Note:** An Access database is easy to back up because all its components (the data, tables, forms, and so on) reside in a single file. The name of your database is the first part of the filename, and the Access database file extension should always be .MDB to maintain consistency with the recommendations of Microsoft.

Backing Up in Windows

If you haven't started Windows, do so now. If you have Access running, exit Access and return to the Windows desktop.

> **Caution:** If you have one of the sample databases currently loaded, be sure to close the database (with **F**ile **C**lose Database) before you attempt to back up the samples. This process is true of any database you want to back up. Access does not release a file for backing up until you've closed the file. If you are not running Access, you don't have to worry about closing the database. Because Windows makes it easy for you to switch to another session and do perform a task such as a backup, you should be aware that you cannot back up an open database file.

Follow these steps to back up the Northwind Traders sample database:

1. Double-click the Main program group icon if it is not already expanded in an open window on your Windows desktop screen.

2. Double-click the File Manager icon.

3. Select the disk drive icon that contains the Access database. Figure 1.3 shows drive G: selected.

4. Click the Access directory in the list of directories on the left side of the screen. Depending on the size of your File Manager window, you may have to click on the scroll bar to find the Access directory.

5. Click the NWIND.MDB file from the list in the right window to highlight it.

Figure 1.3

Selecting Drive G:.

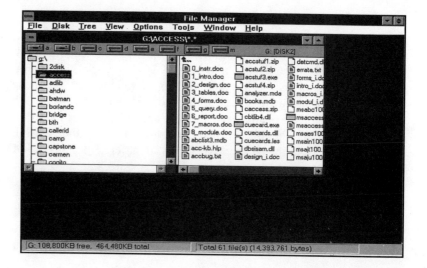

6. Select **File Copy...** from the File Manager's menu. The File Manager fills in the **From** filename for you.

7. Type **NWINDOLD.MDB** at the **To** prompt and press Enter. The NWIND.MDB database file is large and might take a few moments to copy. Once done, you return to the File Manager screen.

8. Back up the ORDERS.MDB and the SOLUTION.MDB databases as you just did for NWIND.MDB.

9. Select **File Exit** to return to the Windows desktop. You now can close the Main program group (press Ctrl+F4) and return to what you were doing. The original databases now are safely backed up on your disk.

> **Caution:** If you like, you can copy the database file to a different disk drive by dragging its filename to a different disk drive icon. If the target disk does not have enough room to hold the database file, Windows prompts you to insert a second disk if needed to hold the entire database file you are backing up.

As an extra precaution, back up the SYSTEM.MDA file as well (to a name such as SYSOLD.MDA). This file keeps track of your system's settings and is extra important if several people share the same Access-based PC.

Backing Up in DOS

If you are in the Windows desktop, you can open a DOS window or exit to DOS before backing up the database. Many people feel that the Windows File Manager is too bulky and slow to be useful when a quick DOS command works just as well. If you've been using Access, be sure to close any database you want to back up before starting the backup procedure listed here.

At a DOS prompt, use the COPY command to copy the database file to a different filename. The following COPY command copies the NWIND.MDB file, located on drive D: in the ACCESS directory, to a file named NWINDOLD.MDB in the same directory:

```
COPY D:\ACCESS\NWIND.MDB D:\ACCESS\NWINDOLD.MDB
```

After a brief pause, the backup is made. If your Access drive or pathname differs from the one here, make the adjustment in the COPY command. In the same manner, also back up the ORDERS.MDB and SOLUTION.MDB databases.

> **Caution:** Make sure the target disk drive has enough free space to hold the database file. You can execute a CHKDSK command first to see how much free disk space remains on the target disk drive to which you are copying. For further information on CHKDSK, refer to your DOS reference manual.

If you want to copy your database to a floppy disk (and you should back up all your databases regularly to a floppy disk unless you have a tape drive, in which case you use the tape drive's software) and the database is larger than will fit on one floppy disk, use the BACKUP command rather than COPY. BACKUP prompts you to insert a second floppy disk if the first one cannot hold the entire database. Be sure that your target diskettes are formatted before beginning BACKUP.

> **Tip:** You can type any command, disk drive letter, or filename at the DOS prompt in either upper- or lowercase letters.

As an extra precaution, back up the SYSTEM.MDA file as well to a filename such as SYSOLD.MDA. This file keeps track of your system's settings and is extra important if several people share the same Access-based PC.

The Building-Block Approach of This Book

The rest of this book devotes itself to the Access Basic language in one form or another. Access Basic cannot be taught in the typical style of other programming languages. In a way, you have to learn the trees before you can see the forest. Most chapters of this book (after some preliminary groundwork) deal with various aspects of the Access Basic language on a piecemeal basis. You may not see the "big picture" at all times. In other words, you have to learn some details of Access Basic, such as variables, before you can see them fully used in a working application.

With some programming languages, such as QBasic and C, you can learn some introductory elements of the languages and begin writing simple programs that accomplish some task such as calculating and printing payroll amounts. Because Access Basic is so closely tied to an existing database application that you create through the database window controls supplied with Access (the Table, Query, Form, Report, and Macro object's tool window), you will not see a full-featured usage of every topic taught in this book until you have read through several chapters.

Therefore, take each chapter as a building block for the next, knowing that you have to learn the "what it is" before learning the "why you do it." If you have read other books in the *By Example* series, such as *Turbo Pascal By Example*, you may notice that this book has to deviate a little in its methods used to teach Access Basic.

Summary

This chapter introduced you to Access Basic and gave you an overview of a program and why you need to learn a programming language. Maybe someday, you'll be able to speak to computers in your own language, but until then, you must learn a programming language. Luckily, Access Basic is easier to learn than some other programming languages. Actually, if you know how to use Access for everything *but* programming, you may find that you need to program only occasionally.

Access provides several low-level routines that you don't have to worry about as you would have to in other programming languages. If you've never written a program before, don't worry because this book starts at the beginning. You can be an advanced Access user but know nothing about programming before reading this book.

In the following two chapters, you review macros to help strengthen your Access Basic programming skills. After answering the review questions, turn the page and set your thinking caps to *learn!*

Review Questions

Answers to review questions are in Appendix B.

1. What is a program?

2. TRUE or FALSE: Computers can think.

3. How has Access Basic improved over other languages such as C?

4. How does Access make backing up a complicated database easier than most database programs?

5. Why must you learn a programming language if you want to "talk" to your computer?

6. Why is backing up the sample databases, such as NWIND.MDB, now important (as opposed to backing it up after you complete the examples in this book)?

7. What is event-driven programming?

8. TRUE or FALSE: Access is a true object-oriented programming language.

9. What are the three ways to automate Access?

10. Why must you close a database before backing it up?

Introduction to Macros

Macros are database objects, just like forms and tables are database objects. Macros provide the easiest way for you to automate your Access database. Any steps you find yourself performing over and over are good candidates for making into macros. As a matter of fact, much of what Access developers do without using macros should be automated with macros, but they rarely get around to creating all the macros that would help them.

Suppose that you are developing a fairly complex Access database application that may take several days or weeks to complete. Rather than opening the database every time you start Access, create a macro that does it for you. When you finish the application, you can unhook the automatic macro easily so that the database doesn't always open when you start Access.

> **Note:** Macros in Access are completely different from macros in other applications. A macro in Access is not just a recorded series of keystrokes for automating repetitive tasks; it performs many functions that otherwise require code. Using macros in Access can be even more efficient than writing code to do the same thing.

This chapter introduces the following topics:

◆ Macro fundamentals

◆ Reviewing existing macros

◆ Creating macros

◆ Running macros

◆ Testing macros

This chapter begins a two chapter section about macros so that you are familiar with creating macros and using them before you leap into Access Basic.

> **Tip:** You can execute Access Basic code from a macro.

Getting Ready for Macros

Macros are a series of automated actions.

Macros are the perfect introduction to programming with Access Basic. If you have never written a program in your life, you'll find that a macro is like a miniature program with steps of instructions (called *actions*) that perform in a sequential step-by-step manner.

> **Tip:** Macros save you time by automating common tasks, but macros (when properly written) also help prevent errors by ensuring that each step of the macro is done in the order needed and exactly as needed.

Macros can automatically open tables and forms, run queries, print reports, and display data on-screen. A macro can update a table with new values (although in a more limited way than Access Basic provides), close databases, search for data, and more.

The actions in a macro run when you execute it. You have three primary ways to execute macros:

◆ When you start Access

◆ When you specifically run a macro you've written through menus or with the database window buttons

◆ When a macro is triggered by certain events on a form or report

Access provides
47 macro actions.

Because any step inside a macro—the macro's actions—performs one part of the overall macro, a macro's individual actions work similarly to the Access Basic commands you learn in this book. Therefore, a macro's individual actions are like Access Basic's individual commands. Each combines to form a macro or a program. Access Basic provides 47 individual macro actions, which you find listed along with their names and descriptions, in Table 2.1.

> **Caution:** Don't feel that you have to learn every macro action that Access supplies. You rarely use all of them. Depending on your database needs, you may find that you routinely use five or six of the actions in your own macros, sometimes use a few more, and never use some of the others.

Table 2.1. The Access macro actions with descriptions.

Action	Description
AddMenu	Adds a pull-down menu to a customized menu bar.
ApplyFilter	Filters or sorts data in a form or report by limiting the query or SQL WHERE clause.
Beep	Causes the computer to beep the speaker.
CancelEvent	If a macro is started by an event (such as a mouse click on a form's button), CancelEvent cancels that event.
Close	Closes an Access window.
CopyObject	Copies an object (form, query, report, or any other database object) from one location (such as the current database) to a different database.
DeleteObject	Deletes an object (form, query, report, or any other database object).
DoMenuItem	Executes a menu command.
Echo	Can show or hide the results of a running macro.
FindNext	Finds the next record that matches the previous FindRecord action.

continues

23

Table 2.1. Continued

Action	Description
FindRecord	Finds the first record that meets a search criteria (not including the current record).
GoToControl	Moves the focus to a field or control on a form, datasheet, or dynaset.
GoToPage	Moves the focus to the first field on a specified page.
GoToRecord	Moves the record currency to the specified record.
HourGlass	Displays the waiting hourglass mouse cursor.
Maximize	Enlarges the active window.
Minimize	Reduces the active window to an icon.
MoveSize	Moves or resizes the currently active window.
MsgBox	Displays a message box with the specified message.
OpenForm	Opens a form in one of three views: design, print preview, or datasheet.
OpenModule	Opens the specified module.
OpenQuery	Opens a select or crosstab query as well as runs an action query.
OpenReport	Opens a report in design or print preview view. Also prints a report, restricting records if you need to do so.
OpenTable	Opens a table in datasheet, design, or print preview view.
OutputTo	Exports database data to Excel, word processing *RTF* (for rich text format), or an ASCII text file.
Print	Prints the active object in the currently open database.
Quit	Exits Access.

Action	Description
Rename	Renames a database object.
RepaintObject	Completes a pending screen update for an object, finishing calculations, if needed.
Requery	Updates data in the active object.
Restore	Restores the size of a maximized or minimized window.
RunApp	Runs a Windows or DOS-based application from within Access.
RunCode	Executes an Access basic function procedure.
RunMacro	Runs another macro.
RunSQL	Runs a Microsoft Access action query using the SQL language.
SelectObject	Selects a specified database object.
SendKeys	Sends keystrokes to an active window.
SendObject	Sends a database form, module, or report as electronic mail.
SetValue	Sets the value of a report's or form's field, control, or property.
SetWarnings	Turns system messages on or off.
ShowAllRecords	Removes any filter from an active form and displays all the records.
StopAllMacros	Stops all macro execution.
StopMacro	Stops the currently running macro.
ShowToolbar	Shows or hides a toolbar.
TransferDatabase	Imports or exports data between two databases.
TransferSpreadsheet	Imports or exports data between the current database and a spreadsheet file.
TransferText	Imports or exports data between a database and a text file.

Note: Again, these individual commands go inside a macro. By grouping certain actions into a macro, you are, in effect, writing a little program similar to the programs you write in Access Basic. The macro actions, however, are extremely specific, and the Access Basic programs that you write are more flexible and powerful. You can call macros from your Access Basic programs to make them even more powerful.

Looking at a Macro

Before diving into the creation of a macro, you might want to look at some existing macros to familiarize yourself with the macro definition screen. Many people jump right in and create a macro before ever seeing one. Creating a macro makes more sense if you look at one of these screens first.

Example

Take a moment to open the sample Northwind database. Choose **File Open Database...** and open NWIND.MDB file stored in the SAMPAPPS directory. In the database window, click the Macro button to see a list of macros that come with the sample database. You see that several macros are supplied with the database.

Tip: As with all of the scrolling lists in Access, you can see more of the list at once by double-clicking the window's title bar (which reads `Database: NWIND`) to expand the window to fill your entire screen.

Highlight the `Print Current Record` macro from the list and click the **Design** button. You see the Macro Print Current Record window as shown in Figure 2.1. The first column labeled Action contains a list (in this case there are only two) of actions that execute in the order in which they appear. The Comment column describes the macro writer's comments about each of the actions and how those actions apply to the macro.

The Print Current Record macro selects the current record and prints it. Just as with fields you add to a table, each of the macros contains properties called *arguments* that you can specify in the window's bottom pane. Only a few of the actions, such as `Beep` and `CancelEvent`, don't require arguments. The argument list changes depending on the action you select.

Position the cursor over the `DoMenuItem` action and look at the four argument boxes listed in the lower pane. Pressing the down-arrow key takes you to the next action (`Print`), and you see that `Print` requires six arguments (the range to print, the starting and ending pages, the resolution of the printed output, the number of copies, and whether or not you want to collate the pages).

Figure 2.1

Looking at the macro definition table.

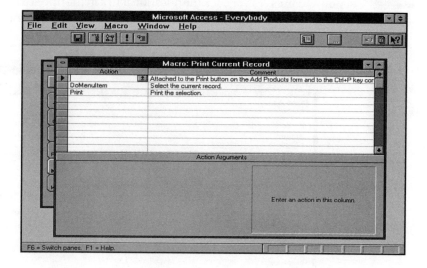

Comment a lot.

The comments are for you (and others who might need to work with the macro definition), not for Access. As with field descriptions, the comments are notes you make to yourself that describe in English what is going on in the macro's action.

> **Tip:** Use abundant comments all throughout your Access database. Any time you can supply a comment or a description, do so. The action might make sense to you without any comment, but if someone else takes over the database during your absence, he or she will appreciate the comments. You learn more about commenting as you move into the straight Access Basic coding in the next part of the book.

Getting Help

The on-line help is available for you at any time. The help system in Access virtually replaces the reference manuals that come with Access. Although the help screens are not tutorials on their topics (that's what books like this one are for!), they do provide all the information you need to use macros, including a list of each macro's arguments and a description of the macros.

Example

With the Print Current Record macro still on-screen, move the cursor to the Print action and press F1 (or click the question mark in the upper-right part of the screen). You'll see the help screen shown in Figure 2.2. To exit help, double-click the Close box.

Figure 2.2

Macro help is only a keystroke or a click away.

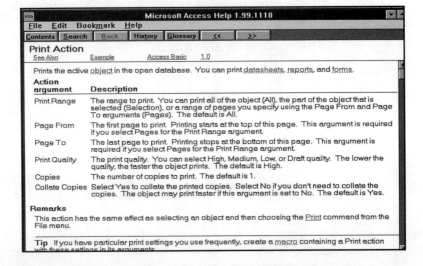

Note: Feel free to search through the help screen, clicking the cross-referenced green terms to find related help topics. You may be surprised at the knowledge you can pick up by using the Access hypertext help system.

Looking at the Toolbar

Before going much further, you should familiarize yourself with the macro window's toolbar. As you probably already know, the Access toolbar (the row of buttons directly beneath the pull-down menus) changes depending on the object you are working on. The toolbar looks different if you change a table's definition, for example, from what it looks like if you change a form's definition.

The macro toolbar provides shortcuts.

Figure 2.3 shows you the macro toolbar, with each tool labeled. The rest of this and the subsequent chapters refer to the toolbar at times, and if you acquaint yourself with the toolbar now, you will make things easier later.

Note: Although you can perform most of the toolbar's actions using the pull-down menus, the toolbar gives you a quick way to point and click common macro operations rather than searching through the menus looking for the same thing.

Figure 2.3

The toolbar and its buttons.

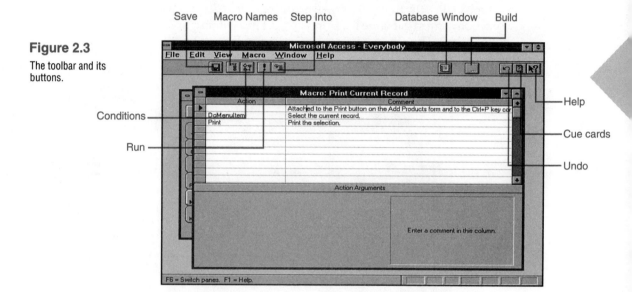

For now, close the Print Current Record macro's definition window (by double-clicking its Control button) and return to the database window.

Creating a Macro

As with most of Access's routine chores, you don't have to memorize commands to create a macro. You have two ways to create the macro: you can use the Access pull-down menu (by choosing File New Macro) or use the database window. Because the database window is the control center for all of an Access database, you may be most comfortable using the database window.

The following examples show you two ways to create a simple macro: by selection and by dragging and clicking. Neither method requires you to memorize any commands.

Example

The first macro you create here is an easy one. The macro beeps and opens the Northwind Trader's customer table in print preview mode.

Click the Macro button and then choose **New**. A new macro definition window opens up. You now can enter the actions for this macro. You can request that Access list the macro action names rather than your typing the commands and risking typos. Click the first cell's down arrow or press Alt+down arrow to display a list of action names (the same list as in Table 2.1 but without the descriptions provided in the table). The action list opens as shown in Figure 2.4.

Figure 2.4

Selecting from a list of actions provided by Access.

Action box ——

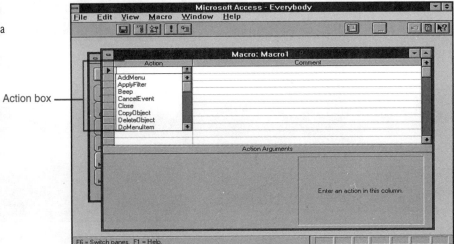

Select the Beep action and press Tab or Enter to move the cursor to the Comment column. Type **Ring the bell** for the first action's comment and press Enter. Because the Beep action requires no arguments, you don't have to do anything in the lower pane of the window for the first action.

Display the action list again. This time, select OpenTable. After you press Enter, the lower pane reveals three action arguments for the OpenTable action. Without your going any further, it should be obvious that the OpenTable action needs to know exactly which table you want to open. You specify the table name in the argument pane.

You can enter the comment, or press F6 to move down to the lower pane and finish the arguments before entering a comment. For this example, go ahead and press F6 to move to the lower pane. The cursor resides in the first argument's box (the Table Name).

> **Note:** Access really tries to make things simpler for you. Notice that another selection arrow sits to the right of the Table Name box. Rather than having to remember the name of the tables you want to open, Access displays a list of all tables in the database, and you have to select only one.

Select the Customers table from the list and press Enter. When you do, the cursor moves down to the View box. Scroll the View box, select Print Preview, and press Enter. The Data Mode determines what the user can do when the table appears. Protect the table's data by choosing Read Only. Press F6 once again to return to the top pane and type the following comment for the second action: **Open and preview the Customer table**. After typing the comment, your screen should look like the one in Figure 2.5.

Figure 2.5

After creating your first macro.

Control button

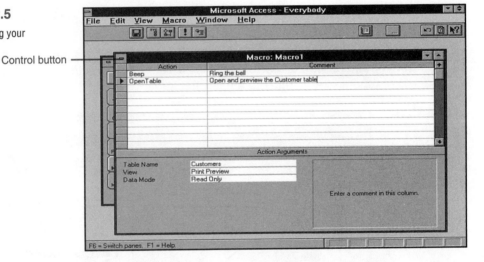

Normally, you save the macro so that it is part of the database. Instead (have faith here), double-click the Macro window's Control button to close the window (Ctrl+F4 also closes the window). Now Access displays a message box that warns you that you haven't saved the macro. Choose No to closing without saving the macro. You will re-create the macro differently in the next example.

Example

The second way to create a macro is to use the drag-and-drop facility. Access is one of the best implementations of the Windows environment that has been written. Here you see how to take advantage of this integration by re-creating the same macro in this example as you created in the preceding example. This time, you do it with even less typing.

In the database window, click the Macro button and then select **New**.

> **Caution:** If you are in the habit of expanding the size of a window to full-screen, don't do that for the macro definition window now. In a moment, you use the database window that is sticking out from under the newly opened macro window.

You may drag your action into place.

As before, select Beep as the first action and type **Ring the bell** for the comment.

With the cursor on the next line, click anywhere in the database window hidden beneath the macro definition window. The database window then becomes active and pops up over the macro window you were just in. Move the database window over to the lower-right side of the screen so that you can still see the Action and Comment columns of the macro definition table.

Click the Table button in the database window to display a list of tables in the window. Next, click the Customers table name and drag it to the second action line's box. Release the mouse button. Access automatically selects the OpenTable action for you and fills in Customers as the Table Name property in the lower pane. Your screen should look similar to the one in Figure 2.6.

Figure 2.6

Access helps you by filling out as much of the action as possible.

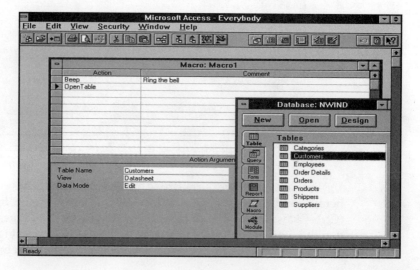

> **Tip:** If you drag a form name, Access assumes that you want to use the
> `OpenForm` action. If you drag a query name, Access assumes that you want
> to use the `OpenQuery` action. If you drag a report name, Access assumes
> that you want to use the `OpenReport` action (get the idea?). If you drag
> another macro name, Access runs that macro (a nesting of macros) with the
> `RunMacro` action.

Because the view you want here is not the datasheet view, press F6 to jump down
to the lower pane and change the View box to Print Preview and the Data Mode box
to Read Only as you did in the preceding example. Type **Open and preview the
Customer table** for the comment and press Enter.

Before you can return to the database window or run the macro, you need to save
the macro. Choose **File** **S**ave. In the Save As dialog box that appears, type **Customer
Ring List** for the macro name. As with most object names in Access, the name can
be up to 64 characters in length. Choose OK to save the macro. After saving the
macro, close the macro definition window (press Ctrl+F4), and you see your new
macro listed with the others if you click the Macro button.

Running the Macro

The macro you just added to the database is a simple one that does not rely on other
events taking place. Many macros interact with other macros and objects, and very
few of them are as simple as the one you created in the preceding section.

The macro you just created is not tied to any event or form, and the following
examples show you different ways to run the macro. The next chapter shows you
additional ways to run macros by tying them to events inside forms and reports.

Example

The most obvious (but not always the fastest) way to run a macro is to run it from
the database window. Click the Macro button and select `Customer Ring List`.
Choose **R**un in the database window, and the macro is off and running! You hear
a beep followed by a display of the Customers table in print preview mode.

> **Note:** The macro is finished when its last action completes. Therefore, the
> Customers table sits there looking back at you, waiting for you to initiate
> some operation. The Customer Ring List macro has done its job.

Press Ctrl+F4 to close the print preview window and return to the database
window.

Example

You also can run the macro by double-clicking its name from the database window. This method is perhaps the fastest way of executing a macro that you write. You have to admit that double-clicking the name is a lot easier than opening a table and changing to print preview mode. Plus, you get a beep as well!

Example

You can execute a macro from the macro definition screen itself by clicking the Run tool button on the macro toolbar. Open the Ring Customer List macro definition again (by clicking **Design** in the database window). When you see the two action lines, click the Run tool button (the tool buttons were labeled in Figure 2.3). Access rings the bell and previews the Customers table.

> **Note:** Running the macro from the macro definition screen comes in handy while you're developing a macro. To see the effect of the addition, you can run all the actions each time you add another one.

Press Ctrl+F4 to close the print preview window and press Ctrl+F4 once again to return to the database window.

Example

You can run a macro in *Single-step* mode one action at a time. Although the Customer Ring List macro is short, it provides a good introduction to *debugging* (getting the errors out) macros.

> **Tip:** The type of single-stepping provided for macros is available for Access Basic programs too, as you see later in the book.

Open the Ring Customer List macro definition again (by clicking **Design** in the database window). When you see the two action lines, click the Step Into tool button on the toolbar (the tool buttons were labeled in Figure 2.3). Nothing seems to happen, but the Single-step button turns red indicating that the single-step mode is on.

Run the macro (by clicking the Run tool button), and you find that rather than running the macro, Access displays the Macro Single Step dialog box shown in Figure 2.7. The dialog box shows the next action to execute, which in this case is the Beep action. Choose **Step** to execute that action (this macro truly is in slow motion) and hear the beep. The next action line's dialog box appears.

Figure 2.7

The Macro Single
Step dialog box.

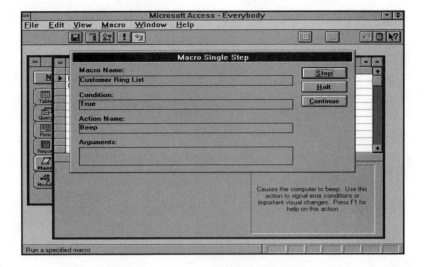

Once you step again, the macro is completed because it consists of only two lines.

Tip: If, at any time, you single-step a macro for the first few actions and then decide that you want to see the remainder of the macro execute without single-stepping, select **C**ontinue rather than **S**tep. Selecting **H**alt ends the macro's execution and returns you to the macro definition screen.

Summary

You've made it through the beginnings of macros and of programming in general. As you learned in this chapter, a macro's actions are step-by-step instructions that work together to accomplish some task within Access.

Creating macros is easy. Many times, you can drag and drop to add actions to a macro that you're creating. The actions used in this chapter are relatively easy. The mechanics of creating macros was this chapter's focus; the following chapter delves deeper into some more advanced means of creating and using macros and explains some of the more complex actions that are possible.

Review Questions

Answers to review questions are in Appendix B.

1. What is a macro?

2. What is an action?

3. TRUE or FALSE: The toolbar changes as you select different objects in the database window.

4. Name two advantages macros provide.

5. Why is commenting macro actions important?

6. What are an action's properties called?

7. What is the method used for debugging macros?

8. What are the two ways to get actions into a macro's definition column?

Review Exercises

1. Add a Beep action to the end of the Customer Ring List macro.

2. Add the Quit action to the end of the macro and run it. Oops! The Quit action exits you from Access entirely. Remove the Quit action once you've seen it work.

3. Add an action that minimizes the Customers table print preview window so that it stays around the desktop (minimized) until you need it. Double-click the Customers icon to enlarge the window. (*Hint:* If the icon gets covered up, you can enlarge it by selecting the Customers table from the **W**indow pull-down menu.)

CHAPTER 3

Macro Actions in Forms and Reports

Now that you've seen the fundamentals of macros and how to create simple ones, you are ready to delve deeper into using them with forms and reports. Most often, you won't want to run a macro from the database window. If you are writing a macro for an end-user who has no knowledge of Access, the end-user will not need to know how to start a macro, so you have to program macros to start automatically.

To understand the usage of macros in forms and reports, you need to learn a few additional elements of Access. Built-in functions (as opposed to the functions that you write in Access Basic) help streamline your work by providing common routines. In addition, you may want to explore an additional macro topic called *conditional macros*. A conditional macro is a macro that executes only if a certain condition is true.

This chapter introduces the following topics:

- Built-in functions
- Conditional macros
- Macros in forms
- Linking macros and form buttons
- Reporting with macros

The majority of this chapter deals with macros and forms. Once you master macros inside forms, you should find the transition to using macros with reports very easy to master.

Some Words about Built-in Functions

Call functions from macros and Access Basic programs.

You can call several built-in functions from macros and within Access Basic programs. A function name is usually (but not always) followed by a set of parentheses with possible values (called *arguments*) inside the parentheses. Capitalizing the function's first letter, such as IsNull() and Int(), is common. Because built-in functions are supplied for you, you don't have to write Access Basic code to represent the actions inside the built-in functions. When you write your own function procedures, you are, in effect, adding your own functions to the supply of built-in functions.

Figure 3.1 illustrates the job of functions, whether they are built-in functions or those you write in Access Basic. A function takes the list of arguments you send it and does something with that list. Once a built-in function does its job, a value is returned from the function, and that value is used in the macro or the Access Basic program that executes the function.

Note: Another term for executing a built-in function is *calling* the function. When you call a function, you send it arguments, and the function executes and returns a value that you can work with in a macro.

Figure 3.1

A function receives one or more arguments and returns a single value.

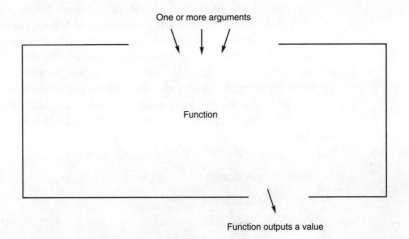

One or more arguments

Function

Function outputs a value

Caution: Neither the built-in functions nor the Access Basic functions can return more than a single value. For instance, a function cannot return a list of values.

This chapter offers only an introduction to the built-in Access functions. Beginning in Chapter 21, "The Domain's D...() Functions," this book provides an in-depth discussion of all the built-in functions. So many of the built-in functions are useless until you begin writing Access Basic programs that the majority of them are not discussed until Chapter 21.

Example

The LCase$() function returns the lowercase equivalent of its argument. Given Figure 3.1's box-analogy of a function, if you throw an uppercase word into the LCase$() function's box, the LCase$() function returns (produces, spits out, whatever boxes do) the same word in all lowercase letters.

> **Note:** If you pass to LCase$() an argument that already contains some lowercase letters or some nonalphabetic letters, LCase$() does not change any of those characters.

The following function call therefore produces the word access:

```
LCase$("ACCESS")
```

Most of the built-in functions work on fields. If a field named Title is passed to LCase$() as follows:

```
LCase$([Title])
```

the function returns the lowercase equivalent of whatever word or phrase is in the Title field.

As you can see, if you pass a field name to a function, you should always enclose the field name inside square brackets.

Example

The Right$() function takes two arguments. Although you see a deeper discussion of Right$() in Chapter 23, you should have little trouble understanding it here because Right$() does just what its name says: Right$() returns the rightmost portion of a string of characters. The first argument must be the string of characters (which can be a field holding a string of characters), and the second argument is the number of characters you want Right$() to pick off and return to you.

> **Note:** As with most Access functions, Right$() does not change its arguments in any way.

The following `Right$()` function call returns the rightmost five characters of its first argument:

```
Right$("Paula Mason", 5)
```

As you can see, this `Right$()` function returns the name `Mason`.

Example

The `Choose()` function accepts an index value followed by a list of data values. `Choose()` returns one of the values in the list determined by the index. Often, the index is a user's response from a menu or a field's value from a form. The index must range from 1 to a maximum of 13, representing the number of values in the list.

> **Tip:** In a way, the `Choose()` function acts like the IRS lookup tables (but it's not as anguishing!). The index determines what value from the list is returned in the same way that your adjusted salary determines what tax rate you pay.

Taking the IRS table analogy a step further, suppose that your database contains a field named `Status` that contains 1, 2, or 3, depending on the following possibilities:

1. If the client is single

2. If the client is married filing separately

3. If the client is married filing jointly

The following `Choose()` function returns the appropriate description based on the value in the Status field:

```
Choose([Status], "Single", "Married (separately)", "Married (jointly)")
```

Conditional Macros

The `Choose()` function is a good introduction to conditional macros. `Choose()` returns different values based on the first argument. If the first argument is 1, the next argument (the second one) is returned. If the first argument is 2, the third argument is returned and so on. `Choose()` returns a value based on a certain condition, namely its first argument.

Access provides conditional functions, macros, and statements.

As you progress through *Access 2 Programming By Example*, you learn a lot about conditional execution of functions, macros, and Access Basic statements. Perhaps the most powerful technique that Access Basic brings to the database is its conditional statements. An Access Basic program executes certain sections depending on the result of a condition, just as Choose() returns a value depending on the value of an argument.

Conditional macros provide a foundation from which you can study conditional execution. In a nutshell, a conditional macro executes only if a certain condition (also called *criterion*) is true. Macros depend on functions to test the condition.

Example

When a macro contains a condition, Access opens an extra column in the macro definition window. Follow these steps to see a conditional macro. The macro is linked to a form's command button; therefore, the macro executes as a result of the user clicking on a form button.

1. Open the NWIND.MDB database if it is not already open.

2. Click the Macro button in the database window.

3. Select the Review Products macro and click the **D**esign button. You see the screen shown in Figure 3.2.

Figure 3.2

A conditional macro definition contains an extra column for the condition.

Ellipsis ————

Conditional macro column

[Screenshot: Microsoft Access - Everybody]

Condition	Action	Comment
		Attached to the Review Products button on the Suppliers f...
	Echo	Freeze screen while macro is running (Echo off).
IsNull([Supplier ID])	MsgBox	If no current supplier on Suppliers form, display a message...
...	StopMacro	... and stop the macro.
	OpenForm	Open the Product List form and show current supplier's prod...
	MoveSize	Position the Product List form in the lower right of the Suppl...

Action Arguments

Enter a conditional expression in this column.

F6 = Switch panes. F1 = Help.   NUM

4. Click Echo, the first action's box. (The first row is used just for a comment that tells which form's command button the macro is linked to. Most Access programmers use the first row of each macro to explain how the macro is triggered.) In the next section you open this form and watch the execution of this macro. The lower pane (where the action's arguments are listed) shows that the echo is turned off. (The Echo On argument is set to No—obfuscated wording to be sure!)

> **Note:** Not every action in the Review Products macro is conditional. Only two actions, the MsgBox and StopMacro actions, are conditional. The first action, Echo, always executes, as do the last two. The second and third actions execute only if the Supplier ID field is null (which means that the field has no value because the user didn't enter one). Notice the ellipsis (...) in the Condition column for the third action. The developer of the NWIND database could have typed **IsNull([Supplier ID])** again, but using the ellipsis is a shortcut for repeating a condition.

> **Tip:** Most macros linked to command buttons contain the Echo action that turns off the display of the macro's individual actions. If you place this action at the top of the Action column, you can keep the screen free of unwanted messages as the macro executes.

5. Click the second action's row to see the arguments for the MsgBox action. The MsgBox displays error messages, warnings, or just helpful advice depending on the needs of the macro. This MsgBox action tells the user to select a supplier and then click this macro's command button again. This action executes only if the Supplier ID is blank, which means that the user needs to select a Supplier ID. Also, notice that the action beeps the speaker, getting the user's attention when this message box appears.

IsNull() is a built-in function that returns a value, but a value unlike the ones you saw earlier in this chapter. IsNull() is one of several built-in functions that return a true or false result (in the same way that a Yes/No data type contains either a true or false value).

> **Tip:** Always remember that help is a keypress away. If you press the F1 Help key (or click the Help question mark button on the toolbar and drag the question mark to the `MsgBox` action), you see the help screen shown in Figure 3.3 (after maximizing the help window). At the bottom of the help screen, you see four icons you can display inside the message box. (You can scroll the screen by clicking the scroll bar to bring all four icons into full view.) The Type action argument determines which, if any, of these icons you want displayed. The `MsgBox` action defined here shows `None` next to the action argument's type, so no icon appears when this message box is displayed. Close the help screen when you are done with it.

Figure 3.3

The help screen for the *MsgBox* action.

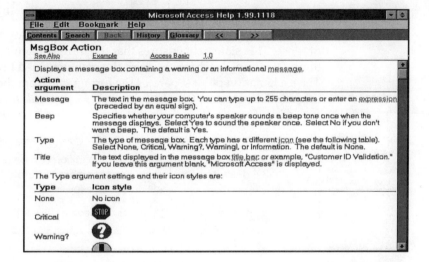

6. Click the `StopMacro` action. No arguments are available for `StopMacro` because the macro just stops dead in its tracks and lets the user do something else. This action stops the macro if the Suppliers ID field is empty; otherwise, the remaining macro actions execute.

> **Caution:** You don't need a `StopMacro` action at the end of a macro because Access knows when the end of a macro is reached. `StopMacro` is almost always used in a conditional macro to stop the macro early if a certain condition is met.

7. Click the OpenForm macro. The OpenForm macro opens a form in one of several views. (Table 2.1 in Chapter 2 gives a brief description of each of the actions in case you need a handy reference to the actions.)

Think for a moment what is needed when you open a form. You have to tell Access which form to open, the view you want to look at, and possibly some kind of query so that a selected group of records or fields appear on the form. The OpenForm's action arguments at the bottom of the screen enable you to dictate all these argument values. The Product List form is opened in datasheet view. No filter is applied, but a condition must be met before a record is reproduced on the form. Here is the condition shown for this action:

```
[Supplier ID] = Forms![Suppliers]![Supplier ID]
```

This seemingly complex statement only looks complex, but it makes a lot of sense. This statement ensures that the form containing this macro, the Suppliers form, synchronizes with the newly opened Products List form. The exclamation point separates the form name from the field name. In English, this statement says: *"Select only those records from the Product List form whose Supplier ID matches that of the Supplier ID on the Suppliers form."*

> **Tip:** Even when explained, this Where condition can be confusing. Figure 3.4 describes the parts of this statement in more detail. The format of these kinds of Where conditions is as follows:
>
> ```
> [controlName]=Forms![formName]![controlName]
> ```

Figure 3.4

Picking apart the Where condition.

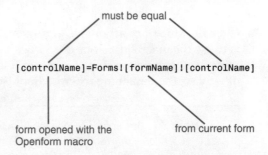

In one sense, relating two forms together with a macro's Where condition is just like creating a relation between two tables. The relation keeps the tables in synch when you want to query data from both of them, and the Where condition keeps two forms in synch when you want to display a second form based on an underlying form's value.

8. Click on the MoveSize action. MoveSize specifies the exact placement of the form just opened and places the Products List form in the lower-right corner of the Suppliers form window.

9. Close the form and return to the database window in preparation for the next section.

You've now followed the details of one of the most complex macros possible, and yet you probably found that there was little exceedingly difficult about it once you saw the pieces broken down.

A Form's Macros in Action

Before you learn how to create a macro in a form, review an existing form that contains several working macros, all connected to buttons on the form. After you watch some macros respond to the user's pressing of form buttons, you look at the form's definition to see how your macros execute "behind the scenes."

Example

Here you have a chance to run the macro you just followed in the preceding section.

1. Open the NWIND.MDB database if it is not already open. Click the Form button and highlight the Suppliers form. Press Enter or choose the Open button. Access opens the Suppliers form and displays the data-entry form shown in Figure 3.5. The primary focus of this discussion is the form's use of command buttons linked to macros inside the form.

2. Find all 29 command buttons on the form. They include the 26 letters at the bottom of the screen.

3. Click the Review Products command button. You see a Product List window open in the lower-right corner of the screen. By clicking the command button, you execute a macro linked to that button. You now see the execution of the same conditional macro (the Review Products macro) that you learned about in the preceding section. As you click the Review Products button, look back at the macro's actions described earlier to see how they execute.

Figure 3.5

A form with command buttons linked to macros.

Command buttons

Command button   Command button

> **Note:** End-users of the database may not know enough to run macros from the database window, but they can learn to click command buttons easily enough.

The Product List's suppliers are all from Supplier number 1 because the Suppliers Supplier ID field shows a 1. If you close the Products List window and type a different Supplier ID on the Suppliers form and then click the Review Products form a second time, the listed products match the new Supplier ID.

4. Close the Products List window by double-clicking its window Control button (or press Ctrl+F4).

5. Click the Add Products command button to see the Add Products form open on-screen. This form contains four macro-linked command buttons of its own labeled Next, Print, Clear, and Close. For this example, don't add any new products.

6. Close the Add Products form by clicking the Close command button. If Access displays a warning message box, click the OK button to ignore the warning.

> **Tip:** Although you're not yet looking at the internals of these forms' macros, what macro action do you think just ran when you clicked the Close command button? The `Close` action would be a pretty good guess! As you use example forms, think about what must be happening beneath the form and try to determine which actions the macros must be performing. That way, you learn the macro actions faster (refer to Table 2.1 in Chapter 2).

7. Click some of the letter command buttons at the bottom of the form. Try clicking the C button and then the R button to list suppliers whose names begin with those letters. There is not a supplier name for every letter of the alphabet. Click the Q button to see that there is no supplier whose company name begins with Q. Once you are done, keep the form on-screen for the next section.

Looking under the Hood

You have learned all but the final step in adding macros to your forms. So far, you've seen the following:

♦ The 47 actions available for macros

♦ How to write conditional macros containing actions that may or may not execute

♦ How to execute macros that are linked to command buttons on forms

The final step is to see how to actually link the command button on a form with the macro you want executed when the user clicks the button.

The following examples examine the contents of the Suppliers form macros that you used in the preceding example.

Example

1. Click the Design view tool button (the leftmost tool on the toolbar above the Suppliers form). The screen changes to the design view, so that you can see the definition of the form.

2. Double-click the Review Products button. Doing so opens up the Command Button window shown in Figure 3.6.

Figure 3.6.

Looking at the Command Button window for the Review products button.

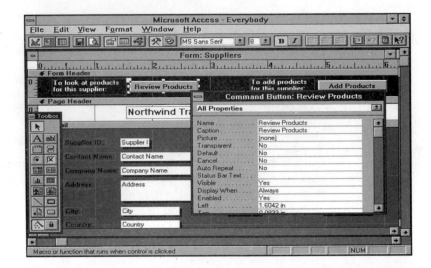

3. Scroll the window's contents until you see On Click.

4. The Command Button property you're interested in here is the On Key Up property. (If you look to the right of the On Click property, you may see Review Products in the box. Review Products is the name of the macro you looked at earlier in this chapter and executed in the preceding section.) Linking a macro to a command button simply requires that you type the macro's name in the On Key Up property of the button.

Note: It is a coincidence that the Review Products button runs a macro named Review Products. Although keeping the same names helps you remember what goes where, the command button could have a Control Name, Control Caption, and On Click macro with entirely different names rather than the same three names.

Tip: You can attach macros to command buttons (sometimes called *push buttons*) on a form by dragging the desired macro name from the database container onto the form; this process automatically creates a command button with the macro name for its caption.

5. Close the Command Button window and double-click the Add Products button to see that the Add Products macro executes for this button.

6. Close the Add Products button window and scroll down the screen until the form's footer section appears. Double-click some of the letter buttons as well as the All button to see that almost the same-named macro, `Filter letter`, executes, where `letter` is a letter from A to Z or `Show All` for the last button.

> **Tip:** If you need to widen the window to see the entire width of the Command Button properties, drag the left side a bit more to the left.

7. Close the Command Button window and close the entire Suppliers form to return to the database window.

> **Caution:** If Access displays a dialog box asking if you want to save changes to your form, choose No. You might have accidentally moved a command button or changed a property. Refusing the dialog box's request to save the form keeps the original sample database intact.

Reporting with Macros

Once you master forms with macros, using macros with reports is a cinch. You can add a macro that asks for a certain range of names to print, tells the user how many pages will print, or whatever else your application demands. Generally, macros respond to reporting events at three times:

♦ When the report is first opened to print

♦ When the report is closed after printing

♦ When a line (whether a detail footer or header) is formatted for printing (using the OnFormat property) but before the actual printing occurs

When designing your reports, you can add a macro to the opening or closing of a report by choosing **V**iew Properties from the report's design menu and adding a macro to the On Open and On Close properties. To add a macro to one of the sections in the report, double-click on that section's title bar.

Example

This example creates a macro that executes when a report prints.

1. Click the Reports button and select the design view for the Sales by Year report.

2. Click the sixth toolbar button to display the View Properties dialog box. Scroll to the OnOpen property. You see that the Open Dialog macro executes when the report is opened for printing, and the Close Dialog macro executes when the report is closed after printing. Both of these macros belong to the group named Print Sales by Year.

> **Note:** A *macro group* is a collection of related macros. When you want to execute a macro in a group, specify the group name followed by a period followed by the specific macro you want to execute, as done here with the specifyers `Print Sales By Year.Open Dialog` and `Print Sales By Year.Close Dialog` commands.

3. Close the Report properties dialog box.

4. Double-click the Page Header title bar. Macros can execute two times while a report prints: either while the report is being formatted to print or while the report is actually printing (or being previewed). The Page Header runs a macro named Format from the Hide Page Header macro group when the header is formatted. No macro runs when the header is actually printed because the On Print property is left blank.

5. Close the report's definition to return to the database window.

Summary

Now you've seen just about everything there is to see about the creation and use of macros. In this chapter you learned that you can link a macro to a form or report easily. Most database macros execute as a result of a command button being pushed on a form.

This book delves so deeply into macros and their uses because you can use an Access Basic program just about everywhere you can use a macro. In place of running macros, each of this chapter's macros could have been an Access Basic program. Before you dive directly into Access Basic, it is very important to make sure that you understand how and when Access Basic programs execute. Starting with macros is easiest because they are already built into Access. Now that you've concluded the first part of *Access 2 Programming By Example,* you can concentrate on the Access Basic specifics, moving away from the overall usage of Access and getting into individual commands. You now know the context of how those programs are used in an Access form or report because you understand macros so well.

Review Questions

Answers to review questions are in Appendix B.

1. What is a conditional macro?

2. What is a macro group?

3. How many return values can a function return?

4. What is meant by a function argument? Give an example of one.

5. When would you use a macro group?

6. What are the events that can trigger a report macro?

7. How are the period and exclamation point used with macros?

8. Describe how a macro is linked to a command button.

9. How does the Where condition synchronize two forms?

10. TRUE or FALSE: The StopMacro action is needed at the end of each macro. Explain why you answer the way you do.

Review Exercises

1. Without looking through your Access reference manual, what do you think the following function returns?

```
Left("Jim Joe Bob", 3)
```

2. Open the Print Sales by Year macro group and study its contents. Try to figure out how these macros help the Sales by Year report do its job. (This macro group is used by the Sales by Year report you studied in this chapter's last example.)

3. To the Suppliers form, add two extra command buttons that are labeled A-N and O-Z. You can add them beneath the existing alphabetic letters. Write two macros that execute when these buttons are pushed. The macros should display the companies in the first half and last half of the alphabet according to the buttOn Key Uped.

Part II

Getting a Feel for Programming

CHAPTER 4

Working with Modules

You are ready to jump on the true Access Basic bandwagon. The macro review from the preceding chapters should come in handy throughout this book because you can make many analogies between Access Basic programs and macros. But, as mentioned in Chapter 1, you might see only parts of the picture for a while.

Unlike many programming languages, Access Basic is difficult to teach sequentially. That means it is difficult to teach you an introductory concept, then build upon that concept, and then build upon the second, creating a nice and neat hierarchy of knowledge. You have to learn some things about Access Basic and then put them aside for a while until you learn other things that seem totally unrelated. In the long run, you will see the big picture, but you can expect a piecemeal approach for a while.

This chapter describes some of the Access interfaces that you need to understand before you look at Access Basic code specifics. Here you use the sixth database window button, labeled *Module*, probably for the first time in your Access career.

This chapter introduces the following topics:

♦ Using the Module button

♦ The programming environment of Access Basic

♦ Using the editor

You use *modules* for everything you do in Access Basic.

> **Tip:** If you've written a program in other programming languages, you will find that a module in Access Basic is just like a program in other languages.

Looking at a Module

Open the NWIND database if it is not already open. The sixth button, Module, is the starting point for writing your own Access Basic programs.

> **Caution:** Be sure that you are familiar with the following Access objects before spending a lot of time with Access Basic: tables, queries, forms, reports, and macros.

Example

Before creating an Access Basic module, you should become familiar with an existing one that comes with Access Basic. You might not understand everything going on in this example at this time, but that's okay.

1. Click the Module button. You see the list of modules open in the list at the right. The NWIND database comes with only a single module named Utility Functions.

2. Click the Design button. A module definition window like the one shown in Figure 4.1 opens.

> **Note:** As you know, if you click the database window's Table button and choose **D**esign, you see a table definition screen (called the *table design view*). If you click the database window's Form button and select **D**esign, you see a form definition screen (called the *form design view*). See a pattern here? Even though the module definition window shown in Figure 4.1 seems very different from the definition design views you have seen, the module definition window is where you define a module.

Describing the Module Window

Because the module window is so different from the other definition windows, take a few moments to learn the parts of the window and get a feel for its interface. Understanding the Access Basic code that appears is not critical at this time, so hang loose and get familiar with the window.

The biggest part of the module window, the white pane that takes the most space, is where you enter your Access Basic programs, just as a word processor contains a large blank area where you can enter text. The next example walks you through some of the fundamental elements of the module definition window.

Example

1. Look at Figure 4.1, which illustrates all the parts of the module screen.

Figure 4.1

Examining the module definition window.

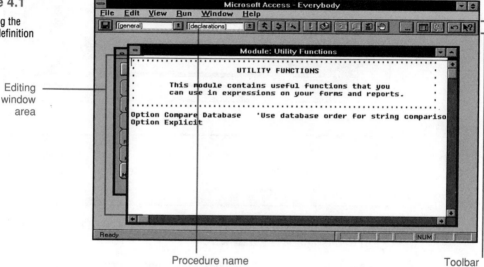

2. You learn that a module contains many pieces called *procedures*. The procedure shown in Figure 4.2 does not do much work, but it is complete.

> **Note:** A module is like a box that contains many parts. You can look at only one part (procedure) at a time.

To see that the procedure on-screen is just one of several, select **F**ile Print Preview. Access displays a preview of what the entire listing of the printed module looks like (see Figure 4.2). Look around the preview and zoom in (with the magnifying glass pointer) to the sections that you want to view more closely. Before you finish this book, you'll be familiar with the entire module.

Figure 4.2

Viewing the entire
module from **F**ile
Print Preview.

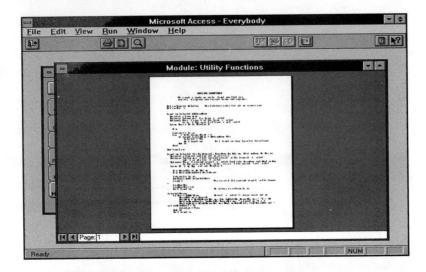

> **Tip:** To see a printed listing of all the procedures in the Utility Functions module, select **F**ile **P**rint. Don't forget to make sure your printer is turned on and has paper.

3. Close the preview window when you are done with it by choosing Close to return to the database window.

4. To see a different procedure, click the Previous Procedure or Next Procedure toolbar buttons. Click the Previous Procedure button a couple of times. Access displays a different procedure within the module. If you click the Next Procedure button twice, you're back to where you began. Click ahead on the Next Procedure button a couple of times and then back again.

> **Note:** Although the procedures follow one another when viewed or printed, Access treats them like a card file with one procedure per card. As you click Previous Procedure and Next Procedure, Access flips to the previous or next card.

The very first screen you saw when you opened the module window was the declarations section. For now, don't worry about what *declarations section* means. However, remember that the declarations section is always considered the first procedure in a module. (This procedure was listed at the top of the preview you printed in step 2.) Therefore, when you click the Previous Procedure button while viewing the declarations section, there really is no previous procedure. Access is wrapping around the bottom of the module, showing you the last procedure in the module.

> **Tip:** Using Ctrl+up arrow and Ctrl+down arrow or PgUp and PgDn also takes you back and forth between procedures.

5. Procedures have names. The declarations section is always called the *declarations section,* but each of the other procedures is assigned a name by the programmer when he or she writes the module.

Rather than clicking the Previous Procedure and Next Procedure buttons, you can move quickly to the exact procedure you want to see by clicking and selecting the Procedure list box. When you click the down arrow of the Procedure box, Access displays a scrolling list of every procedure in the module (see Figure 4.3). Select IsLocked to see that procedure's code in the module window.

Figure 4.3

Displaying a list of procedures to view.

6. Because the IsLocked procedure is longer than the window size (even after maximizing the window), use the scrolling elevator bar on the right side of the code to scroll the rest of the procedure into view.

Using the horizontal scroll bar, you can see the right side of long lines, if there are any in the procedure.

> **Caution:** When you write module code in the future, remember the extra work needed to use these scroll bars. If you keep your procedures short and each line contains fewer than 70 characters, you won't have as much work when viewing them later (and your procedures will be easier to test as well). Unfortunately, you cannot break a long statement in the middle (as you can in many other languages) so it continues on the next line. Therefore, you can have some rather long Access Basic statements. If you can keep the lines short (so they fit within a single screen's view), you can read them more easily.

7. Return to the declarations module so that you're ready for the next example.

Working with the Editing Window

The procedure code window pane shown in the middle of the module definition window is where you create Access Basic programs that you write. Access contains a simple *text editor* (a text editor is like a simple word processing program without the word-wrapping capabilities). You have several ways to edit text in the text editor, and the following example explains how.

Example

Although Microsoft Access may never replace Microsoft Word or others as your choice for word processing capabilities, Access does contain enough editing commands to enable you to add and change the programs that you write. The following example modifies one of the procedures in the Utility Functions module, so you see by example how to enter and modify your own.

1. Find and display the IsLocked procedure's code by selecting it from the Procedure list as you did in the previous example.

2. Press the down-arrow key once to move the cursor to the second line in the module (the line that begins with ' Accepts:).

3. Type the letters **abc**. As you type, the text to the right of the new letters shifts over. Access begins in *insert* mode, which means all letters shift right if you type letters in front of them.

4. Pressing the Insert (or Ins on some keyboards) key turns on *overtype* mode. Press Insert now and type **def**. As you type, def replaces three letters.

As with most Windows applications, especially word processing programs, the Insert key switches between insert mode and overtype mode every time you press Insert.

> **Tip:** The shape of the cursor tells you whether you are in insert mode or overtype mode. When in insert mode, the cursor is a vertical bar, but when in overtype mode, the cursor is a small box. In addition, the word OVR appears at the bottom of the screen while in overtype mode.

5. Back up the cursor over the a that you typed. Press Delete (or Del on some keyboards). The letters under the cursor disappear, and the text to the right shifts over to fill in the deleted letters.

6. Practice editing by putting the line you changed back to its original state. Here is how the line should read:

```
'      Accepts: a dynaset and two string variables
```

7. You can copy, cut, and paste text between an Access Basic module and the Windows Clipboard. Select text by clicking and dragging or by pressing the Shift+arrow keys. Figure 4.4 shows five lines of text selected.

Figure 4.4

Selecting five lines of text.

Selected text ⎯

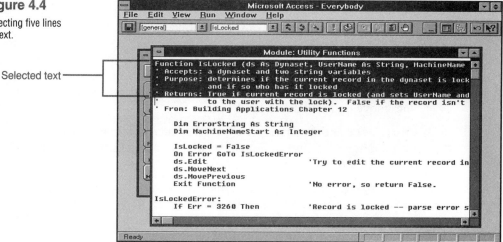

8. Cut the text to the clipboard by pressing Ctrl+X. Ctrl+X is the shortcut key for **Edit Cut**. The text disappears and moves to the Windows clipboard (an area of memory that Windows manages), where the text stays until you replace it with other text.

> **Caution:** Do not press the Delete key to cut text to the Clipboard! Delete is the shortcut key for Edit Delete. When you delete text with Edit Delete, Access deletes the text without saving it to the clipboard. The only way to get deleted text back is to type it in again.

9. When you press Ctrl+V, Access puts the cut text from the clipboard right back in place. Ctrl+V is the shortcut key for **Edit Paste**. The cut-and-paste feature makes moving text from one location to another easy.

> **Tip:** If you want to copy the same text several times throughout a program, press Ctrl+C (the shortcut key for **E**dit **C**opy) rather than Ctrl+X. When you copy text to the clipboard, the text remains in place in the module, and a copy of the text is sent to the Windows Clipboard.

Example

Some additional text-editing features of Access are useful to know but not required. Given what you now know about the Access Basic editor, you can maintain any program that you may ever write. Nevertheless, the more editing features that you learn about, the more effective an Access Basic programmer you will be.

1. Move the text cursor to the start of the following line:

```
On Error GoTo IsLocked
```

2. Press Ctrl+Y, and the line disappears. Every time you press this key combination, you delete a line of text. When you delete a line, the other lines move up to fill in the deleted line.

3. Press Ctrl+Z and watch closely. Ctrl+Z is the shortcut for the **Edit Undo** menu option. The **Undo** command undoes your last edit, which in this case is the deletion of the line.

4. Press Ctrl+N. Pressing this key combination opens a blank line into which you can insert new text. When you press Enter, you see another way to insert blank lines. An Enter keypress always inserts a blank line as long as the insert mode is active.

5. You can search and replace text using the Edit menu. To look for the words `Dim cur`, choose **Edit Find...** and Access displays the Find dialog box shown in Figure 4.5. Type the words **Dim cur**, but don't press Enter yet. As long as you leave the Search buttons on Current **Module**, Access looks only through the current module for the search text. Because this database has only one module (named Utility Functions), the option doesn't do much here. (Leave the Current **M**odule active for this example.)

Figure 4.5

Getting ready to search for text using the Find dialog box.

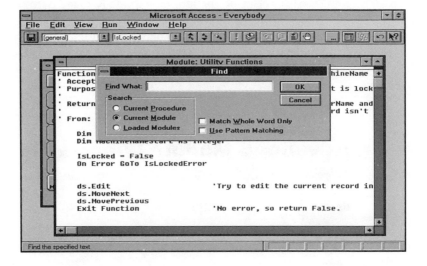

If you select Match **W**hole Word Only, for example, Access displays a successful find only if it finds `Dim cur` but not `Dim currChar`. (For now, don't worry about the meanings of these cryptic word searches.) You also can select **U**se Pattern Matching to search for wildcards in your text. Although several wildcards are available in Access, the * and ? work just like their DOS counterparts. (`a?c` finds `abc`, `acc`, `a4c`, and so on, and `a*c` finds `ac`, `aac`, `aaac`, `a4433c`, `akdkenreocncc`, and so on.) For this example, leave these options alone.

6. Press Enter or click OK to begin the search. Access begins the search and finds the text `Dim cur` in the `Proper` procedure. (The search would be limited just to the `IsLocked` procedure if you had selected Current **P**rocedure in the Edit Find... dialog box.)

> **Tip:** If you're searching for text that occurs multiple times throughout a module, press F3 to repeat the last search. F3 is the shortcut key for the Edit Find Next menu option. Shift+F3 (shortcut for Edit Find Previous) searches backwards from the cursor's position in the module looking for the search text. The `Dim cur` text happens to appear only once in this module.

7. Press Ctrl+up arrow to return to the IsLocked procedure.

8. Replacing text is almost as easy as finding text. Choose **Edit Replace...** to display the Replace dialog box. Next to the **Find** What prompt, you type the text to search for, and next to the **Replace** With prompt, you type the text with which you replace the found text. Choosing the **Verify** button makes Access query you when it finds the text to replace so that you can make sure you really want to replace the found text. The **Replace** All button instructs Access to replace every occurrence of the text without asking your permission at each replacement. For now, select Cancel to leave the Utility Functions module as is.

Advanced Module Window Control

There are additional ways you can control the editing window to make your editing even easier. One of the most powerful features of the Access module text editor is its multiwindow capability.

Example

Suppose you want to look at one procedure while typing another. You can jump back and forth between the procedures, but opening a second editing window makes things even easier.

> **Note:** In the editor's multiple windows, you can look at two views of the same procedure, two procedures from the same module, or two procedures from different modules.

1. With the IsLocked procedure displayed, choose **View Split Window**. Access opens a second editing window. The declarations section appears in the top window, and the IsLocked window appears below, as shown in Figure 4.6.

2. Pressing the F6 key sends the cursor from one window to the next. Press F6 a few times to watch the cursor move between windows. (You also can move the cursor to either window by clicking with the mouse.)

3. Move the cursor to the top window and press F2. F2 is the shortcut key for the **View Procedures** menu option. You then see a dialog box from which you can select a module and a procedure within the module. Because the NWIND database contains only a single module, you see only a single module name at the top of the dialog box.

Figure 4.6

Editing two
procedures
at once.

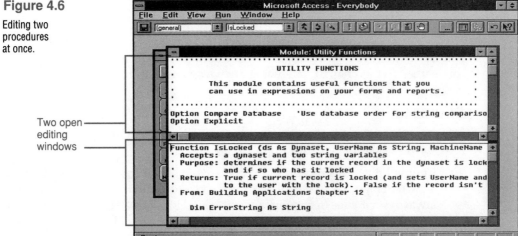

Two open
editing
windows

4. Select the NullToZero procedure. Access shows the NullToZero procedure in the upper window, and the IsLocked procedure is still in the lower window. If you want, you can cut and paste between the two windows.

> **Note:** Each window is separate with its own set of scroll bars that scroll independently of the other window.

5. Close the newly opened window (the top one) by selecting **V**iew Split Window again. The top window goes away, and the IsLocked window now fills the screen as before.

6. Click the Split Bar and drag it down to the center of the IsLocked window. The Split Bar is the thin horizontal line right above the first line in the procedure and just below the title bar.

7. Release the Split Bar. Then you see the two procedures again, and NullToZero is back in the top window. Using the mouse to display two windows often is faster than going through the View menu. To remove the top window by using the mouse, drag the Split Bar underneath the title bar again and release the mouse button.

Adding Your Own Procedures and Modules

You can create your own procedures and modules easily by using the information you learned in this chapter. Following are two examples.

Example

This example adds a new procedure to the Utility Functions module still open on your Access desktop.

1. Choose Edit New Procedure... to display the New Procedure dialog box shown in Figure 4.7. Access asks for the type of procedure (procedures are always either subs or functions as explained in Chapter 1) that you want to add. For this example, leave Function selected. Access also needs to know what you want to name the new procedure.

Figure 4.7

Adding your own procedure using the New Procedure dialog box.

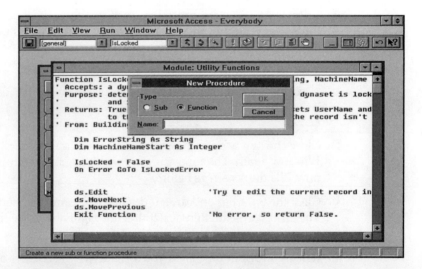

2. Type **MyProc** next to the Name prompt and press Enter. Access opens a new editing window and adds the first and last line needed in every function. (If you tell Access to add a Sub, Access automatically displays the first and last line needed in all sub procedures.)

> **Tip:** You also may add functions and sub procedures by simply typing Function *name* or Sub *name* in a module.

3. Don't type any text. If you do, without knowing Access Basic, you could easily mess up the sample database. (If you want to practice, go ahead but don't save the module when you close it in the next step.)

4. Close the module by pressing Ctrl+F4. If Access asks if you want to save your changes, select **No** and Access returns to the database window.

Example

To create a new module (as opposed to a new procedure inside an existing module), you use the familiar database window where you begin creating everything in Access.

1. Click the Module button in the database window if it is not already active.

2. Choose the **New** button. Access opens the module's declarations section (remember that all modules require a declarations section). You now can add to the declarations section or add a new procedure using the steps you learned in the preceding example. For now, don't add a procedure. Not knowing Access Basic makes adding code difficult.

3. Close the newly created module. If you did not type anything in the module's declarations section and if you didn't create a new procedure for the module, Access does not save anything. If you typed something, choose **No** when Access requests if you want to save the new module.

Summary

This chapter took you on a thorough tour of the Access Basic text editor. If you have used a word processing program, you can use the Access Basic text editor. In this chapter you learned how to edit and create modules and procedures within those modules.

The editing power of Access Basic probably is more than you ever need, but that's good. It's better to have extra power than not enough. The multiple window views, cut and paste capabilities, and function selection ability become second nature as you progress through the rest of *Access 2 Programming By Example.*

The following chapter takes you on a short trip into Access Basic's on-line help. As an Access developer, you've no doubt already used the on-line help. The next chapter explains some help topics that are specific to Access Basic programmers.

Review Questions

Answers to review questions are in Appendix B.

1. How do you begin editing or creating a module?

2. TRUE or FALSE: You can add new modules to an existing procedure.

3. After you look at one procedure's code in a module, what are two ways to look at a different procedure?

4. TRUE or FALSE: When you look at two procedure windows at one time, if you scroll the top window, the bottom one scrolls also.

5. What does the Split Bar do?

6. What are two ways to move the cursor between windows in a multiwindow procedure display?

Review Exercises

1. Open the Utility Functions module and determine which procedure contains the following line:

```
Mid(theString, ptr, 1) = LCase(currChar)
```

2. After you find the procedure in the preceding exercise, insert the following lines before the one mentioned in Exercise 1:

```
' I am getting used to this editor
' I'll practice 'til I'm blue
' Because I want to be an Access Master
' And makes lots of money too!
```

3. Create a new module and add a function procedure named NullToZero. Copy the code from the NullToZero procedure into the Utility Functions module. Then save the new module under the name mymod. (*Hint:* Display the modules at the same time using a multiple editing window.)

CHAPTER 5

Getting Help while Programming

Learning all the ins and outs of every Access Basic command is difficult. You are no doubt already familiar with the help system inside Access. When you write Access Basic programs, however, some particular ways to get help are not available or needed during regular non-programming Access development.

This chapter explores some of the ways that you can use the on-line help system to assist and accent your programming talents. You should take the time to read through this chapter's descriptions and do this chapter's examples even if you're a seasoned Access on-line help user. You'll see ways to use the on-line help that may come in handy as you learn the programming statements of Access Basic.

This chapter introduces the following topics:

♦ Reviewing the help fundamentals

♦ Searching for help with an Access Basic command or function

♦ Access Basic and the context-sensitive help system

♦ Copying help text into your application

The on-line help system is thorough, and you rarely need the language reference manual that comes with Access once you master the on-line help.

Reviewing Help

Help is always a keystroke away. To get help at any time, you can press F1, select from the Help pull-down menu, or click the help's question mark tool in the upper-right corner of the screen.

> **Note:** You can get to the same help subject in several ways. Some people like to use the keyboard for everything, and some prefer the mouse.

Example

Start Access if it is not already started. Do not open a database. If a database is open (you know because the database window appears on-screen), choose File Close Database to close it.

Even though you are starting with a blank screen, you see the Help menu option and the question mark help tool. Access is waiting to help you get started. Now choose Contents from the Help menu. Access displays an overview of the on-line help system shown in Figure 5.1.

Figure 5.1

The Help Contents screen.

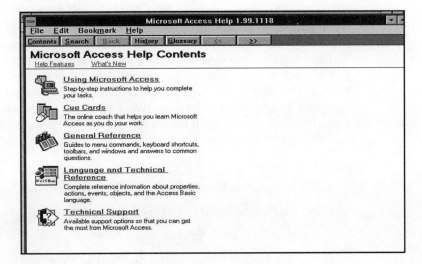

Tip: If you click the Help question mark tool, Access turns the mouse cursor into a question mark pointer. If you point and click (with the question mark pointer) to any command, function, button, menu selection, or other screen element with the question mark tool, Access displays context-sensitive help on that particular topic.

During your previous work with Access, you've probably worked with four of the five help contents topics: Using Microsoft Access (a general introduction to the Access system), Cue Cards (active on-line help that guides you through the steps of different database tasks), General Reference (common questions, keyboard shortcuts, and other general-interest tips), and technical support (describes the support services available to you as a user of Microsoft Access). The Contents help screen describes these four divisions along with the fifth, Language and Technical Reference, which describes the ins and outs of the Access Basic languages as well as other database objects and features.

Caution: Don't confuse Cue cards with the AccessWizards. The Cue cards are a series of help screens that guide you through the development of an object such as a form or report. The AccessWizards (there are two, the FormWizards and the ReportWizards) are more than just help. AccessWizards ask you questions and create forms or reports for you based on your answers.

Access cross-references many help topics.

When you see a help screen, keep the following points in mind: green text indicates a cross-reference of some kind. The Contents help screen contains many cross-references. When you select a cross-referenced topic by clicking it, Access displays help specific to that topic.

Note: When you move the mouse cursor over a cross-referenced topic, the mouse cursor changes to a hand shape with a pointing finger that indicates help is available for that topic.

Example

Click the Language and Technical Reference cross-reference. Access displays the first of many help screens related to the Access language (see Figure 5.2). Now click the Access Basic Data Types topic towards the bottom of the help screen. Notice that some of the cross-referenced topics are underlined with straight lines (such as Integer), and some are underlined with dots (such as type-declaration suffix).

Figure 5.2

Looking at more help topics.

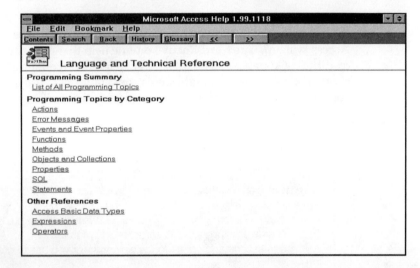

When you select a cross-referenced topic that is underlined with a straight line, Access takes you to a different help screen. Select Integer, for example, and Access shows you a new help screen describing the integer data type.

Now click the **B**ack button to return to the Access Basic Data Types help screen.

A cross-referenced topic that is underlined with dots does not take you to a different help screen. Instead, Access displays a small message box on top of the current help screen with more information about the cross-referenced topic. The new box may contain a definition of the cross-referenced topic or a box of menu selections from which you can choose.

Click the type-declaration suffix cross-reference to see the help menu for that topic. Then press Esc to remove the help message that popped up. Press **B** once more to return to the Language and Technical Reference screen.

Example

One of the most helpful Access Basic help screens is available from the help screen you are now viewing if you completed the preceding example. At the top of the screen, you see the cross-referenced topic List of All Programming Topics. Click this cross-reference, and Access displays the all-important Programming Topics help screen shown in Figure 5.3.

Figure 5.3

The Programming Topics help screen.

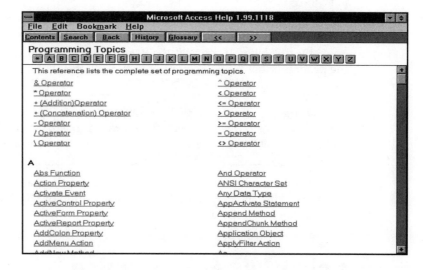

You can find anything on the Programming Topics help screen.

Every single Access Basic command, built-in function, special symbol, and other programming elements are listed on this gigantic control center of a help screen. The cross-references are listed in alphabetical order. To get help on any topic, click the topic's name. Because the topics are numerous, you see only a portion of the topics on a single screen.

> **Note:** Remember that this Programming Topics help screen is available from the **H**elp **C**ontents menu. You'll probably use help from the Programming Topics help screen often.

> **Tip:** You can remove the cross-reference help by clicking **B**ack at the top of the screen, by clicking on the underlying window's background, or by pressing the Esc key.

To get to the rest of the topics, you can click the vertical scroll bar at the right of the screen. Scroll through the topics now to get a feel for the vastness of the help.

> **Tip:** Enlarging a help window to full-screen size helps bring its scroll bar into better focus.

The alphabetic buttons at the top of the screen take you directly to any topic if you know the first letter. If you click the P button, for example, the help system displays the programming topics beginning with the letter *P*.

> **Note:** The asterisk button to the left of the A button goes to the top of the Programming Topics help screen where the special symbols are listed. The A button begins display at the topics that begin with the letter *A*.

As with any help screen, you can remove the Programming Topics screen by double-clicking the help window's Control button or choosing **F**ile **E**xit from the menu at the top of the window.

Help while Programming

Although the Programming Topics help screen and all the other **Help Contents** screens are extremely useful, you don't have time to look around for help when you are in the middle of a program. Suppose, for example, that you want to use a certain Access Basic command, but you forget exactly how you should type the command.

Context-sensitive help is available.

The context-sensitive help throughout Access works also in Access Basic. When you want help with a certain command, move your cursor over that command and click the help toolbar button or press F1. Access Basic looks at the word under the cursor and displays help on that word.

Example

This example shows you how the help system guides you as you program. The nice thing about help (unlike the Cue Card system you used to learn the fundamentals of Access) is that help stays out of your way until you are ready to use it. Follow these steps to watch some of the help system in action:

1. Open the NWIND.MDB database.

2. Click the Module button and choose **D**esign. You see the declarations module in the editing window.

3. Press PgDn to display the IsLoaded function.

4. Move the text cursor over the Dim statement in the middle of the window. It doesn't matter where the cursor is within the word. You can move the text cursor by pointing and clicking or by pressing the arrow keys. You must press F1 to display help. The Dim help screen appears, as shown in Figure 5.4.

Figure 5.4

Getting help with the *Dim* command.

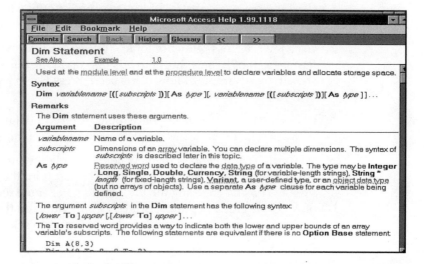

The format of this help screen matches the format of every one of Access Basic's command and built-in function help screens. At the top of the screen is the topic's title, Dim. Because Dim is an Access Basic statement, the word Statement follows Dim. If you look for help on a function or operator, Function or Operator follows the topic's title accordingly.

Note: If there are differences between the printed documentation and the help file, the help file usually is correct because it was updated prior to the release of Access.

After the title comes a brief description of the topic. The *syntax* of the topic is shown next. You learn more about syntax in the next chapter, but for now, think of syntax as the spelling and ordering of a command and its related elements.

Extensive remarks, which sometimes span several screens, follow the syntax section. You can scroll through the remarks by clicking the scroll bar.

Example

Under the Access Basic Dim topic's title, you always see the cross-references See Also, Example and 1.0. Understanding an Access Basic command often requires your looking at related commands and seeing an example of how you might use the command.

1. Click the See Also cross-reference to see a list of five topics related to the Dim command. Then press Esc to remove the box of related topics.

2. Click the 1.0 cross-reference topic. You see Dim information related to the first version of Access, 1.0, help box pop up in the middle of the screen, showing an example of how Dim is used. Press Esc to remove the 1.0 help box.

3. Click the Example cross-reference topic. You see a detailed help box pop up in the middle of the screen, showing an example of how Dim is used.

The buttons at the top of the new help box might seem strange, but they are helpful (at least two of them are). You can print the example directly from the box by choosing the Print button. For some reason, the designers of Access decided to put the printer Setup button on the help screen as well. If your printer is not set up already, you can select Setup to modify the printer's setup.

> **Note:** If you have two printers attached to your computer, you could use one for printed reports or one for mailing labels in your Access Basic application. And by selecting the appropriate printer via the Setup button, you could use the other printer to print the help's example. Maybe the developers of Access knew what they were doing after all when they added the Setup button!

The Copy button is most useful but deserves its own example; that comes next.

Copying Help Code

Use the help screen code.

All throughout the Access Basic help screens are several examples of every command and function. If you want, you can copy help examples from help screens directly into your own program.

Example

To copy help examples into your program, follow these steps:

1. With the example help box still on-screen, click the Copy button. Access displays the Microsoft Access Help Copy dialog box shown in Figure 5.5.

Figure 5.5

Getting ready to copy text from help to the program.

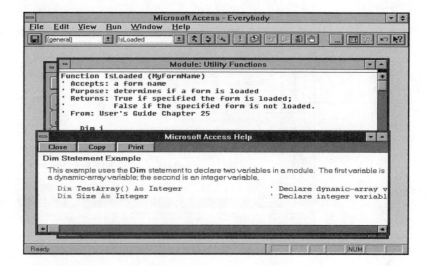

As you can see, the entire example help box appears in the Copy dialog box, but you want to copy only the example code itself. Scroll the vertical scroll bar until you see the two lines that begin with Dim. These lines are the ones that you copy into the module.

2. Highlight the two code lines by clicking and dragging the selection with the mouse. (Keyboard users can use the Shift+arrow keys to select text.)

3. Click the Copy button, and the Copy dialog box goes away.

> **Note:** The text has not yet been sent to the module. The copied text is now on the Windows clipboard.

4. Remove the help screen by choosing **File Exit**. You then see the module's text editor again.

5. Move the cursor so that it rests on the blank line above the Dim statement.

6. Press Ctrl+V (the shortcut key for **Edit Paste**). Almost magically, the example Dim lines are inserted into the program. The module's code is updated to hold the copied text, as shown in Figure 5.6.

Figure 5.6

After copying the example text.

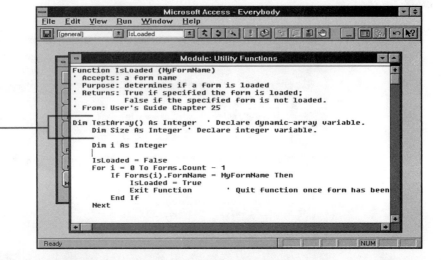

Newly inserted lines from Copy

```
Function IsLoaded (MyFormName)
' Accepts: a form name
' Purpose: determines if a form is loaded
' Returns: True if specified the form is loaded;
'          False if the specified form is not loaded.
' From: User's Guide Chapter 25

Dim TestArray() As Integer   ' Declare dynamic-array variable.
    Dim Size As Integer ' Declare integer variable.

    Dim i As Integer

    IsLoaded = False
    For i = 0 To Forms.Count - 1
        If Forms(i).FormName = MyFormName Then
            IsLoaded = True
            Exit Function          ' Quit function once form has been
        End If
    Next
```

Tip: Often, copying text that is *close* to what you need is faster than typing the text from scratch. Although walking through this example and copying the text takes a while, doing so becomes second nature after only a little practice.

7. Close the module (choose **File Close**) without saving the changes and return to the database window.

Summary

In this chapter you learned that the on-line context-sensitive Access help is extremely helpful for Access Basic programmers. Not only does the Programming Topics screen provide help for every Access Basic command, function, and symbol, but you get help on any command just by pointing with the mouse and pressing F1 while writing code in the text editor.

The Access Basic help screens provide uniform help for all the commands, functions, and symbols in Access Basic, showing you not only the syntax of each topic but also a code example. Using the help's copy feature, you can copy help code directly into your own Access Basic programs instead of having to type the entire line yourself.

In the next chapter you learn how to structure Access Basic programs so that they follow the format required by Access.

Review Questions

Answers to review questions are in Appendix B.

1. List at least three different ways the Access help system can aid you as an Access Basic programmer.

2. What are three ways to display help?

3. How do you know if a help topic is cross-referenced somewhere else?

4. What are the two kinds of cross-references and how do they differ?

5. What does *syntax* mean?

6. TRUE or FALSE: You can print the example code from the help screen.

Review Exercises

1. Find and display the help screen for Opening, Copying, and Saving modules.

2. Look through the Access Basic help screens until you find the syntax and remarks for the Let statement. Return then to the help's Contents screen.

3. Open a new procedure in the Northwind Trader's Utility Functions module. Copy the help code from the following help topics: Type, GoSub, and GoTo. Once you have done so and are happy with the results, close the text editor without saving your changes.

CHAPTER 6

Breaking a Program into Functions and Sub Procedures

An Access Basic program is like a macro. The program is a set of instructions, just like a macro is a set of actions. Your Access Basic instructions are more low level than macro actions, however. But being more low level is an advantage, not a disadvantage. Macro actions behave in the way that the designers of Access intended them to behave. You have no control over the actions other than being able to pass various arguments to some of them.

An Access Basic program is like a powerful macro without its commands set in concrete, as actions are. The commands supplied with Access Basic do little on their own, but when put together into an Access Basic program, you can make them do anything you want.

This chapter introduces the following topics:

♦ Programming terminology

♦ The job of a compiler

♦ How errors can affect your program

♦ The importance of program maintenance

Access Basic instructions require more thought on your part than macros. Because Access Basic instructions are more primitive, you must plan your programs in advance and write them in such a way that makes them easy to maintain and change if needed. This short chapter teaches you the importance of breaking your programs into separate sections so that the sections are more manageable. In one sense, a section of a program is like your own macro action that you write and dictate instead of using one supplied by Access.

> **Tip:** An Access Basic program is like a musical score. The individual notes are primitive and don't do much on their own (just like Access Basic's individual instructions), but you can combine the notes into powerful concertos.

Just a Little More Terminology

Compile your program so Access can run it.

You now know that a program is a set of detailed instructions that do what you want them to do. When Access takes your instructions and follows them, Access is *running,* or *executing,* your program. The program that you write and the program that Access executes, however, are different because Access requires you to send your program through a *compiler* after you write your program. Only after a program is *compiled* can Access really run it.

> **Note:** The program that you write is called the *source program.* A source program is human-readable, not computer-readable.

As you learned in Chapter 1, a computer is nothing more than millions of binary on and off switches of electricity. The complex combination of turning them on and off eventually produces an application such as Access. Sounds incredible, right? Before your program can execute, it must be converted into 1s and 0s, which represent those on and off states of electricity.

A compiler takes your source code (also called a *high-level program* because Access Basic is known as a *high-level,* or human-readable, language) and converts that source into the *low-level* language of compacted commands that Access Basic can work with. Figure 6.1 shows the conversion process.

Figure 6.1

Only a compiled
Access Basic
program can
execute.

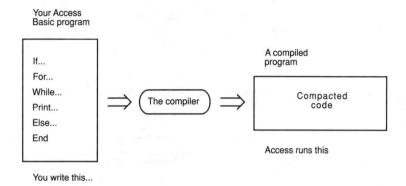

> **Note:** In ancient days of computers (50 years ago), computer programmers actually entered their programs into the computer as 1s and 0s. They flipped a panel of switches that represented on and off binary states of electricity. Using a keyboard and typing English-like Access Basic commands makes your job a lot easier as a programmer! You also can get much more done in less time.

After you write your Access Basic program, you use the pull-down menus on the module's text editor screen to compile the program.

You might wonder how macros work when you don't have to compile them. Unlike Access Basic program instructions, macros don't have to be compiled. Macro actions are already compiled, which is the primary reason you cannot change the work that a specific action does. The actions' source code is not available to you (Microsoft keeps it locked away!).

Your Memory

Throughout this book you'll read a lot about memory. As you probably already know, memory inside your computer is called *RAM* (*random-access memory*). RAM memory is volatile, which means its contents are erased every time you turn off your computer. Therefore, you must save data to the disk drive (which is nonvolatile) when you want to keep that data.

Figure 6.2 shows the contents of your memory when an Access Basic program runs. A great deal is happening between your program and the computer! Of course, the database data that you work with is stored on the disk drive. Access is concerned about writing data to your disks as soon as you enter data into a database. Throughout your Access Basic programs, however, you may often keep some data in memory so that you can make a calculation with the data or print it.

Figure 6.2

The contents of memory with an Access Basic program.

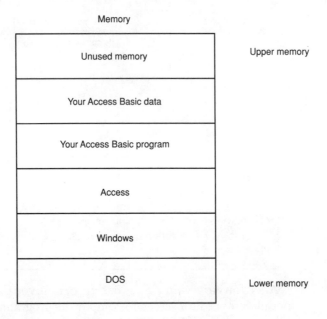

Memory

Unused memory	Upper memory
Your Access Basic data	
Your Access Basic program	
Access	
Windows	
DOS	Lower memory

Example

Figure 6.3 shows an Access Basic program listing with labels that illustrate its parts. The program is in source code form. You know it is source code because you can read the program's instructions. At this point, don't feel that you have to understand any of the program. This section simply gives you an overview of some of the grammar and linguistic aspects of an Access Basic program.

> **Caution:** I suspect that you want to rush into things and start on Access Basic right now. You've sat through five and a half chapters without learning Access Basic! Actually, you've been learning Access Basic from a high-level standpoint throughout this first section. Have patience; you have just a couple more *overview* subjects to deal with before you dive into the language. Too many newcomers to programming drown in specifics and cannot see the forest for the trees. In this book you get the forest first, and the trees (the details) will fill out starting in the next chapter.

Figure 6.3

Looking at the parts of an Access Basic program.

```
Option Compare Database ─────────── Declaration
SubJarProducts ( ) ─
    Dim db As Database, SomeData As Dynaset, criteria
    Set db = CurrentDB( )
    Set SomeData = db.CreateDynaset("Products")
    criteria = "[Quantity Per Unit] Like '*jar*'"
    SomeData.FindFirst criteria
    Do Until SomeData.NoMatch
        Debug.Print SomeData! [Product Name]
        SomeData.FindNext criteria
    Loop
    SomeData.Close
End Sub ─

Function Century (someDate) ─
    If IsDate(someDate)
        Century = ((Year(someDate) - 1) \ 100) + 1
    Else
        Century = Null
    End If
End Function ─
```

Statements

Module

Built-in function

Sub

Function

Programs execute step by step.

Access Basic programs generally execute *sequentially*. That is, the first program instruction executes, and then the second, and so on. Later in this book you learn how to repeat sections of code. You also learn ways to force a program to run out of its normal instruction sequence. Unless you override the normal order, however, a program runs in the order of its statements.

Tip: A computer obeys your commands and in the order you issue them. Therefore, you must be careful and plan ahead before writing a program.

Syntax Grammar 101

Not only does Access Basic follow your instructions' order, but Access Basic follows your instructions' *syntax*. Syntax is the grammar (spelling and linguistics) of Access Basic. Your computer is just a machine. How many people always understand your orders the very first time? But people can think, unlike computers. Your computer's instructions, therefore, must have no syntax mistakes. If you misspell a command, no matter how close to the correct spelling that command is, Access Basic coughs and lets you know that nothing can continue until you fix the problem.

Caution: Access Basic cannot find all your program's errors, just the syntax errors. If you program a *logic error*, that is, an error that is syntactically correct but something that the program just shouldn't do at the time, Access Basic follows those incorrect instructions and produces incorrect results. Access Basic follows your commands blindly, and it does not second guess you and do what you should have programmed.

If you make syntax errors, Access Basic tells you when you compile that program.

As you learned in the early chapters of this book, an Access Basic program is called a module. In Chapter 4, you learned how to use the Access Basic text editor to enter, change, and save your program module. Figure 6.3 shows an entire module and its contents (albeit a small module). A module is broken into procedures that you write. And, as you already know, there are two types of procedures: function procedures and sub procedures; this book often refers to them as functions and subroutines. Figure 6.3 (refer to the preceding figure) contains one of each.

Note: A built-in function is not a function procedure. Built-in functions are supplied by Access Basic, and you learned a little about built-in functions in Chapter 3.

Function procedures can return values.

As with built-in functions, your function procedures can return values, although they do not have to. As a matter of fact, when you write a function procedure that does not return a value, you also could write that same code in a sub procedure. The only difference (other than some syntax) between a function procedure that does not return a value and a sub procedure is that a sub procedure is limited in where it can be called (from other procedures only). On the other hand, you can call a function procedure from forms and other objects from where a sub procedure cannot be called. Therefore, most of this book is concerned with function procedures because they can do everything that sub procedures can do, as well as return values when needed and be called from forms, just as macros can.

Why Divide?

Technically, an Access Basic program, no matter how much it accomplishes, can be one long module with a single long subroutine or a function procedure that you write. You don't have to break a program into separate procedures.

A book does not have to be broken into separate chapters either. Without the chapter divisions, however, the book would grow tedious. Too many pages lumped together gives you the sense of a never-ending story. Despite the writer's best efforts, keeping a reader's attention without some upcoming break is almost impossible.

A program is never finished.

Good programmers break their programs into separate procedures simply because the program is easier to write and maintain. *Program maintenance* is the process of changing and updating a program through the years. The world changes and business changes and so must programs. Companies merge and spin off, and the companies' programmers must update programs accordingly. If you break your program into separate procedures and then you (or someone else) later must change that program, you'll be more able to focus on those changes, and the rest of the program won't get in your way.

Throughout this book you see the term *program maintenance* mentioned often. Building good programs is important for your future. Programming departments across the land are full of programming backlogs with no end in sight. Well-written programs are critical for successful computer systems (and for programmers who want to keep their jobs!).

Summary

In this chapter you learned that programs execute in a step-by-step order. Syntax and logic errors can creep into your code, so you must be careful. Your computer is just a machine and cannot think, unlike people. Because your computer follows your orders exactly, you must be exact. Despite the high-level nature of Access Basic, you are allowed extremely little freedom in the syntax of your programs. So be sure to type command names exactly.

Access Basic programs, called modules, are usually broken into separate procedures, which let you maintain your programs more easily later. You learn all about the procedure divisions throughout this book.

In the next chapter you begin to explore a new concept that you've never seen before in Access. Variables are the storage locations for the Access Basic programs you write, and you learn how to create, name, and use variables in your programs.

Review Questions

Answers to review questions are in Appendix B.

1. What is another name for an Access Basic program?

2. Why must you be careful writing Access Basic programs?

3. What is program maintenance?

4. What is the difference between a function procedure and a built-in procedure?

5. How do good programmers write programs?

6. Why is program maintenance important?

Review Exercises

1. Use Figure 6.3 to answer the following questions:

   A. How many modules are listed?

   B. How many procedures are listed?

   C. How many sub procedures are listed?

   D. How many function procedures are listed?

2. Is the following statement an example of a syntax error or a logic error?

   Wee went two the fare too sea the bares.

3. The following statement has two errors, a syntax error and a logic error. Find both of them.

   There are twwo errorrs in this sentence.

Part III

*Primary Access Basic
Language Elements*

CHAPTER 7

Numeric Variables and Constants

When you learn any new programming language, you should begin with variables; Access is no exception. Variables hold the data that your programs process. Although all of your true database data resides on the disk, that disk data must be brought into memory variables before your programs can do anything with them.

Actually, this chapter explores data in general, not just variables. Unlike beginning programmers of many programming languages, you should have no trouble understanding that data takes on all sorts of shapes and sizes called *data types*. A data type can be an integer, long integer, single-precision, or many other kinds of data types that you have already been assigning to your database fields.

This chapter introduces the following topics:

♦ What variables and constants are

♦ Naming and using numeric variables

♦ The types of numeric variables

♦ The Let assignment statement

♦ The types of numeric constants

This chapter builds on your current knowledge of field data types as much as possible.

Data in General

An Access Basic program takes data and processes it into meaningful results. Within every program are the following:

◆ Commands

◆ Data

Variables change but constants never do.

The data is made up of *variables* and *constants*. Data is also on the disk, but the program itself directly works with data in variables as Figure 7.1 illustrates. As its name implies, a variable is data that can change (or vary) as the program runs. A constant is data that remains the same during a program run.

Figure 7.1

Data from the disk must be brought into variables for Access Basic to do its job.

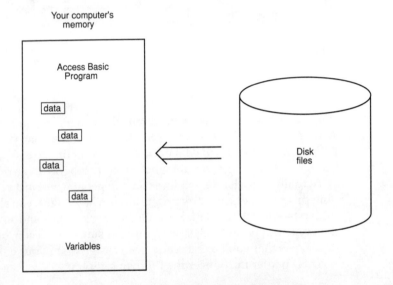

Note: This chapter focuses on numeric variables and numeric constants. If you are not a "numbers person," don't fret. Working with numbers is the computer's job. You have to understand only how to tell the computer what you want it to compute, and the computer does all the math.

Example

Your weight, salary, and address are all values that change over time. Your first name, date of birth, and Social Security number never change. Therefore, your weight, salary, and address are variable data, and your name, date of birth, and Social Security number are constant.

Variables

A *variable* is a place in memory where a data value resides. Think of variables as though they are boxes that hold values in your computer's memory. The value that the variable holds can be a number, a special character, a word, a sentence, or an entire paragraph of text. You can have as many variables as your program needs to hold data that changes due to calculations of the user's input. When you are ready for a variable, you only have to refer to a new one, and Access Basic makes sure you get the variable.

Variables have characteristics similar to, but simpler than, Access table field characteristics that you already know about from your work in Access. Because you are responsible for making up your own variables when you need them, you must understand each of the variable's characteristics so that you can choose one that fits your data. The characteristics of variables are as follows:

♦ Each variable has a name.

♦ Each variable has a data type.

♦ Each variable holds a value.

The following sections explain these characteristics. Again, most of these Access Basic introductory topics should be easy for you because you've seen similar concepts in your Access development already.

Variable Names

An Access Basic program might have many different variables. Each variable must have a different name so that you can tell the variables apart from each other and, more importantly, Access can tell them apart. All variable names must be unique, just like post office boxes have unique addresses.

> **Note:** If Access Basic allowed you to have two variables with the same name, Access would have no way to know which variable you were referring to when you requested the value of one of the variables by its name.

Learn how to name variables.

Variable names can be as short as one letter, or they can be a maximum of 40 characters long. Variable names must begin with a letter of the alphabet; after the initial letter, a variable name can contain letters, numbers, and the underscore character.

Tip: Most Access Basic programmers separate parts of a variable name from each other with a combination of uppercase and lowercase letters.

Note: A variable cannot be the same name as an Access Basic reserved word (a command, built-in function, or property).

Example

The following variable names are valid:

```
Age      index      acct92      acct_92      monthOfBirth
```

Example

Access Basic does not distinguish between upper- and lowercase letters in a variable name. Therefore, all of the following refer to the same variable name:

```
sales94      SALES94      sALES94      Sales94
```

The following names are different from each other because of the underscore in the first variable:

```
Sales_94      Sales94
```

Example

None of the following variable names are valid:

```
94_sales      empl Salary      f%^tqy762      Let
```

94_sales is not valid because a variable name cannot begin with a number. empl_Salary is invalid because a variable name cannot contain spaces. f%^tgy762 is also invalid because of the special characters in the name. Let is an Access Basic command, so it cannot be a variable name.

Tip: Use meaningful variable names. You can call a salary variable pear, but salary is a much better name because its name reflects what the variable is intended for.

Variable Types

As with fields in your database tables, variables have data types. A variable's type determines what type of data that variable can hold. Table 7.1 lists the different numeric data types that Access Basic recognizes.

Table 7.1. Access Basic numeric data types.

Data Type Name	Variable Suffix	Example
Integer	%	4, 0, –9, 423
Long	&	4323434, 994455, –595667
Single	!	4.0, 0.121, –123.46
Double	#	92938849.5433, –212.343948322

Although you probably understand each of these data types from your Access work, the following review might be helpful to shed some focus on the different data types.

An Integer is a number without a decimal place (its content is a whole number). Integers (as all numeric data types) can be negative or positive. Long values can be larger or smaller (more extreme) than regular Integers. Single and Double values are called *real numbers*. They have decimal points and a fractional part to the right of their decimal points. Single-precision values keep accuracy to six decimal places, whereas double-precision values keep accuracy to 14 places.

Data type suffix characters always go at the end of variable names if you use them (and you do for a while in this book). The suffix is not part of the name because variable names cannot contain special characters. If you attach a variable suffix to the end of a variable name, Access Basic automatically knows what data type the variable is. If you do not attach a variable suffix at the end of a variable name, Access Basic might assume other things, as you learn in the next chapter.

> **Caution:** After you first use a data type suffix at the end of a variable name, you must continue using the suffix for the rest of that variable's life. To Access Basic, all of the following are different variable names:
>
>   a#   a%   a!   a&

The data type determines what kind of number the variable can hold. For example, a Long can hold larger integers than an Integer variable. Table 7.2 lists the ranges of values each variable data type can hold. You cannot, for example, store 32,769 in an Integer data type because 32,767 is the largest number that an Integer variable can hold.

Table 7.2. Ranges of each data type.

Data Type	Range of Values
Integer	–32,768 to 32,767
Long	–2,147,483,648 to 2,147,483,647
Single	
Positive numbers	1.401298×10^{-45} to 3.402823×10^{38}
Negative numbers	-3.402823×10^{38} to $-1.401298 \times 10^{-45}$
Double	
Positive numbers	$4.94065645841247 \times 10^{-324}$ to $1.79769313486232 \times 10^{308}$
Negative numbers	$-1.79769313486232 \times 10^{308}$ to $-4.94065645841247 \times 10^{-324}$

Note: The variables described in this chapter are all *numeric* and can hold only numbers. In the next chapter you learn about variables that hold other types of data.

Don't overtype a variable.

In this and other chapters, you learn how to store data in many differently typed variables. Many data types are available because you should match a variable's data type to the data the variable may hold. Therefore, you should not store a person's age in a Long variable because an Integer suffices and is more efficient. Larger precision variables consume more memory and are less efficient to use than short precision variables, so use the shorter data types unless you need the storage available in the longer variables.

Example

The following are single-precision variables because of the ! suffix:

```
a!    totalPayroll!    distance!    sales93!
```

If you calculate atomic weights of chemicals, for instance, you should probably store them in variables whose names end in a # like the following to achieve the most accuracy:

```
co#    oPh#    lBh#    nmAwE#
```

Access Basic Constants

Unlike a variable, a constant value does not change. You used constants when you typed numbers into database fields. The values that you put in variables are constants. The number 57 is always 57, and you cannot change what 57 is. You can change a variable, however, by putting another value into it.

Numeric constants can be positive or negative. Constants have data types and ranges, just as variables do. Table 7.3 shows the types that are available as numeric constants.

Table 7.3. Types of numeric constants.

Data Type	Range
Integer	–32,768 to 32,767
Long	–2,147,483,648 to 2,147,483,647
Single	-3.40×10^{38} to 3.40×10^{38}
Double	-1.79×10^{308} to 1.79×10^{308}

Caution: When you type constant numbers that will be stored in Access Basic variables, do not type the commas in the numbers as you are allowed to do when entering data into numeric fields.

Assigning Values to Variables

Now that you know about variables and constants, you probably wonder how to get values into variables. You simply put values in variables with the *assignment statement*. The format of the assignment statement is

```
[Let] variableName = expression
```

Let is optional.

When you see an Access Basic statement's format and square brackets enclose part of the statement, that part of the statement is optional. Therefore, you don't have to use the Let command when assigning values to variables. Because assigning values to variables is so common in Access Basic, the designers of the language decided to make Let optional.

In the assignment statement, the *variableName* is any valid variable name that you make up. The equal sign is required and must go after the variable name. The *expression* is a value or an expression that equates to a value (you learn more about expressions later). Because a variable holds a value, you can assign one variable to another. The *expression* can also be an object reference such as a field name.

> **Tip:** Think of the equal sign as a left-pointing arrow. Loosely, the equal sign means that you want to take whatever is on the right side of the equal sign and store it in the variable on the left side.

Table 7.4 lists the fundamental Access Basic *operators*. An operator is a symbol or word that performs some operation, usually mathematical, on data. The four operators listed in Table 7.4 work the way you'd expect them to. The expression on the right side of the assignment statement's equal sign can contain math expressions that include these operators. You learn more about the math operators in Chapter 12.

Table 7.4. The fundamental math operators.

Operator	Name	Example
*	Multiplication	3 * 8
/	Division	24 / 6
+	Addition	4 + 6
-	Subtraction	13 - 5

Example

If you want to keep track of your current age, salary, and dependents, you can store these values in three variables and include them in your program. These values might change later in the program, for example, when the program calculates a pay increase due to a Yes/No field being triggered from a table. Good variable names might be age%, salary!, and dependents%. To assign values to these three variables, you might write a program that looks like the following:

```
Let age% = 32
Let salary! = 25000.00
    Let dependents% = 2
```

Example

Because Let is optional, you can rewrite the three assignment statements from the preceding example as follows:

```
age% = 32
salary! = 25000.00
    dependents% = 2
```

Example

To see how to assign one variable to another, suppose you stored your tax rate in a variable earlier in this program, and you decide to use your tax rate for your spouse's tax rate as well. You then can code the following:

```
spouseTaxRate! = taxRate!
```

The value that you assigned to taxRate! would, at this point in the program, be *copied* to a new variable named spouseTaxRate!. The value in taxRate! is still there after this line finishes.

Example

Remember that a variable can hold only one value at a time. Therefore, you cannot put two values in the same variable. For example, the following code assigns mileage% one value, then assigns gallons% a value, and then reassigns mileage% another value. Because a variable holds only one value at a time, the original value of mileage% is replaced in the third line.

```
mileage% = 100
gallons% = 20
    mileage% = 150
```

The capability to change values in variables is important, but this example stretches the rule. You have no good reason to put 100 in mileage% when you don't use mileage% for anything before putting another value in mileage% two lines later. When you use variables in more powerful programs, you will see that you often have to put several values into the same variable you used previously.

Example

The following assignment statements calculate results and store the results in variables:

```
pi# = 3.14159
radius# = 5.0
areaCirc# = pi# * radius#
length! = 29
    doubLength! = length! + length!
```

Note: Access Basic initially stores **0** in all uninitialized numeric variables. If you use a variable before assigning any value to that variable, Access uses the zero in the variable. Although Access Basic initializes all variables to zero, you should assign a zero to any variable that you want to hold a zero. By doing so, you make your intentions clear, and anyone looking at your program knows that you intended for the zero to be there.

Summary

Congratulations! Although you may not see the big picture yet, you have made big progress toward writing your own Access Basic programs. Numeric variables form the fundamental building blocks of the rest of Access Basic. The next chapter shows you nonnumeric variables and explains how to declare variables without needing the data type suffix characters at the end of variable names.

Review Questions

Answers to review questions are in Appendix B.

1. What is a variable?

2. TRUE or FALSE: A variable is more temporary than disk storage.

3. How do variables differ from constants?

4. Which of the following are incorrect variable names?

actPay94!   94actPay!   act Pay94!   act_pay_94!

5. TRUE or FALSE: A variable can be any of the following data types: Integer, Double Integer, Single, or Long.

6. TRUE or FALSE: The following statements are equivalent:

Let a% = 100

and

a% = 100

7. How many values can a variable hold at the same time?

8. TRUE or FALSE: Double variables hold larger values than Single, so always use Double to be safe. Explain your answer.

Review Exercises

1. Write the statements that store your weight (you can fib), height in feet, and shoe size number in three variables. Use the Let statement.

2. Rewrite the statements in the preceding exercise without using Let.

3. Write the statements that store the length of a pool (in feet) in one variable, and the width in another, and the calculated surface area (length times the width) in a third variable.

4. The variable factor! holds a cost-reduction percentage for your company's sales force. Write an assignment statement that reduces factor! by one-half. (*Hint:* You must use the variable factor! on both sides of the equal sign.)

CHAPTER 8

Working with All Data Types

In the preceding chapter you learned about numeric variables and numeric constants. Access Basic supports many other data types, such as Currency and String, that you see in Access table fields. Access does not directly support Date/Time, Yes/No, Text, or Counter (which are Access field data types), but you can simulate them in Access Basic, as this chapter explains.

This chapter also shows you additional ways to *declare* variables. When you declare a variable, you tell Access Basic that you want the variable to take on a certain data type. In the preceding chapter you learned about the data type suffixes, and if you've ever programmed in other versions of the BASIC programming language (such as QBasic or QuickBasic), you may have used the suffixes before. With Access Basic you can use the suffix characters for compatibility, but you also can use additional ways to declare variables that sometimes lend themselves to Access Basic programming better than the suffix characters.

This chapter introduces the following topics:

♦ The String data type

♦ The Currency data type

♦ Access's special field types and Access Basic's equivalents

♦ The Variant data type

♦ The Deftype statement

♦ The Dim statement

♦ Symbolic constants

The String Data Type

A *string* is a group of zero or more characters. You can possibly have empty strings, also called *null strings,* so a string might contain nothing depending on the program's need at the time. A string is like Access's Text data type. Access Basic does not support the Text data type (unlike the database portion of Access), but it does support the String data type, and the two are basically interchangeable.

Note: In Access, empty strings often are called zero-length strings.

The *$* is the *String* data type suffix.

The data type suffix of String variables is the dollar sign, $. Therefore, all of the following are string variables:

```
myName$      company$      address1$      Employee$
```

Note: Strings may consist of numbers such as a Social Security number or a phone number. Never attempt to perform any math with a string, even if that string contains only numeric digits. Reserve strings for any data (letters, digits, or anything else) on which you'll never perform a calculation and keep all other numeric data values in numeric variables.

Example

If you want to keep track of a customer's name, address, city, state, ZIP code, and age in variables, you might make up the following variable names:

```
custName$
custAddress$
custCity$
custSt$
custZip$
custAge%
```

Notice that the customer's age is numeric, so it is stored in an integer numeric variable. Although the ZIP code holds only numeric digits, you don't add two ZIP codes together in this example, and so you store it in a string variable. You might want to calculate an average age of your customers for market research, for example, so you use a numeric variable for the age.

Example

If you want to keep track of an employee's salary, age, name, employee number, and number of dependents, you might use the following variable names:

```
empSalary!
empAge%
empName$
empNumber$
empDependents%
```

You should store only the name and employee number in string variables. You should store the salary, age, and number of dependents in numeric variables.

Storing Data in String Variables

You put data in string variables with the assignment statement, just as you do with numeric data. You can assign either a string constant, another string variable, or a Text field value into a string variable with the assignment statement. The format of the assignment for string variables is

```
[Let] strVariable$ = "String constant"
```

or

```
[Let] strVariable1$ = strVariable2$
```

As with all Let statements, the word Let is optional. Each variable (*strVariable$*, *strVariable1$*, and *strVariable2$*) can be any valid string variable name or Text field name. The equal sign is required. Any string constant or another string variable name can follow the equal sign.

Enclose string
constants in
quotation marks.

Notice that string constants are always enclosed inside quotation marks. The quotation marks are not stored in the string variable; only the data between the quotation marks are stored in string variables.

Example

To keep track of a book's title, author, and edition, you might store the data in three string variables as follows:

```
Let bookTitle$ = "In Pursuit of Life"
bookAuthor$ = "Francis Scott Key"
bookEdition$ = "2nd"
```

> **Note:** Because `Let` is optional, this book does not use `Let` again.

Example

You can assign a string variable's value to another string variable, as the second line in this example demonstrates:

```
empLastName$ = "Johnson"
spouseLastName$ = empLastName$
```

> **Note:** You do more with using field values in assignment statements once you get further into the book.

Example

You can put an empty string (a null string) into a string variable by putting two quotation marks, with no space between them, after the equal sign as in the following:

```
e$ = ""
```

The variable `e$` contains a null string with zero length. Access Basic initializes all string variables to null strings before you use them.

> **Tip:** You might want to start with a null string if you build strings one character at a time—for instance, if you are receiving data sequentially from a modem or building a string based on characters typed one at a time by the user.

> **Caution:** You cannot use the Access Basic reserved word **NULL** to assign string variables to a zero-length string. Instead, use the empty quotation marks.

Example

Even if you store a string of numeric digits in a string variable like the following:

```
num$ = "19"
```

you cannot do math with the variable. If you attempt something like this:

```
ans = 45 + num$
```

Access Basic issues an error message (Type mismatch) because the data type of the num$ variable is not numeric, and you cannot add it to a number.

String Concatenation

You cannot perform math on string variables, even if the string variables contain numbers. You can perform another type of operation on string variables, however: *concatenation*. Concatenation is attaching one string to the end of another or combining two or more strings into a longer string. You can concatenate string variables, string constants, or a combination of both, and assign the concatenated strings to a string variable.

The + concatenates strings.

The string concatenation operator is the plus sign. Access Basic knows not to confuse the concatenation operator with the addition operator because of the operator's context; if it sees string data on either side of the plus sign, Access Basic knows to concatenate the strings. The ampersand (&) also is a string concatenation character. The ampersand does not provide the ambiguity that a plus sign provides, but the plus sign is more common in other dialects of BASIC. Programmers moving to Access Basic from another version of BASIC might be more comfortable with the plus sign.

> **Caution:** String variables can hold strings as long as (approximately) 65,535 characters. If you work with lots of text data, be sure that you don't attempt to concatenate strings that would combine to be more than 65,535 characters in length. Although you probably will never have strings that long, you could if you were manipulating data from a large database. In Chapter 23, "String Functions," you learn about string functions that can help you manage string lengths.

Example

If you store an employee's first name in one string variable and last name in a second string variable, you can store the full name in a third string variable by concatenating the two string variables with a space between them, as follows:

```
firstName$ = "Don"
lastName$ = "Carlos"
fullName$ = firstName$ + " " + lastName$
```

> **Caution:** Without the separating space, the two names print back-to-back.

Example

The default database filename extension is .MDB. Therefore, if you ask the user for a database filename, you can append the needed .MDB extension by concatenating it as follows:

```
fullFile$ = userFileName$ + ".mdb"
```

The Currency Data Type

Currency variables use the @ suffix character.

As with fields, variables can hold fixed-point dollar and cent amounts with the `Currency` data type. `Currency` variables are accurate to four decimal points, although dollar amounts comprise the almost-exclusive use of `Currency` data, so most of your `Currency` variables extend just to two decimal places. The suffix for the `Currency` data type is @. Here is the range of the `Currency` data type:

−922,337,203,685,477.5808 to 922,337,203,685,477.5807

Example

A previous example used a single-precision variable to hold a salary amount. Salaries are always expressed in dollars and cents, so a better name for an employee's salary variable would be

```
empSalary@
```

instead of

```
empSalary!
```

The *Variant* Data Type That's Not a Data Type

The `Variant` is a data type, but it is unlike the other data types you have seen. For veteran programmers in other dialects of BASIC, the `Variant` data type is used but never made as explicit as it is made in Access Basic.

A Variant data type can hold *any* data value of *any* of the following types:

♦ Number

♦ String

♦ Date/Time (just like the field data type)

♦ Null

Table 8.1 lists the ranges of values that the Variant data type variables can hold depending on the kind of data that you assign to them.

Table 8.1. The *Variant* data type ranges and values.

If You Store This	The Variant Range Is
Date/Time	January 1, 100 to December 31, 9999
Numbers	
Positive numbers	$4.94065645841247 \times 10^{-324}$
	to $1.79769313486232 \times 10^{308}$
Negative numbers	$-1.79769313486232 \times 10^{308}$
	to $-4.94065645841247 \times 10^{-324}$
Strings	Any string from 0 to 65,535 characters long

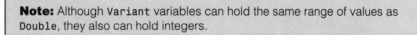

Note: Although Variant variables can hold the same range of values as Double, they also can hold integers.

You specify Variant variables (until you learn a different way later in this chapter) by not using any data type suffix at all. In an Access Basic program, variables that have no data type suffix characters are assumed to be Variant (unless you override the Variant data type with Deftype as described later).

Example

All of the following variable assignments use Variant variables because no data type suffixes are used:

```
a = 1
b = "Hi"
c = #01/02/94#
d = #March 27, 1995#
e = 109.43
f = -123344.543
g = e + f
h = #11:02:12#
```

> **Caution:** Be sure to enclose times and date values within the pound signs as you do in field name criteria; otherwise, Access Basic might assume that the values are strings.

Example

The same Variant variable can hold one data type and then a completely different data type within the same program. Access Basic looks at your assigned data type and converts the Variant variable to that data type at the time. For example, the following code first assigns a string to the variable v and then assigns a number:

```
v = "A string"
v = 433.45
```

Example

Unlike String variables, a Variant variable can hold four kinds of seemingly empty values: 0 (which is considered null for numeric variables); an empty string, " " (which has a string-length of zero); an *Empty* value (which all Variant variables hold until you assign something else to them); and Null (a reserved word in Access Basic that you work with throughout this book).

The variable ev, therefore, holds the data type of Empty (the variable has literally no value—not 0, not " ", and not Null), but after the following statement, the variable holds something else:

```
ev = 0
```

To put an empty string into ev, you do the following:

```
ev = ""
```

To put the Null value into ev, you do this:

```
ev = Null
```

If You Need Another Type...

Many fields have equivalent variable types.

As you have seen, no Access Basic data types correspond to the following Access field data types:

♦ Counter

♦ Date/Time

♦ Memo

♦ OLE Object

♦ Text

♦ Yes/No

You have no way to store the OLE Object and Memo data types in Access Basic variables. In the previous section you saw that the Variant data type holds almost anything. Other variable data types can hold these field values as well (except OLE Object and Memo). You can substitute Access Basic variables for field values as follows (assuming that you aren't using the Variant type):

♦ Store database Counter values in Long variables

♦ Store database Date/Time values in Double variables

♦ Store database Text values in String variables

♦ Store database Yes/No values in Integer variables

> **Note:** Knowing the equivalent data types becomes important when you learn to compare variables to each other and to fields in your database tables. You might have data already in certain variables that you want to compare to fields in a table. You learn all about comparing data in Chapter 16, "Comparing Data with IF."

A Better Way to Declare Variable Data Types

After all this chapter's and the preceding chapter's discussion on data type suffixes, rarely do you, as an Access Basic programmer, use data type suffixes! The reason so much time has been spent is two-fold: The data type suffix characters are part of the language, and you should understand them. Perhaps a more important reason is that many Access Basic programmers have moved to Access Basic from another dialect of BASIC such as QBasic. The data type suffixes, especially the dollar sign on string variable names, are used frequently, and only recently has the BASIC-like programming community been switching to a "suffix-less" mode of variable declaration.

You have two ways to declare variables of specific data types without using the data type suffixes:

◆ Using the `Deftype` statement

◆ Using the `Dim` statement

The following sections address these two methods.

Using *Deftype*

The first letter in a variable name determines the variable's type.

The `Deftype` statement sets the data type for variables so you don't have to use a data type suffix character. The `Deftype` statement determines which variables are specific data types by the first letters in their names. The seven formats of the `Deftype` statement are as follows:

```
DefInt letterRange [, letterRange]
DefLng letterRange [, letterRange]
DefSng letterRange [, letterRange]
DefDbl letterRange [, letterRange]
DefCur letterRange [, letterRange]
DefStr letterRange [, letterRange]
DefVar letterRange [, letterRange]
```

The second half of the `Deftype` statement determines what data type (`Integer`, `Long`, `Single`, `Double`, `Currency`, `String`, or `Variant`) the variables within the `letterRange` are. The `letterRange` is a letter, or two letters separated by a dash, which indicates the starting letter of the variables that should take on that data type.

Although this concept sounds difficult, the following examples demonstrate the `Deftype` statement nicely.

Example

The following statement ensures that every variable whose name begins with *n* in the Access Basic program is of the Integer data type:

```
DefInt n
```

After making this statement, you can never assign a noninteger value to any variable that begins with *n.* The following line is allowed:

```
num = 9
```

But this line is not allowed:

```
name = "Larry"
```

Example

All variables whose names begin with *a, b, c,* and *p* are strings after you make the following statement:

```
DefStr a-c, p
```

Example

Data type suffixes override the Deftype statement. Therefore, the variable salary@ is a Currency variable even though all other variables whose names begin with *s* are integers:

```
DefInt s
salary@ = 542.34
```

Using the *Dim* Statement

Dim stands for *dimension.*

The Dim statement has several uses in Access Basic. One of the locations in which Dim is used most is in variable declarations. Actually, Dim is one of the primary variable data type declaration statements. This statement is used more than either data type suffixes or the Deftype statement. Now that you've seen the other ways to declare variable data types, using Dim is easy.

Following is the format of Dim:

```
Dim variableName [AS type]  [, variableName AS type]
```

> **Note:** Dim has several formats, and you see more of them throughout this book.

In this format, the type can be any one of these data types: Integer, Long, Single, Double, Currency, String, and Variant.

Example

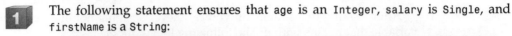

The following statement ensures that age is an Integer, salary is Single, and firstName is a String:

```
Dim age AS Integer
Dim salary AS Single
Dim firstName as String
```

Example

You can declare more than one variable on the same line. The following code is equivalent to the code in the preceding example:

```
Dim age As Integer, salary As Single, firstName As String
```

Example

As with data type suffix characters, variables that you declare with Dim override Deftype statements. In the following two lines of code, the variable salary is a Double data type even though every other variable is a String:

```
DefStr a-z
Dim salary AS Double
```

> **Note:** If you do not declare a variable with a data type suffix character, Deftype, or with Dim, Access Basic assumes the variable is a Variant variable.

> **Caution:** Dim a, b, c As Integer declares a and b as Variant data types and only c as Integer. If you want all three declared as Integers, you must specify each one as follows:
>
> ```
> Dim a As Integer, b As Integer, c As Integer
> ```

Symbolic Constants

Const assigns names to constant data.

If you find yourself repeating the same constant, no matter what the constant's data type is, consider declaring that constant value as a *symbolic constant*. A symbolic constant is just like a constant with a name. Unlike a named variable, however, a symbolic constant cannot be changed at runtime (that's why it's called a *constant*!).

The Const statement assigns names to your program's constants. The format of the Const statement is

```
Const constantName = expression
```

Many Access Basic programmers use uppercase names and underscores for constants, such as MINIMUM_AGE rather than MinimumAge. This distinction from a mixture of case helps you spot variables and constants in a program more easily. Name constants with the same naming rules as variables.

> **Tip:** Declare symbolic constants at the top of a program. If the constant changes, you have to change it in only one place instead of several.

Example

Suppose that a company uses Access to manage its part-time summer high school employees. The minimum age for the high school workers is 16. Rather than using the value 16 throughout a program, you can use the following statement, which appears at the top of the program (in the same area as the variable declarations):

```
Const MINAGE = 16
```

Rather than 16, the program contains several occurrences of minAge. If the minimum age ever increases to 17, you have to change the program in only one place. Therefore, you change the Const statement as follows:

```
Const MINAGE = 17
```

The rest of the program can remain untouched because it uses the symbolic constant MINAGE rather than the value itself.

Example

After the preceding example's Const, you could never use the following line later in that same program:

```
minAge = 18
```

minAge is not a variable, so you cannot change it in the middle of the program.

> **Caution:** Symbolic constants are not variables, so don't try to store data in them.

Summary

You deserve a break! This chapter explained all the various data types available to you in Access Basic. Almost every field data type supported in the Access database system is also supported in Access Basic or an equivalent.

This chapter showed you how to declare variables of many different data types. The primary ways are using data type suffixes at the end of your variable names, the `Deftype` statement, and the `Dim` statement. `Deftype` is more general than the other two because the `Deftype` works on an entire range of variables instead of specific variable names.

If you find yourself using the same constant value in several places in one program, consider naming the constant with the `Const` statement to make the program easier to write and change.

In the next chapter you learn how to print the contents of variables and see how to add descriptive titles before the variables that you print.

Review Questions

Answers to review questions are in Appendix B.

1. What is a string?

2. How do you prepare variables to hold strings?

3. What goes in the `type` part of the `Deftype` statement's format?

4. Within what character must you enclose date and time values before assigning them to a `Date/Time` variable?

5. TRUE or FALSE: A symbolic constant is a variable with a name.

6. What is the data type of the variable `money` after the following statement? What about a variable named `carAllowance`?

   ```
   DefStr g-w
   ```

7. What are the four ways to put null-like values in `Variant` variables?

8. What kind of data can the `Variant` data type hold?

9. Explain why the following is impossible:

```
amount = 25 + "56" + 12
```

Review Exercises

1. Write a statement to store your favorite television show's name in a string variable named `myFav$`.

2. A mathematical Access Basic programmer wants to use a symbolic constant to hold the value of PI rather than typing **3.14159** throughout the program. Write the `Const` statement needed to create a useful symbolic constant.

3. Using `Dim` and then `Deftype` (in a separate section of code), define an integer distance variable, a string pet's name variable, and a double-precision atomic weight variable.

CHAPTER 9

Seeing Your Results

The preceding two chapters began your Access Basic tour, but you haven't seen anything happen yet! Unlike regular programming languages where the language commands are of prime importance, the Access Basic language is one of the *last* elements of Access that you learn. Right out of the gate, an Access beginner starts creating tables and using fancy reports with little effort or knowledge, especially with the help of the Access Wizard technology. Being able to hit the ground running is one of the strengths of Access; having patience while learning Access Basic, however, is more difficult, and you need to see some results of your learning so far.

This chapter focuses on the Access Basic *immediate window*. You can open the immediate window, which displays results of simple Access Basic commands one at a time. You don't even have to compile the Access Basic code as you would have to do if you ran an Access Basic program that contained the same commands. The drawback to using the immediate window is that you cannot run every Access Basic statement there. Of the statements you can run, you see the results of each command immediately after entering it.

This chapter teaches the Access Basic `Print` statement because it is the perfect way to display the contents of variables (and field data, controls, and properties as well) while you are learning Access Basic. Throughout *Access 2 Programming By Example,* you also learn about some debugging uses in the immediate window.

This chapter introduces the following topics:

♦ The `Print` statement

♦ The immediate window

♦ Printing options

The most important lesson you learn in this chapter is how to look at the contents of variables after you store data in them.

Note: Access Basic offers several different uses of the word `Print`: the `Print` statement, `Print #` statement, and `Print` action. The `Print` statement taught in this chapter lets you see variable values so you can get used to using variables.

Looking at *Print*

`Print` sends to the screen whatever is to the right of the word `Print`. The format of `Print` is

```
Print [Spc(n)][Tab(n)] [expression][;][,]
```

The format of `Print` makes it look more intimidating than it really is. The `Spc` and `Tab` portions of `Print` are built-in functions (notice the parentheses with an argument, *n*, inside) and are optional. For the time being, don't worry about `Spc` and `Tab`. The *expression* is any variable, constant, or a combination of both. If you want, you can list more than one variable or constant by separating them with a comma or semicolon, as described later in this chapter.

Tip: The question mark (**?**) is a shortcut for `Print`. Any place you can use `Print`, you can type a question mark instead.

Print can print blank lines.

If you use `Print` on a line by itself, Access Basic prints a blank line. Printing a blank line is a good way to separate lines of screen output from each other.

Before looking at a `Print` example, you need to see how to activate the Access Basic immediate window.

Note: The result from each `Print` is called *output*. Access Basic outputs values based on your `Print` instructions.

The Immediate Window

The immediate window lets you experiment.

The *immediate window* is available only from the module window. Think of the immediate window as a place where you can "try things." In the immediate window, you can assign values to variables and look at the results without compiling a program.

Tip: The immediate window is most helpful when you're trying to debug an Access Basic program. If a program that you write is not behaving in the way you expect, you might try some of the program's statements in the immediate window where you can see the results immediately (that's why it's called the *immediate* window). Using the immediate window, you can see if your expected results coincide with the actual results.

Example

In this example you learn how to open the immediate window. First, open the sample Northwind Traders database if it is not already open and click on the Module button from the database window. Click the **D**esign button. When the module window opens, find the line in the program that reads `Option Explicit`. Then add an apostrophe (') and space before the line so that your screen looks like the one in Figure 9.1.

Figure 9.1

After adding an apostrophe to
Option Explicit.

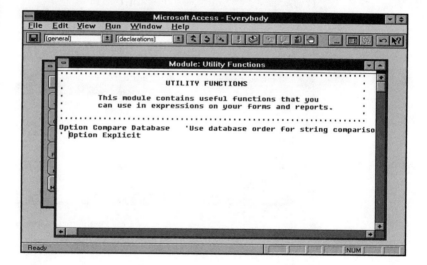

Caution: Don't fret if you don't understand why you're adding the apostrophe; you aren't supposed to understand it at this point! In Chapter 11, "Remarks and Full Program Execution," you learn that you are turning the statement into a *remark*. To look at variables in the immediate window (and to get used to the elementary uses of the `Print` statement), you've got to add the apostrophe before the `Option Explicit` statement; otherwise, Access Basic doesn't enable you to assign values to variables.

You now can open the immediate window. Again, you can open the immediate window *only* from the module window, and you must repeat the apostrophe insertion if you leave the module window and return to it later to use the immediate window. (Don't save the module's program after adding the apostrophe because the program needs the statement to appear without the apostrophe during general use.)

Select View Immediate Window from the pull-down menu. The immediate window opens as shown in Figure 9.2.

> **Tip:** If you want to enlarge the immediate window, drag the window edges to resize them.

Figure 9.2

The newly opened immediate window.

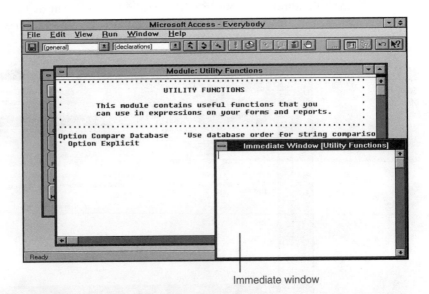

Immediate window

Example

In this example you fill three variables and print their results. First, type the following into the immediate window:

```
age% = 32
salary@ = 25000
emp$ = "Kim Powers"
dependents% = 2
```

> **Caution:** Neither `Dim` nor `Deftype` work in the immediate window, so you must use data type suffix characters to indicate variable data types.

To print the value of a variable, use the `Print` statement. Type the following statements, one at a time, pressing Enter at the end of each one. You'll see that Access Basic prints the value of the variables as you type each statement.

```
Print age%
Print salary@
Print emp$
Print dependents%
```

Now you've written a program! You initialized three variables and printed their results. Your immediate execution window should look like the one in Figure 9.3 when you are done. If something on your screen is different, look back at the lines you typed to make sure you didn't inadvertently change something you shouldn't have changed.

Figure 9.3

After printing the contents of the variables.

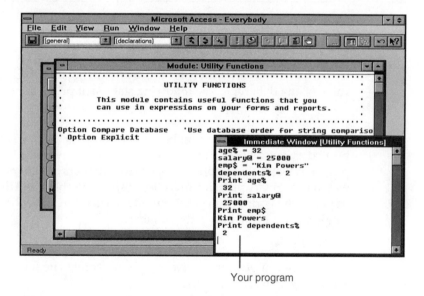

Your program

> **Note:** Don't expect to be overwhelmed by this display. As you enter each line, the immediate window interprets and executes that line. The immediate window is a great introduction and learning tool for Access Basic, and later you'll be glad that you spent some time here.

Example

As an alternative to the preceding example, you could type the following statements, interchanging an assignment with a Print, and achieve the same output:

```
age% = 32
print age%
salary@ = 25000
print salary@
emp$ = "Kim Powers"
Print emp$
dependents% = 2
print dependents%
```

Note: Eventually, you'll get away from the immediate window and include other types of output in your programs. The results will be more meaningful then. Keep in mind that the immediate window is a temporary output display window and works with only one individual Access Basic line at a time.

Printing Constants

Using Print, you can print constants by following the word Print with a constant value of any data type. The following statement prints the number 2:

```
Print 2
```

A blank always follows numbers when you print them, whether the numbers are printed as constants or from variables. A blank may precede a number when you print it. A blank always precedes positive numbers but not negative numbers. In a way, an imaginary plus sign precedes positive numbers, and the negative sign takes its place when printing negative numbers. Therefore, the following statement does *not* produce a blank before the number:

```
Print -15
```

You also can print string constants with Print. The following statement prints Access Programming By Example:

```
Print "Access Programming By Example"
```

Blanks are never printed before or after string constants. The issue of blanks becomes important when you print more than one value per line.

Example

Don't print numbers without descriptions.

The primary reason for using string constants is to label your output. Don't ever print numbers without labeling them. Your Access Basic programs could contain many `Print`s. Rather than simply printing the values of the four variables initialized in the previous example, you should print labels before each one as follows:

```
Print "Age"
Print age%
Print "Salary"
Print salary@
Print "Employee name"
Print emp$
Print "Dependents"
Print dependents%
```

Printing values one at a time in the immediate window seems useless now when run as a single program. These instructions produce the following output with descriptions before each number:

```
Age
 32
Salary
 25000
Employee name
Kim Powers
Print Dependents
 2
```

> **Note:** Notice that blanks do not appear before printed strings.

> **Tip:** If you want to erase the immediate window, select the window's text (by dragging the mouse or using the usual Shift+arrow key combination) and press Del.

Printing More than One Value at a Time

You now know several ways to use `Print`, but you can still do more with this statement. The `Print` statements you've seen so far printed one value per line. You also can print several values on a single line by separating each value with a semicolon or comma. The choice depends on how far apart you want the values printed.

Printing with Semicolons

To print two or more values next to each other, separate the values by using the semicolon in the `Print` statement. When you follow `Print` with values—either variables or constants—and separate those values with semicolons, the semicolons tell Access Basic that you want the values to print right next to each other.

> **Note:** Even when you use semicolons between values, blanks appear before positive values and after all numeric values.

Printing with Commas

To print more than one value separated by several spaces, you might use commas between the values. The comma is helpful in a `Print` statement when you want to print columns of output.

Before seeing examples, you must understand how Access Basic determines the spacing between two printed values separated by commas. Access Basic assumes there are *print zones* every 14 columns. The number of print zones depends on the point size of the text you are using at the time. Figure 9.4 shows the locations of six print zones.

A comma separating `Print` values tells Access Basic to print the next value in the next print zone. Therefore, the following `Print` statement prints `Access` in the fourth print zone (column 43):

```
Print ,,, "Access"
```

Figure 9.4

The Access Basic immediate window print zones.

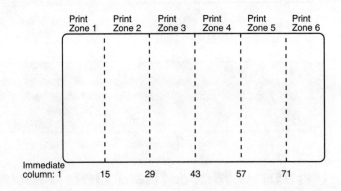

> **Caution:** If your printed data fills more than one print zone, the next value
> prints one extra zone over. For example, if you print a name that has 20
> letters and then follow the name with a comma and another name, the
> second name prints in the third print zone (column 29).

Example

The following statements print the contents of variables next to their descriptions:

```
Print "Age"; age%
Print "Salary"; salary@
Print "Employee name "; emp$
Print "Dependents"; dependents%
```

The extra blank at the end of the Employee name description is necessary. Without it, the name would print right next to the description with no space between them.

Example

The following statements illustrate the use of the comma between Print values. The three lines print the animals' names in four columns. Although the names are different lengths, they begin in the same print zones. The comma means that the next animal name is printed in the next print zone.

```
Print "Lion", "Whale", "Monkey", "Fish"
Print "Alligator", "Bat", "Seal", "Tiger"
Print "Dog", "Lizard", "Cat", "Bear"
```

If you were to put these statements in an Access Basic program and run them, you'd see the following output in the immediate window:

```
Lion        Whale       Monkey      Fish
Alligator   Bat         Seal        Tiger
Dog         Lizard      Cat         Bear
```

Printing with Tab

Tab controls
your spacing.

Printing with commas is similar to using tabs in a word processing program. The commas act as a tab by moving the next value to the next print zone. A print zone, however, is not a real tab because you cannot change its location. Print zones always occur every 14 spaces. But you might want to print a table that prints values in locations different from the print zones. When you do, use the Tab function in your Print statement.

In its parentheses, Tab requires a numeric argument that specifies the number of characters to tab over before printing the next value. Never use Tab by itself; always combine Tab with Print.

> **Tip:** You can put several Tabs in a single Print if you want to print more than one value at a time. Separate Tab and its surrounding values with semicolons.

Example

The following statements print the first column of animal names in screen position 1, the second column in screen position 20, the third in screen position 40, and the fourth in screen position 60.

```
Print "Lion"; Tab(20); "Whale"; Tab(40); "Monkey"; Tab(60);
"Fish"
Print "Alligator"; Tab(20); "Bat"; Tab(40); "Seal"; Tab(60);
"Tiger"
Print "Dog"; Tab(20); "Lizard"; Tab(40); "Cat"; Tab(60); "Bear"
```

If you were to put these statements in an Access Basic program and run them, you'd see the following output:

```
Lion            Whale           Monkey          Fish
Alligator       Bat             Seal            Tiger
Dog             Lizard          Cat             Bear
```

The Tab function is especially helpful for printing tables of data. Although words and values do not always take the same width on-screen (Alligator is longer than Dog), you might want the rows of data to begin printing in the same columns. With Tab, you have more freedom to place data exactly where you want it.

Printing with *Spc*

Like Tab, Spc goes inside Print. Spc specifies how many spaces to skip before printing the next value. Spc keeps you from having to type many string constants filled only with spaces in your output. The following rule of thumb explains the difference between Tab and Spc.

> **Note:** When you use Tab, the cursor always skips to a fixed position, the column inside the Tab's parentheses. When you use Spc, the cursor skips over the number of spaces inside the Spc function's parentheses.

Example

If you always want a fixed number of spaces between numeric or string variables when you print them, use Spc rather than Tab. Tab forces the cursor to a fixed location, regardless of how wide the data is. The following statements show you the difference between Tab and Spc:

```
a%= 7865
b%=1
c!=6543.2
Print "Printing with Tab:"
Print a%; Tab(7); b%; Tab(14); c!
Print "Printing with Spc:"
Print a%; Spc(7); b%; Spc(14); c!
```

If you were to put these statements in an Access Basic program and run them, you'd see the following output:

```
7865   1        6543.2
7865        1                6543.2
```

Closing the Module Window

Before you move to the next chapter, close the immediate execution window and the module window. To close the immediate execution window, double-click its Control button. Then close the module window by choosing **File Close** or double-clicking its Control button. When Access asks if you want to save the changes, select **No** to return to the database window.

Summary

Now that you've seen and used the immediate execution window, you can try statements as you learn them and look at variables when you put values in the variables. You'll rarely use the immediate execution window for printing variables that you just initialized, but you will often print values from variables and fields that are initialized from the database or a macro.

The next chapter explores more kinds of data values available in Access Basic so that you can begin to put some of the pieces together with actual database objects.

Review Questions

Answers to review questions are in Appendix B.

1. What do you use to write output to the screen?

2. TRUE or FALSE: You can print both constants and variables.

3. What is a print zone?

4. How can you print more than one value at a time on the same line?

5. What is the difference between a comma and a semicolon in a Print?

6. How many characters wide is a print zone?

7. What is the difference between Tab and Spc?

8. Why is it important to print descriptions with numeric values?

9. In what column would the word Computer start, given the following Print?

```
Print Tab(20); "Computer"
```

10. In what column would the number 765 start, given the following Print?

```
Print -21; 21; 0; Tab(30); 765
```

Review Exercises

1. Write statements that store and print your weight, height in feet, and shoe size. First, store the values in three variables and then print them with appropriate descriptions.

2. Using the values in exercise 1, print your weight in column 15, your height in column 25, and your shoe size in column 35.

3. Look at a newspaper's financial section and find a table of figures. Try to duplicate the table on your screen, making sure the columns of data line up under the headings. (Of course, your subsequent Print statements keep the lines from directly following one another.) Use Tab, semicolons, commas, or Spc to match the newspaper's columns as closely as possible. Each of the newspaper's characters may differ in width, so you might have to guess and not use the same number of spaces that the paper uses. The more printing you do, the faster you can produce any screen output ever needed.

CHAPTER 10

Variables and Database Objects

This chapter begins to combine Access Basic variables with database objects. After reading this chapter, you will be able to copy database data to variables and send variables to the database. This chapter explores many of the new Access Basic data types that are different from data types of any other programming language. You also see how to refer to specific objects with an Access form, table, report, or any of the other kinds of objects.

This chapter introduces the following topics:

♦ The database object data types

♦ Using the exclamation point notation to specify your objects

♦ Using the dot operator to specify Access-generated objects

♦ Using the Set command to associate database objects to the Access Basic variables that you declare

The representation of database objects in Access Basic variables represents the true power of Access Basic and begins to show you ways to integrate Access Basic into your common database tasks.

Database Object Data Types

In the previous chapters you learned about the `Integer`, `Long`, `Single`, `Double`, `String`, `Currency`, and `Variant` data types. In most programming languages, you would have seen all the data types needed. Access, however, brings new requirements to its programming language. In it, you can represent actual database objects as variables.

Most database objects, such as forms and reports, don't lend themselves well to the usual variable data types. You need a way to represent objects and manipulate those objects as easily as you represent and manipulate other types of data. The eight database object data types available in Access Basic are listed in Table 10.1.

Table 10.1. The Access Basic database object types.

Data Type	Description
Control	A control on a form or report
Database	A database
Dynaset	A query's result that is updatable*
Form	A form or subform
QueryDef	A query definition
Report	A report
Snapshot	A query's result that is not updatable*
Table	A table

Updatable means that if the query's resulting data can be changed, the underlying tables also are changed.

> **Note:** The first column of Table 10.1 lists data types that you must use if you want to declare variables of those types.

The three data types Table, Dynaset, and Snapshot are called *recordset* objects. The term *recordset* describes the fact that these data types refer to a collection of records. With the Set command you learn later in this chapter, you can create variables that refer to tables, dynasets, and snapshots. Table variables refer to the entire tables while dynaset and snapshot variables refer to subsets of tables as defined by your selection criteria. A snapshot variable is a fixed dynaset. If you change a dynaset variable, the underlying table's data changes, but if you change a snapshot variable, the underlying table does not change—just the variable snapshot changes. Examples throughout the book help clarify these issues.

Use *Dim* to declare database object variables.

There are no data type suffixes for the database data types, and there are no Deftype statements either. You must use Dim to declare variables of database data types.

Tip: Because `Dim` is the only way to declare database object variables, perhaps you should always use `Dim` to declare all variables instead of using `Deftype` and suffix characters. Microsoft recommends `Dim`, but many programmers have moved to Access Basic from other dialects of BASIC, and they are used to the `Deftype` and data type suffix characters. You should use whatever declaration methods you prefer, but `Dim` is most consistent.

Example

The following statements declare a database variable, a form variable, and a table variable:

```
Dim dbEmp As Database
Dim fNewEmp As Form
Dim Table As tOrders
```

Example

With the `Dim` statement, you can combine more than one declaration on a single line. The following statement does exactly the same as the preceding example's three statements:

```
Dim dbEmp As Database, fNewEmp As Form, Table As tOrders
```

Before using these three variables, you must associate them with an actual database object as described in the next section.

Note: Many Access programmers make the first letter or two of the object variable's name abbreviate the variable's data type. In other words, all `Database` variables begin with `db`, all `Form` variables begin with `f`, and all `Dynaset` variables begin with `dy`. The next letter, capitalized, begins the name of the variable to distinguish it from other variables of the same data type.

Associating Object Variables to Database Objects

The `Dim` statement only reserves storage in memory for variables and names those variables. `Dim` does not associate variables with any object. Therefore, you must use the `Set` command to associate an actual existing database object with an object variable.

The format of Set is

```
Set variableName = object
```

The *variableName* must be the name of an object variable declared with a Dim statement as described in the previous section. The *object* is either an object name, another object variable, or any function or method that returns an object.

> **Caution:** Set does not do the same thing as the Let assignment statement. Assignment statements are for variables and nonobject data; Set is for assigning database objects to database variables.

Set creates a *reference* to a database object. A reference is like an alias to the object, or just another name for that object. By creating the alias variable, you can use the variable name just about anywhere you can use variables in your Access Basic programs.

Be specific with *Set*.

The *object* used in the Set statement requires notation that enables you to zero-in on the data you want to reference. You used the *object* notation in Chapter 3 while working with macros. Many objects in the same database may have the same name. A control on one form, for example, might have the same name (such as Part No) as a control on a different form. Therefore, when referring to objects using Set, you must be very specific about the data.

> **Caution:** Even if you want to refer to an object whose name does not overlap other object names in your database, you must use the specific naming references described in this section for Access Basic to find the data you need.

Table 10.2 explains how to specify the Set objects for form and report objects.

Table 10.2. Specifying objects.

To Refer to a	Use This Syntax
Form	Forms!formName
	Example: Forms!Item
Form property	Forms!formName.propertyName
	Example: Forms!Item.CanGrow
Control on a form	Forms!formName!control
	Example: Forms!Item!iName

To Refer to a	Use This Syntax
Form Control's property	Forms!formName!control.property
	Example: Forms!Item!iName.Visible
Report	Reports!reportName
	Example: Reports!Inv
Report property	Reports!reportName.propertyName
	Example: Reports!Inv.KeepTogether
Control on a report	Reports!reportName!control
	Example: Reports!Inv!iName
Report Control's property	Reports!reportName!control.property
	Example: Reports!Inv!iName.Visible

> **Note:** Access has a tremendous number of properties for objects. You have no doubt used many of them during the creation of forms and reports that you've developed in the past. Part 1 of your *Access Language Reference Manual* lists all of the properties in a table that you can refer to when needed. You'll never have to reference many of the properties in an Access Basic program, and several properties you'll reference often.

> **Caution:** Although Table 10.1 listed the data types **Form** and **Report** (both singular), you see examples using **Forms** and **Reports** (both plural) in Table 10.2. Table 10.1 lists the data types used with **Dim** to declare variables; Table 10.2 uses **Forms** and **Reports**, which are not data types but pre-defined objects that mean "all the forms in the open database" and "all the reports in the open database," respectively.

Example

Suppose that you want to refer to a form named myForm in your Access Basic program. You first must declare a form variable (with Dim) and then associate that variable to the myForm form as the following statements do:

```
Dim fVar As Form
Set fVar = Forms!myForm
```

Every use of the fVar variable refers to the myForm form.

Note: The `myForm` is known as a *member* of all the forms in the database.

Example

Often, a form's control is bound to a field in the underlying table. Other times, a control is unbound, such as a label on a form that describes data next to it or a title for the form. Notice in Table 10.2 that a control is specified in a form with a separating exclamation point, just as a form is specified. Therefore, the general format `Forms!formName!control` tells Access that a form with the name `formName` contains a control named `control` with which you want to work.

To be more specific, suppose that you want to associate a field name with an Access variable. First, you declare the control variable as follows:

```
Dim ageControl As Control
```

To associate the `ageControl` variable to the field named `age` in the form named `fCust`, you associate the control to the variable as follows:

```
Set ageControl = Forms!fCust!age
```

Tip: To understand a reference to a control more fully, read the reference from right to left. That is, the `age` field in the `fCust` form is being associated to the variable named `ageControl`.

Example

The dot operator indicates an Access-supplied item.

Always specify a property, either a control's property or an object's property, with a dot operator (`.`). Suppose that you want to save the width from a report in an Access Basic variable. A report's width is a property from the report's property window (you can open a report and select View Properties... to see other properties). After you declare the variable, you can save the report property's value as shown here:

```
Dim reportWidth As Integer
Set reportWidth = Reports!myReport.Width
```

Suppose that you want to save the `Caption` property from a report's field named `ProductID`. You must first declare the property variable. Then you must specify the report name, followed by the field (control) name, and finally, the `Caption` property as in the following:

```
Dim prodIDCapt As String
Set prodIDCapt = Reports!myReport!ProductID.Caption
```

After setting the variable to reference the field's caption, you can change the caption from an Access Basic program by assigning it a value, just as you assign a value to any variable (using the assignment statement) as in the following:

```
prodIDCapt = "Look Here!"
```

Caution: Not all properties can be set. Some, such as the AddColon properties, are not even available from Access Basic. Those properties that are available *cannot* always be changed (they can appear only on the right side of an equal sign). Those properties that are available can be assigned to variables of the same data type. For example, the FontName property requires a String data type (or Variant, which can be any data type needed at the time).

Note: The dot operator always precedes objects defined by Access (such as a control or a subform within a form denoted by the predefined Form object) while the exclamation point precedes only objects that you create (such as a form's name).

Example

Once you assign a form or a form's control to a variable, you can use the variable to refer to that variable's property. In other words, you could declare and set the preceding example's ProductID field's Caption property as follows:

```
Dim prodField As Control
Dim prodIDCapt As Variant
prodField = Reports!myReport!ProductID
Set prodIDCapt = prodField.Caption
```

You then assign the Caption a new value in the same way as before:

```
prodIDCapt = "Look Here!"
```

Sticking to Access Basic's Naming Rules

Take a moment to review the variable-naming rules from Chapter 7. You do not name Access Basic variables using the same rules you use to name Access objects such as fields, controls, forms, and reports. For example, field names can have blanks embedded in them, but variable names cannot.

If you need to specify an Access object in an expression that does not fit into the Access Basic naming rules, enclose the name in brackets.

Example

If you want to refer to a field named my age, inside an Access Basic expression you must enclose my age in brackets as follows:

```
Set ageControl = Forms!fCust![my age]
```

The following expression is *not* allowed due to the blank in the field name:

```
Set ageControl = Forms!fCust!my age
```

> **Tip:** Most Access Basic programmers enclose all their object names in brackets because using brackets never hurts, even if they are unneeded.

Additional Reference Notation

A String variable can contain the name of a member. For example, you can assign a form's name to a String variable named formName as follows:

```
formName = "My form"
```

Once you learn how to get input from the user at the keyboard, you can ask the user for a form name as well. There are many reasons (and procedures) for storing an object's name in a variable. Once an object's (or member's) name is stored in a variable, you can use the variable by enclosing it in quotation marks. The following statement refers to the form named My form:

```
Dim fName As Form
Dim formName As String
formName = "My form"
fName = Forms(formName)
```

The fourth line does exactly the same as the following:

```
fName = Forms!formName
```

Even if an object or member's name is not stored in a variable, you can use the parentheses notation. This statement also is equivalent to the previous statements:

```
fName = Forms("My form")
```

You can reference reports in the same way as forms.

> **Note:** Don't use the exclamation point if you use parentheses around an
> object or a variable that contains an object's name.

Looking at Form Values

In Chapter 9, "Seeing Your Results," you learned how to look at variables inside the
immediate window. At any point you also can use the immediate window to look
at form and report values, as the following example shows.

Example

Follow these steps to print a value from a form in the immediate window:

1. With the Northwind Traders database still open, click the Forms button
   and open the Employees form.

2. After the first employee's record appears (Ms. Davolio's), display the
   Window pull-down menu and select Database: NWIND to display the
   database window again. This step leaves the Employee record open.

3. Click the Module button and select **D**esign.

4. Open the immediate window by selecting **V**iew **I**mmediate Window.
   In the window, type the following statement:

   ```
   ? Forms!Employees![Last Name]
   ```

   (Remember that ? is the shortcut for the Print command.) Access displays
   the Last Name field from the Employees form (Davolio), as shown in
   Figure 10.1.

5. Close the open module and form windows.

> **Tip:** To change a value in a form from within the immediate window, assign
> the value another value. Of course, you can add and change form values
> from the form view, but if any fields are hidden from view (such as intermedi-
> ate calculation fields or other fields that appear in the table but not on the
> form), you can display their results from the immediate window while
> maintaining the form's hidden view of those values.

Figure 10.1

Using the immediate window to display a field's value.

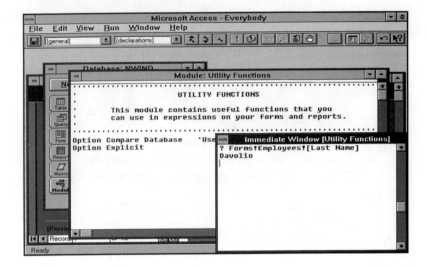

Note: Throughout this book you read about several predefined objects that you can use in your Access Basic expressions. For the time being, you have enough knowledge of expressions to work with the programs presented for the next few chapters. You learn about the Debug and Screen predefined objects later in the book.

Don't Drown in Terminology

Access Basic takes a little wading, not diving, and *Access 2 Programming By Example* tries to let Access Basic sneak up on you instead of throwing everything to you at once. Remember, this book attempts to teach Access Basic programming to those who may never have programmed before. Now you've seen how Access Basic integrates with the data in a database.

Objects within your Access Basic programs can take on any of the eight types described in Table 10.1 (in addition to the predefined Debug and Screen objects). The objects might have any or all of the following:

◆ Properties such as visibility and color

◆ Controls such as fields

◆ Other objects such as forms within forms or controls on reports (objects embedded inside other objects are called members)

♦ Methods, which are like built-in functions or commands that usually take arguments and that are associated closely with certain objects (thus, methods manipulate objects)

You have control of all these items as you program in Access Basic. At this point, remember that you must specify with the ! or . notation (or the equivalent parentheses reference notation) moving from the general object (at the left) to the specific object (at the right).

Example

The *Access Language Reference Manual* contains this complex statement:

```
Debug.Print Forms!TopForm!Container.Form!SubForm.Visible
```

Debug is a predefined object that really means the immediate execution window. Print is a method that belongs to the Debug object. In this case, Print is a routine that prints the object. The data being printed is the Visible property of the SubForm form located on the form inside the Container control of the TopForm form. Whew!

The ! in this expression precedes the database's user-defined value, and the . always precedes an Access-defined value.

Example

Methods manipulate objects.

Learning Access Basic is sometimes difficult because details get in your way. For instance, if you were to see a list of all the methods in this chapter, most would make little sense to you at this time. Methods let you manipulate objects, and this book teaches individual methods when you get to an example that needs one.

Often, methods are used to open tables and databases so that Set finds specific tables. The following statements associate reference variables to the MYDB.MDB database and the MyTable table:

```
Dim aDB As Database
Dim aTable As RecordSet
Set aDB = MyWorkspace.OpenDatabase("MYDB.MDB")  ' Lowercase would
also work
Set aTable = aDB.OpenRecordset("MyTable", DB_OPEN_SNAPSHOT)
```

As your *Access Language Reference Manual* explains, OpenDatabase() is a function that returns an object (that you now reference with aDB in the rest of the program) from your current workspace (specified with MyWorkspace), and the OpenRecordset method generates a recordset object that you can reference (read, edit, and add data to) later in the program.

> **Note:** The two methods in this example are preceded by dots and not exclamation points because the methods are defined by Access, not by you. If you use version 1.0 or 1.1, you'll have to substitute the `OpenTable()` function for the `OpenRecordset()` and eliminate the `MyWorkspace` specifier.

Summary

You may think that this book got hard all of a sudden with this chapter. This chapter can be intimidating if you haven't worked much with the notation presented here. If, however, you've created extensive Access applications with macros and expressions, this material is basically a review of expression notation.

This chapter presented a "chicken before the egg" problem in that you really could not go farther in the book until you saw this notation, and yet the notation is not very useful until you learn some Access Basic commands that can manipulate the expressions. After you've worked through a few more chapters, you might want to return to this chapter to review.

Review Questions

Answers to review questions are in Appendix B.

1. What symbol always precedes objects you define?

2. What symbol always precedes objects Access defines?

3. Name three object data types.

4. Why are brackets sometimes required around object names?

5. TRUE or FALSE: You can specify a `Table` variable in three ways: with `Dim`, with `DefTable`, and with a data type suffix character.

6. When do you use parentheses rather than the exclamation point to separate parts of an expression?

7. TRUE or FALSE: Assuming that `reptName` is a `String` variable containing the string `"My Report"`, the following are exactly the same reference:

```
rName = Reports(reptName)

rName = Reports![My Report]
```

8. TRUE or FALSE: The following are exactly the same reference:

```
rName = Reports(reptName)

rName = Reports!("My report")
```

Review Exercises

1. Write a statement that declares a dynaset variable, a table variable, and a form variable.

2. Write the statements declaring a report variable that refers to a report named MyReport and declaring a control variable on that report which refers to a field named Amount.

3. Look through the Utility Functions module's code samples and find examples of the dot notation, parentheses notation, and exclamation point notation used in the procedures.

CHAPTER 11

Remarks and Full Program Execution

Now that you understand a few programming statements, it's time to put some parts together to form a complete program. You have many more commands to learn at this point, but you're ready to see how full Access Basic programs are compiled and run.

This chapter introduces the following topics:

- Program documentation

- The Rem statement

- The ' remark

- Writing a complete program

- Compiling and running a program

By mastering these concepts, you can be prepared to write longer programs that do more than store and print values.

Program Remarks

You know that a program exists to give the computer instructions to read and follow. You need to understand the programs you write, however. After writing a program, you cannot always remember parts of the program when you are making changes later. When someone else writes a program, working on that program especially is difficult. Someday computer instructions might be written in a spoken language such as English. Until then, you must learn to speak and understand the computer's language.

The Rem statement makes Access Basic code more understandable to humans, although the computer ignores it. Rem is short for *remark*. The format of Rem is

```
Rem any message you choose
```

You can have as many remarks in your program as you want. Many programmers scatter remarks throughout a program. The computer completely ignores remarks; it produces no output, stores no variables, and requires no data as a result of the Rem command.

Example

1

If a computer completely ignores remarks, you probably wonder why you should bother to use them. Rem statements are for people to use so that they can understand programs better. For example, an Access Basic program that produces a fancy colored box with flashing lights around it and your name inside (like a marquee) would take some cryptic Access Basic commands. Before those commands, you might put a remark like this:

```
Rem The next few lines draw a fancy colorful boxed name
```

This remark does not tell Access Basic to do anything, but it makes the next few lines of code more understandable to you and others; this statement explains in English exactly what the program is going to do.

Rem statements also are helpful for putting the programmer's name at the top of a program. In a large company with several programmers, it's helpful to know who to contact if you need help changing the programmer's original code. Remember that Rem does not print that name when you run the program (printing is done with other Access Basic commands), but the name is there for anyone looking at the program's listing.

You also might consider putting the module name of the program in an early Rem statement. For example, the statement

```
Rem Programmer: Pat Johnson, Module: Compute Sales
```

tells who the programmer is, as well as the program's module name in the database. When you are looking through many printed program listings, you quickly can load the one you want to change with the module editor by looking at the Rems at the top of the program.

The Rem Shortcut:'

Because Rem statements appear so often in programs, the authors of Access Basic supplied an abbreviation for the Rem statement. Rather than typing **Rem**, you can type an apostrophe (').

Unlike Rem, apostrophe remarks can appear to the right of program lines to help explain each line. Rem statements have to go on separate lines.

Example

The Northwind Traders Company sample database Utility Functions declarations section contains this seven-line remark:

```
''''''''''''''''''''''''''''''''''''''''''''''''''''''''''''''''''''''''''''''
'                           UTILITY FUNCTIONS                                '
'                                                                            '
'        This module contains useful functions that you                     '
'        can use in expressions on your forms and reports.                   '
'                                                                            '
''''''''''''''''''''''''''''''''''''''''''''''''''''''''''''''''''''''''''''''
```

The apostrophe looks cleaner and is easier to type than a bunch of Rem statements.

Example

The Proper procedure in the Utility Functions module contains remarks that appear on lines by themselves as well as to the right of other programming statements. Here is a section from that procedure:

```
For ptr = 1 To Len(theString)            'Go through string char
➡by char.
        currChar = Mid$(theString, ptr, 1) 'Get the current
        ➡character.

        Select Case prevChar             'If previous char is
        ➡letter,
                                         'this char should be
                                         ➡lowercase.
```

Because the apostrophe is easier to type and can be used where Rem cannot be used, the rest of this book uses the apostrophe remark rather than Rem.

Example

In Chapter 9 you added a remark (before you understood remarks) to the first line in the Utility Functions module. After you added the apostrophe, a line in the declarations section looked like the following:

```
' Option Explicit
```

The Option Explicit statement tells Access Basic to require that all variables be explicitly declared with Dim before you can use the variables for anything. In Chapter 9 you learned how to use the immediate window to look at values of variables. The Dim statement is not allowed in the immediate window, only in fully coded procedures. Therefore, Access Basic does not let you use variables in the immediate window—even if you use the variables' data type suffix character—until you turn the Option Explicit statement into a remark. After you add the remark, Access Basic ignores the Option Explicit statement and enables you to work with nondimensioned variables.

Using Helpful Remarks

Don't overdo remarks.

Although a program without remarks can be difficult to understand, you should use only helpful remarks. Remarks explain what the program code is doing. Therefore, the following remark is not helpful:

```
' Put the value 3 into the variable named numKids%
numKids% = 3
```

Although the preceding remark is lengthy, it does not explain why the value 3 is placed in the statement. Consider the following improved example:

```
' Save the number of kids for dependent calculations
numKids% = 3
```

This remark gives a better idea of what the program's statement (the assignment) is used for. Someone trying to figure out the program would appreciate the second remark more than the first.

This example was simple. However, many Access Basic statements do not require remarks. For example, including a remark to explain Dim empAge As Integer might not be worth much because there is little ambiguity about what is going on; an integer variable that will hold an employee's age is declared.

Remember to put remarks in your programs as you write them. You are most familiar with your program logic when you are typing the program into the editor. Some people put off including remarks in their programs until after they write the programs. As a result, the remarks never get included, or the programmer makes only a half-hearted attempt to include them.

The rest of this book's examples include remarks that explain the programs.

> **Tip:** Access enables you to insert blank lines in your programs to separate
> sections of code from each other. Access Basic programs are also known
> as *free-form*, meaning that statements can begin in any column. Most
> Access Basic programmers include lots of *white space* (blank lines and
> extra spacing here and there) to make programs more readable than they
> would be if the code were scrunched together.

Writing a Program from Scratch

It's time to write a complete program. Remember that a program really is a module
that contains several procedures. Although you could create a new module for this
book's examples, it is easier to add a new procedure to the Utility Function module
and use the data and objects already residing in the Northwind Traders database.

Writing the program requires adding the code for the new procedure, compiling
the module with the new procedure, and then adding the trigger that runs the
program. You can run a program in several ways. The program you write in this
chapter executes as a result of using a form in the database.

> **Tip:** Most of the programs described in *Access 2 Programming By Example*
> are function procedures. Function procedures can do anything that sub-
> routine procedures can do, as well as return values. You use subroutine
> procedures only because functions are designed to return values and,
> therefore, you always have to call them as if they are returning something,
> even if they don't. This means that you might have to assign a function to a
> variable that you'll never use, and the variable's sole job in the program is to
> let the function execute. You can execute a subroutine procedure without
> assigning it to a variable.

Example

The following steps describe how you can add a new procedure to the Utility Functions
module. The procedure is simple; it converts whatever the user types in the Employee
form's Last Name field to uppercase using the built-in UCase$() function. UCase$()
does the opposite of the LCase$() function described in Chapter 3—UCase$() converts
its argument to uppercase letters.

1. Open the Northwind database if it is not already open.

2. Click on the **M**odule button in the database window.

3. Click on the **D**esign button to open the Utility Functions module.

4. To add a new procedure to the module, select **Edit New** Procedure..., and the New Procedure dialog box shown in Figure 11.1 opens.

Figure 11.1

The New procedure dialog box.

5. The Function option is already selected. (To add a new subroutine procedure, you select **Sub** rather than Function.) Type **CapLast** as the **Name** of the function and press Enter. Access Basic opens a new function procedure in the editing window and types the first and last lines of the function procedure shown here:

```
Function CapLast ()

End Function
```

> **Note:** All function procedure names follow the same naming rules as Access Basic variables and must end in parentheses. If the function requires arguments (this one does not), something appears inside the parentheses. The first line in every function is called the *function declaration* and begins with the word `Function` and the function name. All functions must end with the `End Function` line.

6. Between the two statements supplied by Access, type the following program:

```
Dim cLastName As Control        ' A place to hold the last name
' Save the last name typed by the user
Set cLastName = Forms!Employees![Last Name]
' Save the converted name
cLastName = UCase$(cLastName)
```

The first line declares a `Control` variable that will hold a last name from a form's `Last Name` field. The next line (after the remark) sets the field named `Last Name` from the `Employees` form to the variable `cLastName`. The fourth line capitalizes the `cLastName` variable by passing the last name to the `UCase$()` function and then saving the return value from `UCase$()` back in the variable.

> **Note:** It is *vital* you remember that Set associates a variable to an object, unlike an assignment statement that copies a value from one place (such as a variable) to another variable. After associating the Last Name field to the cLastName variable, when you change cLastName, you change the field it is associated to also.

7. Choose File Save to save the module with the new function you just added. After you finish, your screen should look like the one in Figure 11.2.

Figure 11.2

After saving the new function.

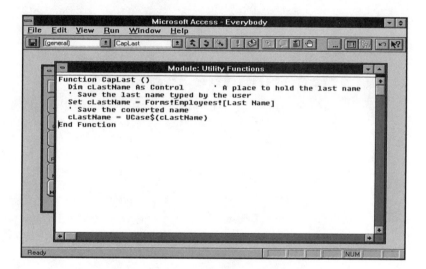

Compiling the Program

Compile and smile!

Before you can execute an Access Basic program's instructions, you must compile the program. Compiling a program requires making a simple menu selection and fixing errors if the compiler finds any. The following example walks you through the compilation steps.

Example

The following steps compile the program you created and saved in the previous example.

1. Select Run Compile Loaded Modules from the menu.

> **Caution:** Nothing obvious happens when you compile a program—at least, you hope, nothing *obvious* happens. Behind the scenes, Access Basic converts your source (and all the other procedures in the module) to binary machine language. If Access Basic encounters any errors, you know because Access Basic informs you of the error with a dialog box. Most of the time, an error occurs because you misspell a command. If you get an error after compiling the program, carefully look over the instructions that you typed and fix any discrepancy you find between the program you typed and the one listed in the previous example.

2. Double-click the module's control button to close the window and return to the database window.

Triggering the Program

Somehow, you've got to hook your new function to the database so that the function executes when something triggers the function's execution. An Access Basic function can be called from another function or from an *event property* such as a mouse click on a form. When you want to run a function from an event property (as you do here), you must use the following format:

```
=functionName([argument1][, argument2][, ...])
```

The `CapLast()` function has no arguments; arguments are optional in many functions. The equal sign before the function name differentiates the name from a macro that might exist with the same name.

> **Note:** You cannot call subroutine procedures from an event property (such as a button push on a form or report), only function procedures. You can run subroutine procedures only from other function procedures or subroutine procedures. Also, if you run a function procedure from an event property and the function returns a value, that return value is ignored. Return values are useful when a function is called from an expression or from another function or subroutine procedure somewhere in the database.

Example

With the Northwind Traders database still open, follow these steps to attach the program you wrote to an event in the Employees form.

1. Click the Form button.

2. Select the Employees form and click the **Design** button.

3. Double-click the Last Name field to display the Text Box properties box shown in Figure 11.3.

4. Scroll the Text Box until you see the On Exit option. Click the On Exit row in the Text Box.

The On Exit event specifies what happens if the user does *anything* to the contents of the Last Name field. Therefore, if the user enters a new Last Name value or changes an existing Last Name in the database using this form, Access looks at the On Exit contents and acts accordingly. To execute the CapLast() function you wrote and compiled in the previous examples, type the following in the On Exit field:

```
=CapLast()
```

Here you tell the Employees form that whenever the user updates the Last Name field, your CapLast() function is to execute. CapLast() converts the entire last name to uppercase letters.

Figure 11.3

Displaying the properties box for the Last Name field.

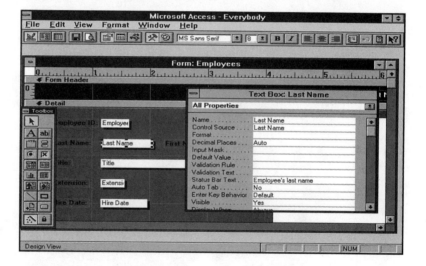

Note: If you use version 1.0 or 1.1 of Access, the Text Box you see will contain far fewer items than the one described. Starting with version 2.0, Microsoft added many more programmable controls to forms in order to reach closer compatability with Visual Basic. Eventually, Microsoft's goal is to consolidate all of the application languages such as Access Basic into a uniform Visual Basic for Applications (*VBA*) language.

5. Choose File Save to Save the form. You now are ready to run the program by triggering the On Exit event. The following example does just that.

6. Choose File Close to save the form and return to the database window.

Running the Program

A form event runs your program.

Now that the program code (the function procedure you wrote) is ready to execute, you can test the code to make sure it works as expected. When the user enters or changes an employee's last name, the CapLast() function procedure ensures that the name is converted to uppercase letters.

Example

To execute the program, you must trigger the event. Follow these steps to see the program execute.

1. Open the Employees form, and you see Nancy Davolio's employee record display with a picture of her on the form.

2. Tab to the Last Name field and press F2 (or you can click on the field) to put the field into the editing mode.

3. Change the last letter from o to a so the name reads Davolia.

4. Press Tab to trigger the On Exit event. Your program converts the entire last name to uppercase, as shown in Figure 11.4.

Figure 11.4

After the *CapLast()* function procedure capitalizes the last name.

Congratulations! You have now completed the cycle that will become second nature as you learn Access Basic.

> **Caution:** Don't save the record with the capitalized last name! You don't want to ruin the integrity of the data this early in the book (you have plenty of time to do that later!). Choose **E**dit U**n**do Current Record to restore the record to its previous state.

5. Click the Design tool (the tool at the far left of the toolbar) to display the design view of the Employees form.

6. Double-click the Last Name field to display the Text Box again.

7. Click the On Exit field and press Del until the box is erased.

8. Choose **F**ile **S**ave to save the form without the function call to restore the form to its original state.

9. Choose **F**ile **C**lose to close the form and return to the database window.

Summary

In this chapter you first learned about remarks using the Rem statement and its more commonly used shortcut, the apostrophe. Remarks are great documenting tools for your programs so you know what they do, and more importantly, others will understand your programs, too.

You then walked through the creation, compilation, and execution of a complete program. The program converted the Employee form's Last Name to uppercase letters. The program was simple, but this book is aimed at newcomers to programming and even a simple first program is quite an accomplishment!

In the next chapter you learn how to perform calculations with your data using the Access Basic math operators. Now that you can initialize and print values, it's time to calculate with them as well.

Review Questions

Answers to review questions are in Appendix B.

1. What does Rem stand for?

2. What does the computer do when it finds a Rem or ' statement?

3. TRUE or FALSE: The following section of a program puts a 4 in the variable named R, a 5 in me, and a 6 in Rem.

```
R = 4
me = 5
Rem = 6
```

4. Why are some remarks redundant?

5. The following statement is meant to trigger the ComputeSales() function and resides inside the Before Update field's property in a form:

```
Run ComputeSales()
```

Why doesn't the statement run the function? How could you change it to work?

6. If you pass arguments to a function procedure, where do you specify the arguments?

7. Which remark format—Rem or '—can go to the right of Access Basic statements in a program?

Review Exercises

1. Using the Rem and the apostrophe format, write the remarks that describe a year-end payroll being printed.

2. Repeat the program presented in this chapter and convert the employee's title to lowercase letters. As done here, be sure to exit the form design view without saving the change to the form.

3. Repeat the program presented in this chapter and convert the employee's first name to just three letters using the Left$() function you learned about in Chapter 3. Once you test the program, unhook the program's code from the event that triggers it (the On Exit event on the First Name control).

CHAPTER 12

Math Operators

If you are dreading this chapter because you don't like math, you can rest easy. Access Basic does all your math for you. It is a misconception that you have to be good at math to understand how to program computers. The opposite is true. The computer follows your instructions and does all the calculations for you.

This chapter explains how Access Basic computes by introducing:

♦ Access Basic math operators

♦ The order of operators

♦ How to store the results of calculations in variables

♦ How to print the results of calculations

Many people who dislike math actually enjoy learning how the computer does calculations. After learning the operators and a few simple ways Access Basic uses them, you will feel comfortable putting calculations in your programs. Computers can perform math operations many times faster than people can.

> **Note:** You've no doubt used many of the math operators in expressions and macros before. Nevertheless, Access Basic programs can enable you to compute much more complex expressions, and with that power comes more responsibility on your part to learn the side effects of long expressions.

The Math Operators

A *math operator* is a symbol used for addition, subtraction, multiplication, division, or other calculations. The operators are similar to the ones you use when you do arithmetic. Table 12.1 lists the Access Basic math operators and their meanings.

Table 12.1. The Access Basic math operators and their meanings.

Symbol	Meaning
*	Multiplication
/	Division
+	Addition
-	Subtraction
^	Exponentiation
\	Integer division
MOD	Modulus (integer remainder)

The first four operators in Table 12.1 work just like their math equivalents, and they work in your Access Basic programs just as they do in the Access database fields and macros. You can precede any variable or number with a plus or minus (these + and - operators are called *unary* operators) to indicate the sign. Some of the remaining operators—\, MOD, and ^—might require a little more explanation.

Integer Division, Modulus, and Exponentiation

The three operators \, MOD, and ^ may be new to you. However, they are as easy to use as the four operators you already know.

\ produces integer results.

You use integer division to produce the integer (whole number) result of a division. Integer division always produces an integer result and discards any remainder. You don't have to put integers on both sides of the \; you can use floating-point numbers, integers, or a combination of both on each side of the \. Table 12.2 shows the results of some sample integer division expressions.

Table 12.2. Integer division results.

Expression	Result
8 \ 2	4
95 \ 2	47
95.0 \ 2	47
95 \ 2.0	47
95.0 \ 2.0	47
95.2 \ 2.4	47

The Access Basic MOD operator does not look like an operator, but it is one. MOD produces the *modulus,* or integer remainder, of division. Table 12.3 shows the results of some simple MOD operations.

Table 12.3. *MOD* operation results.

Expression	Result
8 MOD 2	0
8 MOD 3	2
8 MOD 7	1

You use the exponentiation symbol (^) when you want to raise a number to a power. The number to the left of the ^ is the base, and the number to the right is the power. You can put integers, floating-point, or a combination of both on each side of the ^. Table 12.4 shows the results of sample exponentiation calculations.

Table 12.4. Exponentiation results.

Expression	Description	Result
2 ^ 4	2 raised to the fourth power (2^4)	16
16 ^ 2	16 raised to the second power (16^2)	256
5.6 ^ 3	5.6 raised to the third power (5.6^3)	175.616
144 ^ 0.5	144 raised to the .5 Power ($144^{1/2}$)	12

The Assignment of Formulas

Most of your programs use variables to hold the results of calculations using all the Access Basic operators. When computing values from table fields and other variables, you can build complex expressions using the operations.

Example

The following statements illustrate a payroll computation. The program assigns to three field variables the hours worked, the pay per hour (the *rate*), and the tax rate from a Payroll form. The last part of the code then creates new payroll values from calculations that use some of the math operators.

```
Dim cHrsWorked, cRate, cTaxRate As Control
Dim grossPay, taxes, netPay As Single
' First, save the form's field data in variables
Set cHrsWorked = Forms!Payroll![Hrs Worked]
Set cRate = Forms!Payroll![Pay Rate]
Set cTaxRate = Forms!Payroll![Tax Rate]
' Calculate payroll results
grossPay = cHrsWorked * cRate
taxes = cTaxRate * grossPay
netPay = grossPay - taxes
```

Example

Suppose that you need to divide 95 pieces of candy among four children. You don't want one child getting more than another. After the following calculations are performed, the variable piecesEach holds the number of pieces to give each child and the leftOver variable holds the number of pieces left over after you've given each child candy.

```
piecesEach = 95 \ 4
leftOver = 95 MOD 4
```

> **Caution:** The regular division operator (/) would have produced a fractional result in the first calculation (23.75), and you couldn't give each child three-quarters of a piece of candy.

The Order of Operators

Expressions
compute in a
predetermined
order.

Knowing the meaning of the operators is the first step in understanding Access Basic calculations. You also must understand the *order of operators*. The order of operators (sometimes known as the *hierarchy of operators* or *precedence of operators*) determines exactly how Access Basic computes formulas. The order of operators is exactly how Access Basic computes expressions and is the same as you used in high school algebra. To see how the order of operators works, try to determine the result of the following calculation:

```
2 + 3 * 2
```

Many people would say the answer is 10. However, 10 is correct only if you interpret the formula from left to right. But what if you calculated the multiplication first? If you took the value of 3 * 2, got an answer of 6, and then added the 2 to it, you would end up with an answer of 8, which is the answer that Access Basic computes.

Access Basic performs math in the order specified in Table 12.5. Keep this table in mind as you program Access Basic expressions.

> **Note:** Expressions you enter in any Access field or macro also follow the order in Table 12.5.

Table 12.5. The order of operators.

Order	Operator
1	Exponentiation (^)
2	Negation (-)
3	Multiplication (*) and division (/)
4	Integer division (\)
5	Modulus (MOD)
6	Addition (+) and subtraction (-)

> **Note:** Negation means to change the sign of a variable or number. For instance, `-balance` negates the value in `balance`. Subtraction requires two arguments like this: `total - balance`.

Example

Following Access Basic's order of operators is easy if you follow the intermediate results one at a time. The three complex calculations in Figure 12.1 show you how to work with those results.

Figure 12.1

Three complex calculations showing the order of operators.

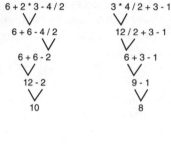

```
6 + 2 * 3 - 4 / 2          3 * 4 / 2 + 3 - 1
        V                          V
6 + 6 - 4 / 2              12 / 2 + 3 - 1
        V                          V
    6 + 6 - 2                  6 + 3 - 1
        V                          V
     12 - 2                      9 - 1
        V                          V
       10                         8
```

```
20 / 3 ^ 2
     V
  20 / 9
     V
     2
```

Example

Looking back at Table 12.5, notice that multiplication and division are on the same level. Being on the same level implies that there is no hierarchy on that level. When more than one of these operators appear in a calculation, Access Basic performs the math from left to right. The same is true of addition and subtraction; the leftmost operation is performed first.

Figure 12.2 shows an example of left-to-right division and multiplication. Because the division appears to the left of the multiplication (and because division and multiplication are on the same level), the division is computed first.

You should understand the order of operators so that you know how to structure your calculations. Now that you have mastered the order, you can see how to override the order of operators with parentheses.

Figure 12.2

Operators on the same level calculate from left to right.

```
10 / 5 * 2 - 2 + 1
     V
  2 * 2 - 2 + 1
     V
   4 - 2 + 1
     V
     2 + 1
     V
      3
```

Parentheses

Parentheses
override operator
precedence.

If you want to override the order of operators, put parentheses in the calculation. In other words, anything in parentheses, whether it is addition, subtraction, division, or whatever, always is calculated before the rest of the line. The rest of the calculations are performed in the normal order.

> **Tip:** If expressions with parentheses are inside other parentheses, such as $((5 + 2) - 7 + (8 + 9 - (5 + 2)))$, Access Basic calculates the innermost expression first.

The formula $3 + 3 * 2$ produces a 9 because multiplication is performed before addition. If you add parentheses around the addition, as in $(2 + 3) * 2$, the answer becomes 10.

Example

The calculations in Figure 12.3 illustrate how parentheses override the regular order of operators. These formulas are the same three shown in Figure 12.1, except their calculations are different because the parentheses override the order of operators.

Figure 12.3

Overriding the order of operators with parentheses.

```
6 + 2 * (3 - 4) / 2          3 * 4 / 2 + (3 - 1)
        V                             V
6 + 2 * - 1 / 2             3 * 4 / 2 + 2
        V                             V
   6 + - 2 / 2                 12 / 2 + 2
        V                             V
     6 + - 1                     6 + 2
        V                             V
       5                           8
```

```
(20 / 3) ^ 2
     V
   6 ^ 2
     V
    36
```

Example

The following function procedure appeared in the first two versions (1.0 and 1.1) of Access. The function, named Century, contains the following line:

```
Century = ((Year(someDate) - 1) \ 100) + 1
```

Year() is a built-in Access function that returns the year of whatever date is stored in the someDate variable (of the Date/Time data type). If someDate contains the year 03/04/90, the Year() function returns 1990. (Year 1900 belonged to the 19th century; the year 2000 belongs to the 20th century, and so on.) Subtracting 1 from 1990 yields 1989. The integer division of 1989 by 100 results in 19. Because a century is always expressed as one more than the year's first two digits, you must add one more to the 19 to move into the 20th century.

Example

The following statement appears to store the average of three values in the variable named av, but the average is not stored. See if you can spot the error.

```
av = 45 + 34 + 82 / 3
```

The problem is that the division is performed first. Therefore, the third number, 82, is divided by 3, and then the other two values are added to that result. To fix the problem, you have to add one set of parentheses, as shown in the following:

```
av = (45 + 34 + 82) / 3
```

> **Tip:** Use plenty of parentheses in your programs to make the order of operators clearer, even if you don't override the order of operators. The parentheses make the calculations easier to understand if you modify the program later.

A Word about Scientific Notation

Scientific notation is a numeric shortcut.

Sometimes Access Basic produces results in *scientific notation,* and you, as a programmer, can enter data in scientific notation; therefore, you need to understand how to interpret scientific notation. Scientific notation is a shortcut notation for representing extremely large or extremely small numbers. You might program Access Basic for many years without using scientific notation, but understanding it means that you won't be surprised if Access Basic displays a number on your screen in scientific notation.

It is easiest to learn scientific notation by looking at a few examples. Basically, you can represent any number in scientific notation, but this representation usually is limited to extremely large or extremely small numbers. Table 12.6 shows some scientific notation numbers and their equivalents.

Table 12.6. Looking at scientific notation numbers.

Scientific Notation	Equivalent
3.08E+12	3,080,000,000,000
–9.7587E+04	–97,587
+5.164E–5	0.00005164
–4.6545E–9	–0.0000000046545
1.654E+3002	1.654×10^{3002}

Positive scientific notation numbers begin with a plus sign or have no sign. Negative scientific numbers begin with a minus sign. To figure out the rest, take the portion of the number at the left and multiply it by 10 raised to the number on the right. Thus, +2.164E+3 means to multiply 2.164 by 1,000 (1,000 is 10 raised to the third power, or 10^3). Also, –5.432E–2 is negative 5.432 times .01 (10 raised to the –2 power, or 10^{-2}).

Example

Light travels 186,000 miles per second. To store 186,000 as a variable in a single-precision scientific notation, type

```
lightSpeed! = 1.86E+5
```

Example

The sun is 93,000,000 miles from the earth. (You're learning space trivia while practicing programming!) The moon is only about 386,000 miles from the earth. To store these two distances in scientific notation, code them as follows:

```
sunDist! = 9.3E+7
mooDist! = 3.68E+5
```

Summary

You now can perform almost any math operation you'll ever need. By understanding the order of operators, you know how to structure your formulas so that Access Basic computes the answer the way you prefer. You always can override the order of operators by using parentheses.

There is much more to computers than math, especially when the primary focus of your programs is databases. Nevertheless, an understanding of expressions is critical to your making Access Basic expressions behave the way you need them to.

Now that you can initialize and compute with variables, you should learn how Access Basic separates and protects the values in variables. The next chapter explains how to break your programs into sections that can recognize only the variables needed within that section.

Review Questions

Answers to review questions are in Appendix B.

1. What are the results of the following expressions?

   A. 1 + 2 * 4 / 2

   B. (1 + 2) * 4 / 2

   C. 1 + 2 * (4 / 2)

2. What are the results of the following expressions?

   A. 9 \ 2 + 1

   B. (1 + (10 - (2 + 2)))

3. Write a line of code that prints the area of a circle (in the immediate window) with a radius of 4. PI is equal to 3.14159. The area of a circle is equal to PI * radius^2.

4. Convert each of the formulas in Figure 12.4 to their Access Basic assignment statement.

5. Rewrite the following numbers in scientific notation format:

   15   −0.000043   −54543   531234.9

Figure 12.4

Formulas to be converted to Access Basic assignments.

$$a! = \frac{3 + 3}{4 + 4}$$

$$x! = (a! - b!) * (a! - c!)^2$$

$$f! = \frac{a!^{1/2}}{b!^{1/3}}$$

$$d! = \frac{(8 - x!^2)}{(x! - 9)} - \frac{(4 * 2 - 1)}{x!^3}$$

Review Exercises

1. Write the code that prints each of the first eight powers of 2 (in other words, 21, 22, 23, ..., 28). Print string constants that describe each printed answer.

2. Store the weights and ages of three people in variables. Write the statements (in the immediate window) that print a table of the weights and ages. Because you are working in the immediate window, the lines of output won't print back-to-back, but that's okay. At the bottom of the table, print the average of the weights and heights (after storing the averages in two variables) and their totals.

Part IV

Adding Control

CHAPTER 13

The Scope of Data

This chapter begins to explore the real-world problems surrounding Access Basic programs. Access Basic programs normally contain several procedures, not just a few individual lines or modules with single procedures. You've already seen the Utility Functions module, which contains several procedures—both function procedures and one sub procedure.

When a module contains more than one procedure, those procedures often have to share data among each other. Creating a variable in one procedure with Dim does not automatically make that variable available in other procedures. If you are going to write Access Basic programs (modules) that are properly broken down into several small procedures, each performing an individual task, you have to be able to give those procedures the capability to share data.

This chapter introduces the following topics:

◆ Declaration and procedure organization

◆ The scope of local, module, and global variables

◆ Private procedures

◆ Creating a new procedure

◆ Checking syntax with the editor

As an Access Basic programmer, you have to know how your module and procedure variables interrelate. This chapter explains how multiple procedures locate variables that are available to them.

Although you saw how to add a new procedure to an existing module in Chapter 11, this chapter shows you how to create a brand new module and add a brand new procedure to it. In the next chapter, you see how to communicate between procedures.

Modules Programs with Procedures

This chapter reviews some module fundamentals before extending that review with new material. You *must* have a firm grasp of module contents before you cover the sharing of variables between procedures in Access Basic.

A *module* is an Access Basic program. One Access database might have many modules (programs), just like an Access database might have many tables and forms. As you've learned in the earlier chapters of this book, Access Basic code is similar to the calculations and operations that you have already used in macro and field expressions, but Access Basic allows much more. Rather than a single expression, you can write a series of expressions and hold results of those expressions in variables for later use. As you learn some of the control statements available in Access Basic in the remainder of this book, you'll see how much power Access Basic modules provide for your database processing needs.

Figure 13.1 shows a graphical outline of an Access Basic database module. Every module contains a declarations section. In the next section of this chapter, you learn all about the statements that can appear in the declarations section. There is only one declarations section per module, and all modules have a declarations section, although you can leave the section blank.

Figure 13.1

A database contains one or more modules, and a module contains one or more procedures.

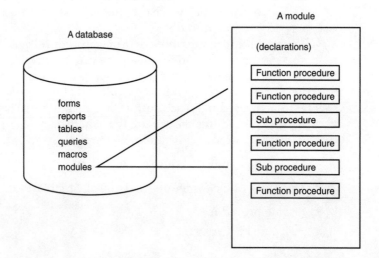

Note: Although an Access database may contain several modules, a single module that contains many procedures is usually sufficient for any database.

The Declarations Section

The declarations section is not a procedure. The declarations section contains statements that affect the rest of the module, but these statements are executed automatically before any procedure in the module ever runs. The declarations section determines how the rest of the module behaves. Variable declarations often appear in the declarations section.

When you first create a new module, Access Basic creates an initial declarations section for you. Access Basic does not create any procedures—neither function procedures nor sub procedures—because Access Basic cannot determine what kind of procedures you need. However, because all modules require a declarations section, Access creates one for you and adds one initial declarations statement. You then can add more statements to the declarations if you need to.

Example

In this example you create a new module in the Northwind Traders database. You should follow this example closely so you know what to expect when you create your own modules.

1. Open the Northwind Traders database if it is not already open.

2. Click the Module button and select New to create a new module. Access displays the new module screen shown in Figure 13.2. Notice that the first declarations section statement, `Option Compare Database`, is placed in the module for you automatically.

Figure 13.2

A newly created module.

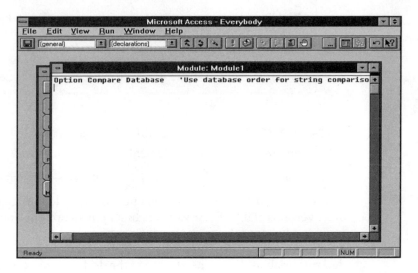

> **Tip:** After creating a new module, you should consider adding remarks telling what the module is used for. If you work with a group of other programmers, put your name in the comments as well, to document your being the one who created the module.

The statement `Option Compare Database` instructs Access to compare data using the option set when you first created the database. Unless you want to override the database's comparison setting (and most of the time you should not), leave the `Option Compare Database` statement at the top of your modules to ensure that the module code compares data in the same way that the underlying database compares data.

If the line were `Option Compare Text`, text comparisons would not be case-sensitive. `Mac` and `MAC` would be considered the same text string. `Option Compare Binary` instructs Access Basic to perform case-sensitive text comparisons so that `Mac` is different from `MAC`.

3. Add the following statement to the declarations section:

```
Option Explicit
```

This statement forces the procedures to declare each variable explicitly with `Dim`. Without `Option Explicit`, all of your variables are of the `Variant` data type unless you declare them with `Deftype` or use data type suffixes.

> **Tip:** Always use `Option Explicit` in every module (it does not span multiple modules in the same database). If you misspell a variable name without the `Option Explicit` statement in the declarations section, Access thinks you are creating a new `Variant` data type. With `Option Explicit`, Access knows when you misspell a variable name.

Other Declarations Statements

Other common declarations statements appear as follows:

```
Option Base     Dim     Global     Deftype     Option Explicit
```

Dim creates local or module variables.

The outdated `Option Base` statement exists only to maintain compatibility with older versions of BASIC. Advanced `Dim` statement options (found later in this book) provide a better replacement for `Option Base`.

You've seen `Dim` used to declare variables; it is probably the best statement to declare variables. If you insert a `Dim` in the declarations section of a module, every variable declared with the `Dim` statement is available to the module.

Being a *module variable* means that the variable is available to any procedure within that module but not to other modules. Therefore, if the following statement appears in the declarations section of the new module:

```
Dim orange As Integer
```

then any procedure within the new module can use orange. If one procedure assigns orange a value, all procedures can use orange also, and the assigned value is still there. However, the module has *no idea* what orange is (unless it contains its own Dim statement for orange, in which case there are two separate orange variables in the same database), and you can use orange only in the module in which it is defined.

If you declare the orange variable inside a procedure, such as you saw in the earlier chapters of this book, only that procedure knows what orange is. No other procedure can use orange. Then orange is known as a *local variable.* If another procedure declares an orange variable (and one can, although doing so is a questionable programming practice), there are two distinct and separate orange variables in the same module, and each can be used (called being *visible*) only within its own procedure.

The Global statement declares *global variables.* A global variable is available to all procedures in all modules in the database. Therefore, if you want to use a variable in more than one module, declare it as a Global variable. The Global statement works exactly as the Dim statement. For example, the statement

```
Global orange As Integer
```

tells Access to declare an integer variable named orange and that orange can be used anywhere in any procedure or module of the database. If one function procedure in one module assigns orange the value of 8, then every other procedure in every module knows that orange holds the value of 8.

> **Note:** Use Global and module-level variables sparingly or not at all. Name clashes can occur easily. Reusing the same variable name for two different purposes is too easy, and if that variable is Global or a module-level variable, you replace a value that was assigned in another location. The opposites of Global and module-level variables are local variables, which are visible (usable) only within the procedures in which they are declared. If you use the same variable name in one procedure as a variable local to another procedure, you do not damage the other's copy of the variable.

Variables have local, module, or global scope.

Because the Deftype statement is usually replaced by the Dim statement in modern dialects of BASIC, including Access Basic, you rarely see any Deftype statements in the declarations section. If you do, however, all variables declared with Deftype in a declarations section are module-level variables. All variables declared with Deftype inside a procedure are local to that procedure.

> **Caution:** Although you should put the `Option Explicit` statement in your declarations sections, leaving it out lets you automatically declare variables just by using them somewhere in the procedures. These variables are all local to the procedures in which they are used and are `Variant` unless you use a data type suffix character.

In conclusion, three kinds of *scope* in Access determine how visible variables are to the rest of the program. Variables declared within a procedure have local scope and can be used only within that procedure. Variables declared in the declarations section with `Dim` or `Deftype` have module scope and can be used only within that module. Variables declared in the declarations section with `Global` have global scope and can be used within any module in the database.

> **Note:** Even procedures have scope. Generally, procedures have global scope and can be called from any other procedure in any other module in the database. If you preface a procedure's first line with the word `Private`, however, the procedure can only be called from within the module in which it is defined.

> **Tip:** Declaring local variables and `Private` procedures becomes especially important when you are working on an Access Basic program with other people. If you and another programmer are writing modules that operate on the same database, you could write a procedure or create a variable that has the same name as the other programmer's module. If your data is local (or has module-level scope) and your procedures are `Private`, name clashes never occur because all of your module's variables and procedures are accessible only within the module that you write. Despite the name-clash advantage, however, most of your procedures cannot be `Private` because `Private` procedures cannot be triggered from the database form or report events, but only from other procedures in the module.

Example

The Northwind Traders database Utility Functions module includes the following two lines in its declarations section:

```
Option Compare Text     ' So string comparisons aren' case-
➥sensitive
Option Explicit
```

Therefore, the designers of the Northwind Traders database wanted all text comparisons to ignore the case of text, and the Option Explicit statement requires that all variables be declared rather than assuming Variant for all undeclared variables, as would be the default without Option Explicit.

Example

Figure 13.3 illustrates all the scoping possibilities that variables and procedures can possess. Notice that both modules' global variables are accessible from within both modules.

> **Tip:** Keep all your Global variables together within one module—unlike the illustrative example in Figure 13.3—so that you can keep track of them more easily. Remember, however, to limit your use of Global variables. Local variables don't get in each other's way as easily as Global variables, and Global variables take memory for the entire module's life rather than during a single procedure's execution.

Figure 13.3

Looking at different kinds of scope.

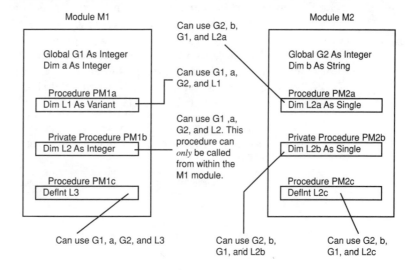

In the figure, the variables a and b have module scope and are visible only from within the procedures in their module. Each procedure contains its own local variable (such as L1 and L2a), and because they are local, only those procedures can access those local variables.

The PM1b procedure is a Private procedure, so it can only be called from another procedure in the M1 module.

Adding a New Function Procedure

Now that you've created a new module, you can add a new procedure to it. The following example adds a function procedure that takes the Region field from the Customers form and changes it. Remember these steps when adding a new procedure that executes from a form or report's event:

1. Write the procedure.

2. Compile the procedure.

   If you do not compile the procedure, Access compiles it automatically when the procedure runs. If there are errors, they are much easier to spot if you compile the program yourself before leaving the editor.

3. Add the procedure event on the form's design view.

4. Test and fix the procedure if there are problems.

Example

The Region field in the Customers form is usually used for a state name, but the Northwind Traders database is used around the world, and not all places have state names. In the following steps you take the region entered (or edited) by the user and convert the region to a two-letter uppercase region code. The program is simple; until you learn Access Basic control statements, these example procedures have to be kept simple. If the user types Utah, the Region field becomes UT; if the user types Tuscany, the Region field becomes TU, and so on.

1. The module declarations window section of your newly-created module should still be on your screen if you are following along from the previous example. Type this line:

```
Function FixRg
```

Access opens a new procedure window with the following lines:

```
Function FixRg ()
End Function
```

> **Note:** All functions begin with a `Function` statement and end with an `End Function` statement. If you were to open a subroutine procedure, you would see the following lines instead:
>
> ```
> Sub FixSub ()
> End Sub
> ```

2. Insert the following program. The variable Rg is local to the procedure because it is not defined in the declarations section.

```
Dim Rg As Control
Set Rg = Forms!Customers!Region
Rg = UCase$(Left$(Rg, 2))
```

The procedure creates a local variable named Rg to hold the form's Region value. The third line first uses the Left$() function (described in Chapter 3) and returns the first two letters of the region, and then UCase$() converts that region to uppercase. The variable Rg is then assigned the new uppercase value. Rg is associated to the form's Region field, so changing Rg changes the field in the form.

3. Select **R**un Compile Loaded Modules to compile the program. If Access encounters an error, it displays a dialog box explaining the error. Then you can fix the error before recompiling again.

4. Close the module window and save the new module under the name **My New Module**.

5. Click the Forms button and select the Customers form. Select **D**esign to display the form's design view.

6. Open the form's Region property window by double-clicking the Region field (not the label, but the field itself). The Region's property box (titled Text Box) appears.

7. Scroll down the Text Box and click the On Exit field and enter the following line:

```
=FixRg()
```

The FixRg() function executes if the user enters a new Region value or edits one already in the database. Now your screen should look like the one in Figure 13.4.

8. Close and save the form. Select **O**pen to display the first Customer's record.

9. Tab to the Region field (that currently is blank) and type **Europe**. As soon as you leave the field (by pressing Tab or Enter), the On Exit event triggers your procedure and the Region is changed to EU.

10. Close the form and return to the database window.

Figure 13.4

After linking the new procedure to the form.

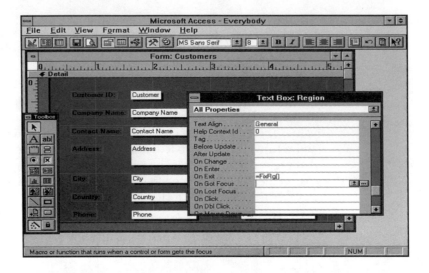

Syntax Checking

The editor can check your spelling.

Unless somebody has reset a **View Options...** parameter that is ordinarily set (called *syntax checking*), Access Basic checks your procedure statements as you type them in the Access Basic editor. In other words, if you misspell a command, such as typing **Dem** rather than **Dim**, Access Basic lets you know then and there that you've made a mistake. Checking your syntax at editing time—rather than at compile time as most programming languages do—makes your compiles much faster.

Example

Open the My New Module module by selecting it from the database window and choosing **Design**. Follow these steps to see the syntax checker in operation:

1. Move the cursor (while staying in the declarations section) under the `Option Compare Database` statement after Option Explicit.

2. Type the following line and press Enter:

```
Dem myVar
```

Access displays the error message box shown in Figure 13.5.

Although the error code is not entirely explicit (a `You misspelled something!` message would be more appropriate in this case), Access does the best it can with the line that you typed. Sometimes the error message can be extremely helpful, and other times the error message is a little misleading. Nevertheless, the error is announced, and you should fix whatever is wrong before moving on.

Figure 13.5

Oops, a typing
error.

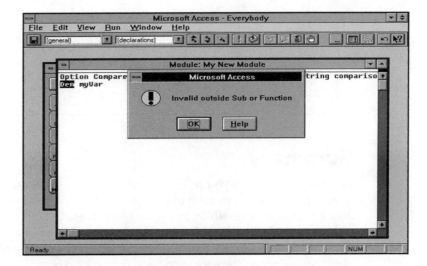

3. For this example, erase the line you just typed and close the module's
   editing window without saving any changes.

Example

You can turn off the syntax checking if you want. Access then takes longer to
compile your programs, but you aren't bothered by the messages as you type your
procedures. Sometimes, you might want to have more freedom inside the editor
than the syntax checker allows. For instance, turning the syntax checker off is useful
when cutting and pasting bits and pieces of code from different programs. The
following steps turn off the syntax checking:

1. Select **View Options...** from the menu.

2. Scroll the **C**ategory list until the Module Design line comes into view.

3. Select the Module Design line. The lower pane reveals two options: Syntax
   Checking and Tab Stop Width.

4. To turn off the syntax checking, change the lower pane's Yes to No. If you
   like, you also can change the number of spaces that the Access Basic editor
   uses when you press Tab, but four (the default) is usually sufficient.

5. Choose OK (or press Enter) to save the option. You can now work in the
   editor and delay the syntax checking until compilation time.

> **Caution:** Many beginning Access Basic programmers are still unaccustomed to the commands in Access Basic. If you're just learning Access Basic, the syntax checking might be helpful to you, so you might want to leave the Syntax Checking set to Yes as you get acquainted with Access Basic.

Summary

This chapter showed you how to create a new module and add a new function procedure to it. Perhaps even more importantly, this chapter explained the difference between local, module, and global variables.

Keeping variables on a local or module level helps maintain their integrity. Understanding when a variable is visible is the prelude to writing programs with many procedures. Although keeping variables local is suggested, local variables do present a problem that you haven't had to address yet. Local variables are visible only within the procedure in which they are declared. Therefore, you should keep all variables local, but *pass them* from one procedure to another. Your variables are then safe but still usable in the procedures that need them.

The next chapter teaches you how to share local variables between procedures and also how to integrate function procedures, subroutine procedures, and macros within the Access Basic environment. You learn in the next chapter how to bypass global variables and use local variables more effectively.

Review Questions

Answers to review questions are in Appendix B.

1. What is a declarations section used for?

2. TRUE or FALSE: Every module requires a declarations section.

3. TRUE or FALSE: A module that contains an `Option Explicit` statement requires that you explicitly declare all variables in your program.

4. Why might you want to turn off the syntax checking?

5. When you create a new module, what statement does Access Basic automatically insert in the declarations section for you?

6. What kind of variable—local, module, or global—has the broadest scope?

7. What kind of variable—local, module, or global—poses the most possible danger?

Review Exercises

1. Write the statement that substitutes for the Option Compare Database statement if you want database comparisons to be made so that upper-case letters always match their lowercase equivalents rather than being different.

2. Change your editor so that the Tab key produces three spaces rather than four. Try the results by typing a few lines of code using Tab to indent some of the lines.

3. Using the outline box-notation of Figure 13.3, draw the following scenario. You are writing three modules. The first module, named Mod1, contains a Proc1 procedure with two local variables. Make the second of Mod1's procedures, named pProc2, Private. The second module, Mod2, contains a module-level variable named m1 and a single procedure named Proc2a that contains a local Integer variable named i. The third procedure declares a String variable named s that is global to all the other modules and one procedure named Proc3 that uses no variables.

CHAPTER 14

Multi-Procedure Modules and Macros

This chapter is one last step to covering the groundwork of building Access Basic applications. This book has put off the *real* Access Basic long enough! Actually, if you're a newcomer to programming, you may have felt buried if global-vs-local data issues had been taught any earlier in this book. If you've already programmed in other languages, perhaps you could have jumped into some of these Access Basic details faster, especially the control statements that begin in the next chapter; but, because you are new to programming, even the idea of variables (which are now simple to you) has to be learned gradually.

This chapter introduces the following topics:

♦ The need for passing data

♦ Returning data

♦ The difference between function procedures and sub procedures

♦ Embedding macros and actions in Access Basic

Although the procedure is the building block of Access Basic, the collection of procedures—the module—is the focus of most of this chapter. Beginning in the next chapter, you see several code examples, some rather lengthy. Until now, you were not ready to see more than a snippet of code here and there. However, the longer examples require one final stop before boarding the Access Basic programmer's train: learning how to share data between procedures.

Clash of the Variables

Locals eliminate name clashes.

Local data is much safer than global data. In the preceding chapter you learned that the location of the variable's declaration is the primary determinant of a variable's scope. When you're writing a system with other programmers, using local variable data becomes even more critical. If two of you use many global variables, and you both happen to use the same global variable, a name clash occurs.

If two global variables named gi are declared, for example, one for your procedures and one for someone else's, Access Basic cannot know which gi you are initializing when you enter the following:

```
gi = 20
```

If you use a global variable and another programmer on the same application uses a local variable with the same name, the local variable always *hides the scope* of the global. Hiding the scope means that the local variable is used during that procedure and not the global variable. When the local variable goes out of scope (which means the variable is no longer available for use once the procedure ends), the global variable is then used whenever the name is referred.

Example

Figure 14.1 helps illustrate what happens when a local and a global variable have the same name.

Figure 14.1

Local variables overshadow global variables with the same name.

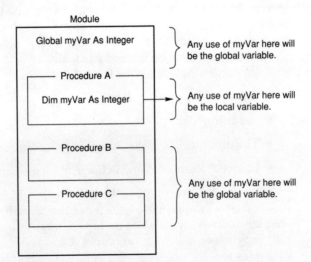

Tip: Use only local variables to solve these problems: name clashes and local variables hiding the scope of globals.

Two or more local variables residing in two separate procedures can have the same name. You never have a problem with name clashes if you stick to local variables. The variables are known only in the procedures in which they *should* be known, and one procedure does not have improper access to other procedures' variables.

Why Share Data?

Local: Good; Global: Usually not good.

Given the premise that local variables are good, and given the fact that local variables can be used (in any manner) *only* in the procedure in which they are defined, a problem arises when you need to write modules that contain more than one procedure. Just because procedures are separate doesn't always mean they have to work with separate data.

One procedure may generate a dynaset variable that *another* procedure is supposed to print. Yet, if the dynaset variable is local in the first procedure, the second procedure cannot use the variable. Neither sub procedures nor function procedures can use each other's local data—at least, not until you set up a sharing mechanism between them.

As with built-in functions that you pass data to (called arguments, as you learned earlier in the book), your procedures can pass data between each other. By passing data, you maintain the advantage of local variables while allowing more than one procedure access to the same data.

When two procedures share local data, one procedure (called the *calling procedure*) passes data to the second procedure (called the *receiving procedure*). (Refer to Figure 14.2.) If the receiving procedure computes or modifies a value that the calling procedure needs, the receiving procedure can return that value back to the calling procedure.

Figure 14.2

Calling procedures pass local data and receiving procedures work with that data.

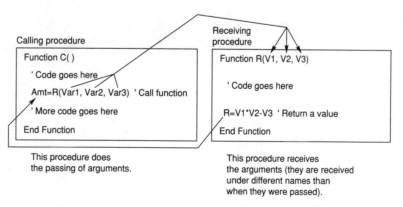

The Receiving procedure named R( ) returns a computed value back to C( ).

By Reference, By Value

If Figure 14.2's procedure named R() changes any or all of its arguments (V1, V2, or V3), the corresponding variables in C() are also changed. They are passed by *reference*, meaning that the passed arguments can be changed by their receiving procedure. If you want to keep the receiving function from being able to change the calling function's arguments, you must pass the arguments by *value*. To pass by value, precede their receiving variables with the ByVal keyword or by enclosing the passed arguments in parentheses.

Example

In the following module (not all of the code is shown so that you can focus on the arguments), the variable r is received by reference while v is received by value in the second procedure (RF()). If the RF() receiving function changes r, the CF() calling function's r is changed as well. If the RF() receiving function changes v, however, the CF() calling function's argument retains its original value.

```
Option Compare Database ' Use regular comparison sequences
Option Explicit         ' All variables be explicitly declared

' Calling function is next
Function CF()
    Dim r, v As Variant   ' Declare local variables named r and v
    Dim i As Integer      ' To hold the return value of function

    ' Code goes here

    i = RF(r, v)          ' Call the function and pass r and v
                          ' i gets RF()'s return value

End Function

' Receiving function is next
Function RF(r As Variant, ByVal v As Variant)
    ' Received r by reference and v by value
    ' Code goes here
    r = 50        ' Change r in both functions
    v = 20        ' Change v just here
    RF = r * i    ' Return a value
End Function
```

Instead of specifying the ByVal keyword in the receiving function's argument list, you can put parentheses around the calling function's variable v to force it to pass by value.

Note: In this book you often see more than one procedure listed with another procedure, with the declarations section appearing before the procedures as shown here. In the Access module window, the procedures are windowed so that you see only one at a time. If you print a module on the printer, the declarations section and the procedures print together, as shown in this book's examples.

Returning Values

Both Figure 14.2's and the previous example's receiving procedures return a value back to the calling procedure. By studying these two examples, you can see how to specify return values. Keep the following rule in mind: To return a value, assign the called function's name the return value before the function ends. In the previous example, the function named RF() returns a value because RF is assigned a value. When CF()'s execution resumes, the return value of CF() is assigned to RF()'s variable named i.

A function doesn't have to return a value.

Recall that a subroutine procedure cannot return a value. You never assign a subroutine procedure's name to an expression. Also, when calling a subroutine procedure, you do not assign the procedure to anything. You can pass a subroutine procedure values, as explained in the next section, but the procedure cannot return a value.

A function procedure does not *have* to return a value, but you must assign its function call to a variable, even if you do nothing with that variable, as if the called function were written to return a value.

Caution: A procedure can be passed many arguments, but a procedure can return only one value. Although the capability to return a maximum of one value might seem limiting, all the built-in functions can return a maximum of only one value. The limitation of a single return value poses no problem, as you'll see. Only function procedures can return values, not sub procedures. If the calling procedure calls another procedure that returns a value, the calling procedure must do something with that return value (such as print it or save it).

Sub Procedures Arguments

Sub procedures work just like function procedures, with the following two exceptions:

♦ Sub procedures cannot return values back to the calling procedure.

♦ When you call sub procedures and pass arguments, you cannot use parentheses around the argument list.

Note: Built-in function's arguments work *exactly* like procedure arguments, but because you didn't write the code for the built-in functions, you don't have to know as much about them to share local variables with them. The Left$() function, for example, cannot work with your local variables or data. That is why you must pass to Left$() the string that you want to work with and the number of characters to return from the left of that string. Left$() (although you can't see the code because it is already compiled and built into the Access system) receives your arguments into its own local variables, works with those variables, and then returns a value back to your program.

Don't use parentheses when calling subs.

A receiving sub procedure still requires parentheses around the *receiving* arguments. You eliminate the parentheses only when you *call* a sub procedure.

Example

Suppose you're writing a procedure that needs to call the following subroutine procedure:

```
Sub Area (Radius As Single)
   Dim cirArea As Single
   cirArea = 3.14159 * Radius ^ 2  ' Compute area of circle
   Debug.Print cirArea      ' Print area in immediate window
End Sub
```

To call this subroutine procedure, you can do the following from another procedure:

```
Area 4.5     ' Call the sub procedure
```

Notice that the 4.5 is not surrounded by parentheses. If you pass no arguments to a subroutine procedure, you only specify the subroutine procedure name when calling it. If you're passing a list of several arguments, you still drop the parentheses from around them when calling the subroutine.

Note: You might wonder what the Debug is doing in this code. Debug is a *predefined* object that you can use for debugging your programs and for printing values in the immediate window. In Chapter 9 you saw how to print values of variables from within the immediate window so you could practice assigning values to the variables. If you want to print values in the immediate window from within a program, preface the Print statement with Debug.

Macros and Your Programs

You can run individual macro actions from within your Access Basic programs. Thankfully, Microsoft lets you use almost all of the actions available for macros directly inside your Access Basic programs. Being able to use the macro actions that you're already familiar with helps speed your Access Basic programming.

Not all actions are available.

Table 14.1 lists the eight macro actions that you *cannot* run inside Access Basic. Access Basic either has an equivalent (and better) way of performing the action, or the action makes no sense to an Access Basic program.

Table 14.1. Eight macro actions not directly supported in Access Basic.

Action	Access Basic Equivalent
AddMenu	Not available in Access Basic programs
MsgBox	The MsgBox function or statement replaces this action.
RunApp	The Shell function replaces this action.
RunCode	You can call a procedure directly from within Access Basic.
SendKeys	The SendKeys statement replaces this action.
SetValue	The assignment statement replaces this action.
StopAllMacros	Not available in Access Basic programs
StopMacro	Not available in Access Basic programs

The Access Basic DoCmd statement runs macro actions in your programs. Here is the format of DoCmd:

```
DoCmd actionName [actionArgumentList]
```

The *actionName* is the name of the action you want to execute from your program. The *actionArgumentList* is optional because not all actions require arguments. If an action requires more than one argument, separate the arguments with commas between them.

> **Caution:** If an action allows for optional arguments and you want to specify only some of the arguments (and take the defaults for the others), you must still use commas as if you had specified the missing arguments. An example later in this chapter clarifies using commas to indicate default action arguments.

As you see from the following examples, an action's syntax is slightly different when coded in an Access Basic program than when coded directly in the macro definition screens. When coding a macro from within a macro's design view, you can point, select, and click to specify arguments and the action's syntax. When writing Access Basic code, you have to type the arguments next to the macro name, which often requires a slightly different syntax than a macro's design view.

> **Tip:** When you get help on an action, you should look at the cross-reference labeled *Access Basic* to find out the action's syntax when used in an Access Basic procedure. The *Access Language Reference Manual*, which comes with Access, also lists the macro syntax and Access Basic syntax of each action.

Example

Consider the following two action statements:

```
DoCmd Hourglass True
```

and

```
DoCmd Hourglass False
```

Before Windows executes any time-consuming task, you usually see the cursor shaped as an hourglass, letting you know to wait a moment. You can do the same in your own programs by turning the cursor into an hourglass shape before a time-consuming calculation or database update and then turning the cursor back into its normal shape (with DoCmd-Hourglass False) when you're done.

The Hourglass action is an example of how actions are slightly modified to work in the Access Basic environment. When you're creating a true macro, the full name for this action is Hourglass On, and you supply either a Yes or No action argument in the query definition window's lower pane. When you're running the Hourglass macro from Access Basic, specify whether the hourglass is on by following DoCmd Hourglass with either True to turn on the hourglass or False to turn off the hourglass and return the cursor to its regular shape.

Example

The previous versions, 1.0 and 1.1, of Access contained a modified Northwind Trader's database module that contained the following subroutine procedure:

```
Sub SizeIt (DocWidth, DocHeight)
' Accepts: two numeric values
  ' Purpose: resizes the active window to the width and height
  'specified
' Returns: nothing

    DoCmd MoveSize , , DocWidth, DocHeight

End Sub
```

The `SizeIt()` sub procedure does just what its remarks describe: `SizeIt()` resizes the active window (the window being worked in by the user when this procedure runs) to a specific width and height specified by its argument list. To make this change, `SizeIt()` calls the `MoveSize` action.

Notice that the first two of the `MoveSize` arguments are unspecified in this procedure. The first two arguments specify the horizontal and vertical positions of the resized window's upper-left corner. Because these two values are unspecified, Access Basic does not move the window from its current position on-screen but just resizes the window to meet the width and height values passed to `SizeIt()`.

> **Tip:** Microsoft recommends that you write these argument-saving subroutine functions when you execute the same action several times but rarely specify all of the action's arguments. These procedures are sometimes called *wrappers* because they wrap around other code, such as the `MoveSize` action, and make the action easier to use.

Running Complete Macros from Modules

A macro action that runs complete macros does exist. The action `RunMacro` runs another macro, similar to the way one procedure can call another procedure. Here is the format of the `RunMacro` action when used in an Access Basic program:

```
DoCmd RunMacro macroName [, repeatCount] [, repeatExpression]
```

If you want the macro to execute several times, one after another, include an integer variable or expression for the second argument. If you want the macro to execute as long as an expression is true (or nonzero), specify the *repeatExpression*. If you don't specify a *repeatCount* but *do* specify a *repeatExpression*, leave a comma for the *repeatCount* argument.

You can specify both a *repeatCount* argument and a *repeatExpression* argument. The macro then runs a maximum of *repeatCount* times but may stop earlier if the *repeatExpression* ever becomes false.

Example

Suppose that you want to run a macro named HelpUser, which requires no arguments from your Access Basic program. The following DoCmd does just that:

```
DoCmd RunMacro HelpUser
```

Example

If you want to run the HelpUser macro four times, add the *repeatCount* argument, as follows:

```
DoCmd RunMacro HelpUser, 4
```

Once you master conditional logic used inside an Access Basic program, you'll be more comfortable learning the third expression, *repeatExpression*.

Example

If the macro that you want to execute is stored in a group, preface the macro's name with the group name, as follows:

```
DoCmd RunMacro myMacros.printTitle
```

Summary

This chapter delved more deeply into the global versus local variable issues. Now you should understand global name clash problems, and even if you don't *fully* understand why using local variables is important, at least you know to use them everywhere you can and what can happen if you don't.

Access Basic lets you use the same local variable name in different procedures. Although you don't want to overdo the practice, using the same variable name for simple processing, such as the counters in loops that you read about later, helps document your code and simplifies the number of variables that you have to keep track of. If, however, you have a global variable and a local variable with the same name, the local variable always hides the global's value. Think of Access Basic as always using the "most local" variable if two variables in the same module have the same name.

If you use local variables, you must provide a way for your procedures to communicate with each other. When one procedure contains local data that another procedure needs to work with, pass the data (called arguments) from the calling procedure to the receiving procedure. The receiving procedure (if it is a function procedure) can return a single value back to the calling procedure as well.

Normally, arguments pass by reference, which means that if the receiving procedure changes the arguments, the arguments are changed in the calling procedure too. If you pass arguments by value (by using the ByVal keyword), the receiving procedure cannot change the calling procedure's arguments.

Finally, you now know how to call both macro actions and complete macros from Access Basic using the DoCmd and RunMacro statements. Therefore, the knowledge that you already have of macros carries over to procedures.

The next chapter, "Program Output and User Input," explains how to display dialog boxes from within your Access Basic programs to send messages to the user and get responses from the user. Being able to interact with the user is important when your programs need to be directed by the user's response.

Review Questions

Answers to review questions are in Appendix B.

1. How do name clashes occur?

2. TRUE or FALSE: In Access you can have two variables with the same names as long as they are both global.

3. How many values can a function procedure return?

4. How many values can a subroutine procedure return?

5. How do the statements DoCmd and RunMacro differ?

6. If your program uses only local variables, name clashes do not occur. Why then must you be able to pass data between functions?

7. Suppose a module contains a global variable named sales, and a procedure within the same module creates a local variable named sales. Which variable, the local or global variable, is changed by this statement that resides inside the procedure:

```
sales = price * quantity
```

8. What is the default method for passing arguments, by reference or by value?

9. What are the two ways to pass values?

10. What does the term *wrapper* procedure mean and how can a wrapper procedure help you?

Review Exercises

1. Using Table 14.1, code the following action in Access Basic (Access Basic does not allow SetValue):

   A SetValue action that sets Forms!Employee!Salary to the expression 46300.

2. Write the Access Basic statement that runs a macro named getUser three times.

3. How do you change the following program so that v is passed by reference and r is passed by value?

```
Option Compare Database ' Use regular comparison sequences
Option Explicit          ' All variables be explicitly declared

' Calling function is next
Function CF()
Dim r, v As Variant ' Declare local variables named r and v
Dim i As Integer    ' To hold the return value of function

' Code goes here

i = RF(r, v)         ' Call the function and pass r and v
                     ' i gets RF()'s return value

End Function

' Receiving function is next
Function RF(r As Variant, ByVal v As Variant)
  ' Received r by reference and v by value
  ' Code goes here
  r = 50       ' Change r in both functions
  v = 20       ' Change v just here
  RF = r * i   ' Return a value
End Function
```

CHAPTER 15

Program Output and User Input

In Chapter 9 you learned how to use the immediate execution window to view the contents of variables. The immediate window is nice for variable display and also for debugging, as you see later in this book, but you're ready to start displaying data the way a Windows programmer prefers—using message boxes.

Not only should you concern yourself with how your output looks but also with the way the user enters data. You are well aware of the ease with which forms enable users to enter data, but once you begin to create powerful Access database systems using Access Basic, you must have a way to ask the user questions so that your programs can act upon the user's responses.

This chapter introduces the following topics:

♦ The MsgBox statement

♦ The MsgBox() function

♦ The InputBox() function

♦ The InputBox$() function

With the MsgBox() and the InputBox() functions, your programs produce professional dialog with your user without being a tremendous burden to program.

Using the *MsgBox* Statement

MsgBox displays your data in a dialog box.

If you've used the MsgBox macro action, the MsgBox statement is fairly simple. MsgBox displays data in a pop-up dialog box and optionally displays an appropriate icon and response buttons for the user. MsgBox also is capable of writing string data to the screen. The string contains the message you want to send. Figure 15.1 shows a sample dialog box generated with MsgBox. From the figure, you see that you control both the message and the title of the dialog box. You also can determine which icon appears and how many buttons appear on the box.

Figure 15.1

A dialog box displayed with *MsgBox*.

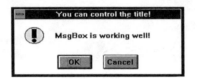

 Note: You can move or close the message box, but you cannot resize it.

You might want to display a message with MsgBox for several reasons. Here is the format of MsgBox:

```
MsgBox messageString [, type] [, titleString]
```

The *messageString* is a string expression (a constant string enclosed in quotation marks, a string variable, or a text control value) that you want displayed in the dialog box. If the string is long, the dialog box expands to hold the whole string, properly breaking each line between words.

 Caution: The message can be no longer than 1,024 characters.

The last two arguments to the MsgBox statement are optional. The easiest kind of dialog box to display is one with only a message and an OK button, as the next example shows.

Example

 The following statement displays the message box shown in Figure 15.2:

```
MsgBox "I am easy to display!"
```

Note: Without the OK button, the dialog box flashes too quickly on-screen and is gone before the user has a chance to read the message.

Figure 15.2

A dialog box
displayed with
MsgBox.

Controlling More of the Message

You control the
buttons in the box.

The *type* in the MsgBox format is a numeric value or expression that controls the number of buttons and the icon that appear in the dialog box. The *titleString* is the string that appears at the top of the box in the title bar. (If you don't specify a title, Access Basic displays Microsoft Access.)

The value you use for *type* is made up of several things. Tables 15.1, 15.2, and 15.3 contain values that make up the *type* parameter of MsgBox.

Table 15.1. Controlling the buttons.

Value	Description
0	Displays the OK button in the box
1	Displays the OK and Cancel buttons in the box
2	Displays the Abort, Retry, and Ignore buttons in the box
3	Displays the Yes, No, and Cancel buttons in the box
4	Displays the Yes and No buttons in the box
5	Displays the Retry and Cancel buttons in the box

Table 15.2. Controlling the icons.

Value	Description
0	Displays no icon in the box
16	Displays the Critical Message icon in the box
32	Displays the Warning Query icon in the box

continues

Table 15.2. Continued

Value	Description
48	Displays the Warning Message icon in the box
64	Displays the Information Message icon in the box

> **Note:** The icons for each of Table 15.2's values are shown in Figure 15.3.

Figure 15.3

The *MsgBox* icons and their descriptions.

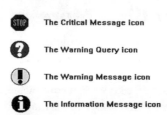

Table 15.3. Controlling the default button.

Value	Description
0	The first button is the default.
256	The second button is the default.
512	The third button is the default.

Table 15.1 describes the layout of the buttons on the dialog box. The previous example did not specify a *type* value, so Access Basic used 0. The dialog box in Figure 15.2 contains only an OK button because it has 0 *type*. If you want a style of buttons different from the single OK button, use a different value from Table 15.1.

If you want an icon to appear inside the dialog box, *add* one of the values from Table 15.2 to the *type* value from Table 15.1. In other words, if you want the OK and Cancel buttons to display (a *type* of 1) and you want the Warning Query icon to display (a *type* of 32), you specify 33 as the *type* (both table values added together).

A dialog box always contains a default button. A default button appears outlined to look as if someone is pressing it. If the user presses Enter without selecting another button, the button defined as the default is selected. Therefore, if you want the Cancel button (the second button described in the preceding paragraph) to be the default button when the dialog box appears, add an additional 512 to the 33 to get a total of 545.

> **Caution:** The MsgBox() function explained later in this chapter can use multiple-button dialog boxes better than the MsgBox statement because the MsgBox() function sends a return value back to the calling code that indicates which button the user chose to end the dialog box.

Example

Suppose that you want to display the dialog box shown in Figure 15.4. (Notice that the center button is the default.)

Figure 15.4

A complex dialog box.

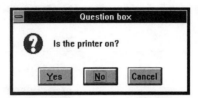

In Access Basic, use the following MsgBox statement to create the dialog box shown in the figure:

```
MsgBox "Is the printer on?", 291, "Question box"
```

Example

Adding the type values together can be cumbersome, but thanks to Access Basic, you don't even have to add. The following MsgBox statement works just like the preceding example because the sum of the type numbers adds to 291:

```
MsgBox "Is the printer on?", 3 + 32 + 256, "Question box"
```

Example

You'll find that a Const named constant helps you display common MsgBox arguments. For example, the following statement

```
Const MB_EXCLAIM = 48
```

Declare named constants for common dialog box options.

declares a constant named MB_EXCLAIM so throughout the rest of the program, you can use the MB_EXCLAIM constant rather than having to remember the value of 48. The following MsgBox statement displays a message box that displays a warning dialog box:

```
MsgBox "Don't select the wrong option", MB_EXCLAIM
```

The *MsgBox( )* Function

The MsgBox statement is useful for displaying messages, but the buttons it can provide are more useful when you use the MsgBox() function rather than the MsgBox statement. The function returns a value that indicates the button chosen by the user. Therefore, after the function displays multiple buttons, you know which button the user chose.

The MsgBox() function works just like the MsgBox statement, and the function accepts the same three arguments. Table 15.4 describes the return values that come from MsgBox().

Table 15.4. *MsgBox()* return values.

Value	Description
1	OK was chosen.
2	Cancel was chosen.
3	Abort was chosen.
4	Retry was chosen.
5	Ignore was chosen.
6	Yes was chosen.
7	No was chosen.

Example

The following assignment statement does a lot:

```
userButton = MsgBox("Are you ready?", 35)
```

When Access Basic reaches this statement, the program waits for the user to answer the MsgBox() prompt by choosing one of the MsgBox buttons. The result of the button choice, a numeric value from Table 15.4, then is assigned to the variable userButton.

The 35 sends the Yes, No, and Cancel buttons to the dialog box (value 3) and displays the Warning Query icon (value 32). If the user chooses Yes, the userButton variable is assigned the value 6. userButton gets a 7 if the user chooses No, and userButton gets 2 if the user chooses Cancel.

Tip: If the user presses Esc at any dialog box that contains a Cancel button, Access Basic acts as though the user chose the Cancel button and returns the value 2 from the MsgBox() function.

In the next chapter you learn how to test the return value of MsgBox() and execute code depending on which button the user chooses.

The *InputBox( )* Functions

The *InputBox()* functions get data from the user.

The InputBox() and InputBox$() functions are the opposite of the MsgBox() function. Whereas MsgBox() displays data for the user, the InputBox() and InputBox$() functions receive the user's input.

> **Note:** The InputBox() and InputBox$() functions generally ask the user for data. Both functions display a dialog box similar to that of MsgBox() (without the icons) that describes what data is being requested.

The InputBox() and InputBox$() functions do the same thing, except that InputBox() inputs Variant data and InputBox$() inputs only string data.

Here are the formats of these functions:

```
InputBox(prompt [, [title] [, [default][, xpos, ypos]]])
```

and

```
InputBox$(prompt [, [title] [, [default][, xpos, ypos]]])
```

The functions' format brackets indicate that if you leave out either the *title* or the *default* (or both), the commas still are required as placeholders.

The *prompt* is a string that you want to appear so that the user knows what you're asking for. The *prompt* can be as long as 255 characters. The *title* is a string that becomes the input box's title. Unlike MsgBox(), with these functions no title displays if you do not specify a *title*. The *default* is a default string that appears inside the typing area. The user can accept the string and press Enter if he or she doesn't want to enter a new value.

The *xpos* and *ypos* indicate the numeric value of the *twips* where you want the input box to appear on-screen. If you've displayed a message or table or form somewhere on-screen, you can position the input box wherever you want it to appear (as opposed to the middle of the screen if you specified no position). *xpos* is the x coordinate (the horizontal position), and *ypos* is the y coordinate (the vertical position).

> **Note:** A twip is 1/1440 of an inch and 1/567 of a centimeter (very small indeed).

Example

Figure 15.5 shows an input box generated from the following `InputBox$()` function (assuming that *UserName* is declared to be a `String` variable):

```
UserName = InputBox$("What is your name?", "Ask a name", "John
➥Doe")
```

The `InputBox()` functions always offer a typing area for the user to enter a value and an OK button so the user can indicate when the input is completed. After the user enters a name (or presses Enter to choose OK and use the default `John Doe`), the variable `UserName` holds the user's answer.

Figure 15.5

Awaiting the user's response.

Summary

You can now display professional-looking dialog boxes from within Access. If you ever want to give the user a little extra message or get the user's attention in a way that a regular database form or report cannot do, display a dialog box with `MsgBox`. `MsgBox` is either a statement or a function. If you need to test to see which buttons the user chooses, you can call the `MsgBox()` function and test the return value.

You also learned how to write programs that accept input from the keyboard. Before this chapter you had to assign variables values at the time you wrote the code or look up variables' values from the database. You can now write programs that prompt for variable data, and the user then enters data when the procedure runs.

Often you see a `MsgBox` statement and `InputBox()` function next to each other in code. The `MsgBox` statement displays information and the `InputBox()` asks questions of the user about that information.

Now that you can get the user's response to your questions, the next chapter explains how to act upon that response. Being able to control a program's execution based on data is vital for true data processing. Your program must be able to respond and make decisions based on values in tables and variables. The next chapter introduces you to *conditional programming logic,* a fancy term for writing programming statements that test data values and act according to the results of the test.

Review Questions

Answers to review questions are in Appendix B.

1. What is the difference between MsgBox and MsgBox()?

2. What is the difference between InputBox() and InputBox$()?

3. Which of the following can you *not* to do a dialog box generated with MsgBox?

    A. Display output for the user

    B. Test to see which message button was pressed

    C. Display warnings to the user

4. Which function do you use to ask a question: MsgBox() or InputBox()?

5. TRUE or FALSE: The Tables 15.1, 15.2, and 15.3 provide the values for three different MsgBox arguments.

6. What is a twip?

7. Why do the InputBox() functions enable you to display output (the *prompt*) when they are input functions?

8. If you don't specify your own title, what happens when Access Basic executes a MsgBox statement?

9. If you don't specify your own title, what happens when Access Basic executes an InputBox statement?

10. Where does the InputBox() input dialog box appear if you don't specify placement coordinate values?

Review Exercises

1. Write a MsgBox statement that displays your name and an OK button.

2. Write a procedure that asks the user for his or her full name. Use the built-in Left$() function to display the first three letters of the name in a dialog box. *Hint:* Because Left$() returns a string, you can use the Left$() function in place of a MsgBox title.

3. Write the MsgBox() needed to generate the dialog box shown in Figure 15.6.

Figure 15.6

How was this dialog box generated?

CHAPTER 16

Comparing Data with *If*

The nice thing about my writing a book for people who have used Access as a database product, even if you've never programmed in your life, is that you already have a fundamental understanding of several issues that most beginning programmers have to be painstakingly led through.

This chapter discusses the If statement, one of the most powerful and useful statements in Access Basic. Even if you have never used If, you are already familiar with testing data for true and false values. You have no doubt created simple queries with conditional statements similar to the following criteria: <3200. If this statement were in the criteria box for a query's Amount field, the query would include only those records whose Amount is less than 3,200. The < is known as a *comparison operator* because it sets a condition that is true only under certain circumstances (in this case, a true results only if the field data is less than 3,200).

The If statement takes full advantage of the comparison operators, and with it you can begin to write programs that make decisions based on data. Most of the time an Access procedure executes sequentially, with one line following the next, unless you add control statements that change the order of the instructions being executed. (An Access procedure doesn't execute sequentially when an If statement causes some statements to be skipped over.) The If statement is one such control statement that determines the order of statement execution at runtime depending on the data being worked with at the time.

This chapter introduces the following topics:

◆ The comparison operators

◆ The `If` statement

◆ The `Else` statement

◆ The `ElseIf` statement

Once you master the `If` statement and its derivatives, the remaining control statements such as loops and `Select Case` are not difficult.

If It's True

The If makes decisions.

`If` has several formats. Here is the format of the most fundamental `If` statement:

```
IF conditional Then
    Block of one or more Access Basic statements
End If
```

Tip: The `Block of one or more Access Basic statements` does not have to be indented as shown in the format, but the indention helps you quickly locate where the `If` begins and ends.

Before you get to the programming side of `If`, take a minute to think of how you use the word *if* in real life. When you begin a sentence with *if*, you're setting up a *conditional* statement (which is a statement that may or may not be true). For example, consider the following statements:

If the day is warm, then I will go swimming.

If the light is green, then go.

If the light is red, then stop.

If I make enough money, then we'll buy a new house.

The clauses following the words *if* and the words *then* are the conditional clauses. That is, if and only if the condition is true do you complete the statement. Breaking down the last statement further gives us the following:

If I make enough money, then we'll buy a new house, but if I don't make enough money, we will not buy a new house.

Making enough money, therefore, is this statement's condition that determines whether the last part of the statement takes place.

Tip: The If's *Block of one or more Access Basic statements* can contain one or more lines with *any* valid Access Basic statements including additional (called *nested*) If statements.

Note: Notice from its format that If takes more than a single line. You are now into the heart of Access Basic, where you see several statements that take more than one line of a program. One shortcut If statement takes only a single line of code (see Chapter 17), but the If shown here requires a matching End If somewhere later in the program.

You might see a one-line If statement. If the *Block of one or more Access Basic statements* takes only a single statement, you can put the entire If on a single line without the End If at the end.

The Comparison Operators

Table 16.1 lists the comparison operators (sometimes called the conditional operators) and their descriptions. As mentioned in this chapter's introduction, you may have used some or all of them before.

Table 16.1. The comparison operators.

Operator	Description	Example
=	Equal to	If Amt1 = Amt2 Then
>	Greater than	If Sales > Minimum Then
>=	Greater than or equal to	If Bonus >= Extra Then
<	Less than	If Quantity < 10 Then
<=	Less than or equal to	If UserNum <= RecordNum Then
<>	Not equal to	If Name <> FullName Then

The comparison operators always appear with two constants, variables, expressions (which point to a field's value on a form or report), or a combination of the three, on each side.

> **Note:** If you want to combine two or more sets of comparisons, use the And and Or operators between the comparisons, as examples later in this chapter illustrate.

If either of the expressions around a comparison operator equates to Null, the If produces a Null result. Null values are available in Access Basic but not necessarily available in other BASIC dialects. Null values indicate invalid data of some kind. Often, your Access Basic program returns Null values when a variable or field cannot be computed because of bad data. To Access Basic, a zero, Null, and blank are three different values. If you want to assign a Null value to a variable, you do so by using an assignment statement and putting Null on the right side of the equal sign and on the left a variable that is to receive that Null value. In Access Basic, Null is a keyword that lets you store Null values.

> **Tip:** Use the built-in IsNull() function to test whether a value contains a Null value. IsNull() returns true or false depending on the value of its argument. Chapter 17 explores IsNull() in more depth.

Example

Assume that four integer variables are initialized as follows:

```
A = 5
B = 10
C = 15
D = 5
```

Conditions are true, false, or *Null*.

The following statements are true:

A is equal to D   `A = D`

B is less than C   `B < C`

C is greater than A `C > A`

B is greater than or equal to A   `B >= A`

D is less than or equal to B `D <= B`

B is not equal to C `B <> C`

The right-hand side of the preceding statements are not Access Basic statements, but they are conditions that can appear to the right of the If statement. Conditional logic is not difficult. Conditional logic always produces a *true* or *false* result (or Null as explained earlier, if either side of the comparison operator contains a Null value).

Example

Assuming the preceding example's four variables still hold their assigned values, each of the following statements about the values is false:

```
A = B
B > C
D < A
D > A
A <> D
B >= C
C <= B
```

Study these statements to see why each is false. A and D are equal to the same value (5), so neither is greater than or less than the other. You deal with conditional logic in everyday life. Think of the following statements that you might make:

The generic butter costs less than the name brand.

My child is younger than Johnny.

Our salaries are equal.

The dogs are not the same age.

Each of these statements can be only true or false. There is no other possibility.

Example

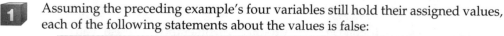

The And and Or work just like their spoken counterparts. Consider the following statement:

If you clean your room *and* if you empty the trash, you can go to the circus.

The *and* makes it clear that *both* sides of the *and* must be true. If the child only cleans the room or if the child only empties the trash, there is no trip to the circus. Given the variables and their values used for the previous examples, the following are true:

```
A = D And B < C
C > A And B >= A
```

> **Tip:** Put parentheses around the individual comparisons to make the code easier to read, as follows:
>
> ```
> (A = D) And (B < C)
> ```

The Or combines two comparisons in a less restrictive manner. Consider this statement, slightly changed from the previous one:

If you clean your room *or* if you empty the trash, you can go to the circus.

The child only has to clean the room *or* empty the trash to go to the circus. (If the child does both, that is fine also.)

The following statement is true:

```
(C = A) Or (B >= A)
```

Even though C is not equal to A, B is greater than or equal to A, so the result of the entire expression is true. If you had used And rather than Or, the entire expression would be false because And requires that both sides be true for the entire expression to be true.

Watch Your Compares

Before you put the If together in complete statement examples, you would be wise to explore exactly how Access Basic compares different types of values. With Access Basic, you can compare numbers to numbers, numbers to strings, strings to strings, and variants to either numbers or strings. Access Basic compares differently depending on what you are comparing.

> **Tip:** If you have programmed in regular programming languages, you may be surprised to learn that Access Basic compares any data, including strings to numbers. Access Basic must allow freedom in data types because you have no idea what the user will next enter in a field, and you must be able to handle whatever the field ends up with.

Example

If a comparison operator compares two numbers of any data type, such as an integer to a floating-point, a true numeric comparison results. All the following comparisons are true:

```
If (4 < 5) Then
If (4 < 5.0) Then
If (4 < 5.4322344433223) Then
If (67.2322 > 67.2321) Then
```

> **Note:** In this and the next few examples, of course, the values being compared (the expression after the If) would normally be variables or fields, but while you're learning about the different types of compares, this book sticks to constant comparison values to make these examples clearer.

The parentheses around the comparison after the Ifs are not required, but they help pinpoint the comparison and make If statements easier to understand.

> **Caution:** The If statements shown in this example and the next few examples are not complete If statements. Understanding the comparison first makes the rest of the statement easier to understand.

Example

1

If both expressions on either side of a comparison operator are strings, Access Basic performs a string compare. The way that strings compare is determined by the Option Compare statement that is set in the declarations section.

Option Compare's determines how strings compare.

If Option Compare Binary is currently set in the declarations section, string comparisons are case sensitive. Therefore, the following string comparisons compare to true:

```
If ("St. Francis Hospital" < "Saint Francis Hospital") Then
If ("abc" > "ABC") Then
If ("12" < "Twelve") Then
```

> **Caution:** Be careful when comparing numbers, letters, and special characters inside strings. To know how strings compare properly, use the ANSI table in Appendix A to determine how individual characters compare.

If the Option Compare Text option currently is set in the declarations section, string comparisons are not case sensitive. The following string comparisons, therefore, compare to true:

```
If ("St. Francis Hospital" = "ST. Francis Hospital") Then
If ("abc" = "ABC") Then
If ("1a2" = "1A2") Then
```

> **Note:** If the `Option Compare Database` option currently is set in the declarations section, you have to see how the database option from the **V**iew **O**ptions... sort order is set.

Strings of zero-length (designated as `""` with no blanks between the quotation marks) always compare less than strings with data.

Example

If you compare a numeric value (field, constant, or variable) to a variable defined with the `Variant` data type, a numeric comparison is made if the `Variant` data contains a number or a string that "looks" like a valid number.

If a variable named v is defined as follows:

```
Dim v As Variant
```

and you store a number in the variable like this:

```
v = 45.6
```

then the following comparisons hold true:

```
If (v = 45.6) Then
If (v < 100) Then
If (-121 < v) Then
```

> **Caution:** Be careful when comparing single- or double-precision numbers with the equality comparison operator (=). Representing exact fractional quantities inside the computer is difficult, and rounding can occur in the extreme decimal places that you don't always see on-screen. Therefore, `45.6 = 45.6` usually compares as true, but `45.6543234 = 45.6543234` does not always compare as true even though the numbers appear to be equal.

If you store a string in the variable as follows:

```
v = "-343.56"
```

then Access Basic compares the following as true because the string stored in v looks like a valid number:

```
If (v > 0) Then
If (v < -500) Then
```

> **Caution:** If the Variant does not contain a valid number and you attempt to compare that Variant variable to a number, a Type Mismatch error appears.

Example

If the Variant data contains a string and you compare that data to another string, Access Basic performs a string comparison. Assuming that v is defined as data type Variant, if you assign it a string as follows:

```
v = "Abc"
```

then Access Basic compares each of the following as true:

```
If v = "Abc" Then
If "Zebra" > v Then
```

Example

If you compare a number to a Variant variable that holds neither a number nor a string that looks like a number, the number *always* compares less than the string. Given the following Variant variable assignments:

```
v1 = "Hi"
v2 = "2322 E. 56th"
```

then the following is true:

```
756 < v1
v2 > 1.8
```

Finishing the *If*

Now that you've mastered the first part of the If statement, it's time to cover the rest of If. The If statement's *body* is known as the code between the If and the End If lines. The following rules hold:

- ♦ If the comparison test is true, the block of statements following If is performed.

- ♦ If the comparison test is false, the body of the If is ignored.

- ♦ Either way, the statement following End If takes over when the If is finished doing its job.

Example

Suppose that you want your Access Basic procedure to display a secret message to the user if the user knows the password. The password is read from a file and stored in the string variable named SystemPass. After asking the user's password, the following If statement determines whether the user sees the message:

```
If (UserPass = SystemPass) Then
    Beep          ' Rings the bell
    MsgBox "The key is in the file cabinet."
End If
```

If the user enters the correct password, the computer beeps and the message box with the secret message pops up.

If, however, the user does not enter the correct password, the body of the If does not execute, and the program then continues after the End If statement.

Example

The IsLoaded procedure in the Northwind Traders database contains the following code:

```
If Forms(i).FormName = MyFormName Then
    IsLoaded = True
    Exit Function        ' Quit function once form has been found.
End If
```

If the If test is true, the two statements in the body of the If execute. This body contains the Exit statement, which forces the If to behave differently, however. When Access Basic runs an Exit Function statement, the entire function immediately terminates. (Without such an Exit statement, the procedure continues executing at the statements following the End If.)

Else: Specifying Otherwise

The complete If statement contains an Else portion that handles comparisons that the If without an Else can take care of. By itself, the If describes what happens if a comparison is true. The Else part of an If—if you include an Else—specifies what happens if the comparison is false. Following is the format of the If with Else:

```
IF conditional Then
    Block of one or more Access Basic statements
[Else
    Block of one or more Access Basic statements]
End If
```

The Else portion is enclosed in square brackets to indicate that it is an optional part of Else. Think of Else as meaning *otherwise*. Here is how you might use an *else*-like *otherwise* in everyday conversation:

> If I set the VCR correctly, we'll watch our movie; otherwise, we'll read books.

The *otherwise* specifies what happens if the condition following If is false.

Example

Here is a function whose body is an If with an Else statement:

```
Function Century (someDate)
' Accepts: a date value
' Calculates the century number of the specified date
' Returns: the calculated century
If IsDate(someDate) Then
        Century = ((Year(someDate) - 1) \ 100) + 1
    Else
        Century = Null
    End If
End Function
```

As the remarks suggest, the function receives a date value from whatever source called the function. The century that matches the date is returned using the IsDate() built-in function. You learn all about the IsDate() function in Chapter 17, but as its name suggests, the function returns the true or false result of a variable being checked. If the variable contains a legal date value, the IsDate() returns a true comparison value, and if IsDate() does not find a good date value, a false value is returned.

Suppose that the calling procedure sends the Century function a good date value, such as 12/31/93 (Access prefers pound signs around dates, so #12/31/93# is more likely the date sent), the century that matches that date is returned. If a bad date value is passed (such as #72/45/94#), the IsDate() returns a false value. Therefore, when the If is false, the Else block of code (one statement long here) executes, and a Null value is assigned as the century indicating an invalid value.

> **Tip:** It might help to remember that only *one* of the two blocks of code following If executes: either the block following If or the block following Else. Both blocks never execute because the If-Else statement is mutually-exclusive and ensures that only one of the two blocks of code executes.

Example

The following simple `If` statement displays a dialog box and tests the user's response to the dialog box buttons (Chapter 15 explained the `MsgBox()` function):

```
If (MsgBox("Are you ready?", 34) = 6) Then
    MsgBox "You pressed Yes"
Else
    MsgBox "You pressed No"
EndIf
```

Example

Any nonzero value equates as true in Access Basic, and zero always equates as false. Therefore, you don't have to use comparison operators to test for true or false conditions.

Suppose that a bonus is paid to any employee who sells a special inventory item. The following `If` statement assigns 500.00 to a bonus variable if the number of special items sold is more than 0:

```
If (QtySpecial > 0) Then
    Bonus = 500.00
Else
    Bonus = 0.00
End If
```

Knowing that a zero condition always evaluates as a false condition, you can specify the following:

```
If (QtySpecial) Then
    Bonus = 500.00
Else
    Bonus = 0.00
End If
```

Here, the first example's `> 0` is redundant (and slightly less efficient) because if the `QtySpecial` has a nonzero value (any value over 0, assuming no negative quantities are allowed), the 500.00 is assigned to `Bonus`. But if a 0 appears in `QtySpecial`, the `If`'s comparison is false, and the `Else` block of code executes.

Example

Any statement can reside in the blocks of the `If`, even additional `If` statements. Consider the following `If` statement:

```
If Not IsNull(anyDate) Then
    Result = DateSerial(Year(anyDate), Month(anyDate) + 1, 1)
```

```
    If Weekday(Result) = 1 Then        ' Sunday, so add one day.
        DueDate = Result + 1
    ElseIf Weekday(Result) = 7 Then    ' Saturday, so add two days.
        DueDate = Result + 2
    Else
        DueDate = Result
    End If
Else
    Result = Null
End If
```

You don't have to understand everything in this code at this point. Basically, if the anyDate data being tested is not a Null value, anyDate contains valid data. A set of nested If statements then tests that data and assigns DueDate (which could be the surrounding function's return value) one of two values depending on what anyDate contains.

Use ElseIf and not Else If.

When an If appears inside another If, the internal If statement is a *nested* If statement. Nested If statements can be confusing to debug, especially if the nested If needs an Else specified and that Else contains another If statement! As this example code shows, Else and If can never go together. You must use the special ElseIf keyword if your Else block of code contains its own If.

In Chapter 20 you learn about the Select Case statement, which shortens nested If statements and makes them easier to write and test.

Checking for *TypeOf*

If you follow an If with the keyword TypeOf, you can find out exactly what kind of object your code is working with. The TypeOf is useful if a function is passed a control variable that represents a control on a form or report, and you want to know what kind of control was passed. You also learn ways to save all the controls on a form and then step through each control, one at a time, inspecting each one and making decisions based on what you find.

Following is the format of the If TypeOf statement:

```
IF TypeOf object Is objectType Then
    Block of one or more Access Basic statements
[Else
    Block of one or more Access Basic statements]
End If
```

The *object* is any control variable name, and the *objectType* is any one of the following control types:

BoundObjectFrame	CheckBox	ComboBox	CommandButton
Graph	Label	Line	ListBox
ObjectFrame	OpenButton	OptionGroup	PageBreak
Rectangle	SubForm	SubReport	TextBox
ToggleButton			

Example

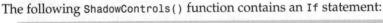

The following `ShadowControls()` function contains an `If` statement:

```
If C.Section = CurrentSection Then
    If TypeOf C Is TextBox Then
        R.DrawWidth = Thickness
        RightSide = C.Left + C.Width + Thickness * 2
        Bottom = C.Top + C.Height + Thickness * 2

        R.Line (RightSide, C.Top + Thickness * 4)-(RightSide,
ÂBottom), 0, BF
        R.Line -(C.Left + Thickness * 4, Bottom), 0, BF
    End If
End If
```

The purpose of this advanced code is to draw a shadow around whatever control is stored in the control variable C. For this discussion, the important thing to notice is that the nested `If` is checking to see what type of control C is and making some calculations and line-drawings based on that control if it is a text box control. If the control is anything but a text box control, nothing is done.

Summary

You now have a tool you can use to write powerful programming statements. With the `If` statement, you can perform a block of statements only if a certain comparison is true. By adding the `Else` option, you can specify the block of code to execute if the comparison is false.

The `If` statement gives your programs the power to make decisions at runtime. Depending on the value of data, whether the user entered that data, the data came from a calculation, or the data was read from a table, your program can analyze the data and execute certain sections of code accordingly.

In the next chapter you see how to extend the test you use after the `If` by looking at built-in inspection functions that return true or false depending on your data's types.

Review Questions

Answers to review questions are in Appendix B.

1. State whether the following comparison tests are true or false:

   A. 4 >= 5

   B. 4 >= 4

   C. "Apple" < "apple" (Assume that the Option Compare Binary option is declared first.)

2. TRUE or FALSE: "Access Basic is fun!" prints on-screen when the following statement is executed:

```
IF (54 <= 50) Then
        MsgBox "Access Basic is fun!"
End If
```

3. Using the ANSI table as a guide, state whether the following string comparisons are true or false:

   A. "Que" < "QUE"

   B. "" < "0"

   C. "?" > "}"

4. TRUE or FALSE: If a decision (made by a comparison test) has more than one possible result, you can use an If-Then-ElseIf.

5. Determine whether the following If comparison produces a true or false result (*Hint:* Perform the innermost parentheses first):

```
If ((5 = (4 + 1)) And ((10 \ 2) <> (5 + 0))) Then
```

6. What is the error in the following code?

```
a = 6     ' a is an integer variable
If (a > 6) Then
   MsgBox "George"
Else If (a = 6) Then
   MsgBox "Henry"
Else If (a < 6) Then
   Print "James"
End If
```

Review Exercises

1. Write a simple procedure (using InputBox) that asks the user for the previous five days' temperatures (stored in the Single variables t1, t2, t3, t4, and t5). Compute the average temperature and print (using MsgBox) "It's cold!" if the average is less than freezing.

2. Add an Else clause to exercise 1 so that the message "It's hot outside" prints if the temperature is above 85 degrees Fahrenheit.

3. Write a procedure that asks for the user's age. If the age is under 21, print the following message:

```
Have a lemonade!
If, however, the age is 21 or more, print the following
➥message instead:
Have an adult beverage!
```

4. Write a procedure that asks the user for three numbers. Print a message telling the user whether any two of the numbers add up to the third.

5. Create a simple database with one table that asks the user for his or her name and age. With FormWizards create a form that prompts for the table's data. Add an After Update control that runs a procedure when the age is entered that prints one of the two messages described in Exercise 3.

CHAPTER 17

Data Type Inspection, *IIf*, and *Choose*

In Chapter 16 you learned about *conditional programs,* that is, programs that perform comparison tests and execute one set of statements or another depending on the result of the tests. Your programs can make sure that the user entered correct data, that a table contains enough information, or that the printer is turned on before you print a report.

This chapter extends your knowledge of conditional logic by describing the Is...() data inspection functions and giving you some shortcuts for the If statement. So much of programming in Access Basic or any other language is devoted to looking at data and making decisions about what to do next based on that data.

This chapter introduces the following topics:

◆ The IsDate(), IsEmpty(), IsNull(), and IsNumeric() built-in functions

◆ The VarType() function

◆ The If operator

◆ The IIf() function

◆ The Choose() function

Data plays such an important part of database programming that you should master this chapter's content, and you'll be well-rewarded once you begin writing Access Basic-based applications.

Inspecting Data

You can test for data types as well as values.

The `Is...()` and `VarType()` functions are called *data inspection* functions. These functions inspect the data *types,* not the contents, of variables. Your Access Basic programs work with many different kinds of data, and you sometimes do not know in advance what kind of data you have to work with. Before you make a calculation, for instance, you want to make sure the data is numeric.

Table 17.1 lists the data inspection functions and offers a description of what they do. Each of the functions receives one argument of the `Variant` data type.

Table 17.1. The *Is...()* data inspection functions.

Function Name	Description
IsDate()	Determines if its argument is a date data type (or if the data can be converted to a valid date)
IsEmpty()	Determines whether its argument has been initialized
IsNull()	Determines if its argument holds a `Null` value
IsNumeric()	Determines if its argument holds a number (or if the data can be converted to a valid number)

Note: Each of the `Is...()` functions accepts the `Variant` data type because it must be able to inspect any data and determine what type it is.

Caution: The `Is...()` functions do not change their arguments to different data types. The `Is...()` functions only test their arguments for specific data types.

Example

The following Century procedure contains the `IsDate()` function. You've seen this procedure before in this book, and understanding the `IsDate()` function is the final step in understanding the entire procedure.

```
Function Century (someDate)
' Accepts: a date value
```

```
' Purpose: calculates the century number of the specified date
' Returns: the calculated century
    If IsDate(someDate) Then
        Century = ((Year(someDate) - 1) \ 100) + 1
    Else
        Century = Null
    End If
End Function
```

Notice that no data type is declared for the parameter someDate, which this procedure accepts. someDate is therefore a Variant data type. Another procedure can call Century and pass Century an argument that is not a valid date. Before using the argument to calculate the century, the IsDate() function returns a true result if someDate contains a date. If someDate does not contain a valid date, the else condition takes over and assigns Null to the function name, returning the Null value back to the calling procedure. You must write the calling procedure so that it tests for a Null value (using IsNull() as explained later in this chapter), and if Null is received back from Century, then Century cannot return the correct century.

Example

An empty variable is one that has not been initialized. Perhaps a procedure has declared the variable but has yet to store data in the variable. Newcomers to Access Basic often wonder why an empty variable is different from a Null value and a zero value. At times, you must have some way to tell whether the user has entered something into fields, and an empty variable signals that nothing has been entered.

The following code is rather simple, but it demonstrates what happens when you apply the IsEmpty() function to variables that have and have not been initialized.

```
Dim V1 As Variant, V2 As Variant, V3 As Variant, V4 As Variant
V1 = 0         ' Zero value
V2 = Null      ' Null value
V3 = ""        ' Null string
If IsEmpty(V1) Then
   MsgBox "V1 is empty"
End If
If IsEmpty(V2) Then
   MsgBox "V2 is empty"
End If
If IsEmpty(V3) Then
   MsgBox "V3 is empty"
End If
If IsEmpty(V4) Then
```

```
    MsgBox "V4 is empty"
End If
```

The only output from this code is the following:

```
V4 is empty
```

You receive this response because all the other variables have some kind of data (they have been initialized).

> **Tip:** Use IsNull() to see if a control or field on a report or form contains data. Use IsEmpty() just for variables.

Example

This IsNull() function checks its argument and returns true if the argument contains a Null value. The value Null is a special value that you can assign to variables to indicate either that no data exists or an error (the way your program interprets a Null value depends on how you code the program). On form and report controls, a field is considered Null if the user enters no data in the field.

> **Caution:** Given that you can assign a Null value to a variable like this: aVar = Null, you might be tempted to test for a Null value like this: If (aVar = Null) Then .... But be warned that such an If always fails. Using IsNull() is the only way to check for a Null value in a variable.

If your Access Basic procedure needs to know whether a form's field named Hours Worked has data, the procedure can check it with an If statement, as follows:

```
If IsNull(Forms!formPayroll![Hours Worked]) Then
    MsgBox "You didn't enter hours worked!"
Else                    ' Thank them for the good hours
    MsgBox "Thanks for entering hours worked!"
End If
```

This statement checks to ensure that the user typed something in the field before moving on.

Example

The IsNumeric() function checks its argument for a number. Any Variant value that can be converted to a number returns a true result in the IsNumeric() function and a false result otherwise. The following data types can be converted to numbers:

- Empty

- Integer

- Long Integer

- Single-precision

- Double-precision

- Currency

- Date

- String if the string "looks" like a valid number

The following code asks the user for his or her age using a Variant variable. The program displays an error message if the number entered by the user is not numeric:

```
Dim Age As Variant
Age = InputBox("How old are you?", "Get Your Age")
If IsNumeric(Age)
    MsgBox "Thanks!"
Else
    MsgBox "What are you trying to hide?\!"
End If
```

The Multitalented *VarType* Function

If you need to know what data type a variable is, use the VarType() function. Table 17.2 lists the return values from the VarType() function, and VarType() returns no other values than the nine listed in the table.

Table 17.2. The *VarType()* return values.

This Value Is Returned	If the Variant Argument Contains This Data Type
0	Empty
1	Null
2	Integer
3	Long
4	Single

continues

Table 17.2. Continued

This Value Is Returned	If the Variant Argument Contains This Data Type
5	Double
6	Currency
7	Date
8	String

Example

The following procedure contains a nested If statement, which prints the data type of whatever data is passed to it.

```
Function PrntType(aVar)  ' Variant if you don't specify otherwise
  If VarType(aVar) = 0 Then
    MsgBox "The argument is Empty"
  Elseif VarType(aVar) = 1 then
    MsgBox "The argument is Null"
  Elseif VarType(aVar) = 2 then
    MsgBox "The argument is Integer"
  Elseif VarType(aVar) = 3 then
    MsgBox "The argument is Long"
  Elseif VarType(aVar) = 4 then
    MsgBox "The argument is Single"
  Elseif VarType(aVar) = 5 then
    MsgBox "The argument is Double"
  Elseif VarType(aVar) = 6 then
    MsgBox "The argument is Currency"
  Elseif VarType(aVar) = 7 then
    MsgBox "The argument is Date"
  Elseif VarType(aVar) = 8 then
    MsgBox "The argument is String"
  EndIf
End Function
```

Tip: The Select Case statement, which you learn in Chapter 20, offers a better method of nesting If statements like the ones shown here.

An *If* Shortcut *IIf()*

The IIf() function performs a succinct version of a simple If-Else statement. Because IIf() is a function, IIf() returns a value, and the value returned depends on a true or false test that you put at the beginning of IIf(). The format of IIf() is as follows:

```
IIf(expression, trueResult, falseResult)
```

If the *expression* is true, the *trueResult* is returned, and if the *expression* is false, the *falseResult* is returned.

Following is an example statement that uses IIf():

```
Dim ans As String
ans = IIf(n < 0, "Cannot be negative", "Good data")
```

This statement does the following: If whatever is stored in *n* is less than 0, the string variable ans is assigned the string "Cannot be negative", but if *n* contains any number equal to or greater than 0, the string "Good data" is stored in ans. (Figure 17.1 illustrates the nature of this IIf().)

If you rewrite the previous IIf() function as an If statement, here is what you do:

Figure 17.1

Dissecting the use of an *IIf( )* function.

```
                            ──────── ans is assigned this
              ┌──────────────────────────┐    ↑
              ▼                           │    │
ans = IIf(n < 0, "Cannot be negative",  "Good data")
       ▲                                      │
       └──────────────────────────────────────┴── or ans is assigned this
```

```
If (n < 0) Then
    ans = "Cannot be negative"
Else
    ans = "Good data"
End If
```

IIf() is more efficient and easier to write than a multiline If statement. However, IIf() replaces only simple If statements, and If statements with several lines of code in their bodies must remain regular If statements.

> **Note:** The IIf() function is similar to the Lotus 1-2-3 @If() function. If you've ever programmed in C, the IIf() function works a lot like the conditional operator ?:.

Example

You cannot divide by zero. Therefore, the following `IIf()` function returns an average sale price or a Null value if division by zero would result:

```
avSales = IIf(Qty > 0, totalSales / Qty, Null)
```

Remembering that a zero value produces a false result, you can rewrite the preceding statement as follows:

```
avSales = IIf(Qty, totalSales / Qty, Null)
```

If you rewrite this statement using an `If`, here is how you do it:

```
If (Qty) Then
    avSales = totalSales / Qtr
Else
    avSales = Null
End If
```

Choosing with *Choose( )*

The `Choose()` function can have up to 14 arguments, more arguments than any other built-in function. Depending on the value of the first argument, `Choose()` returns only one of the remaining arguments.

Following is the format of `Choose()`:

```
Choose(indexNum, expression [, expression] ...)
```

After the second argument (*expression*), you can have up to 12 more just like the second. The *indexNum* must be a variable or field that equates to a number from 1 to the number of *expression*s that are in the function.

If you need to generate a small table of price codes, abbreviations, or product codes, for example, using `Choose()` is more succinct than using an `If` statement. `Choose()`, however, is more limited in scope than `If`.

> **Caution:** `Choose()` returns Null if *indexNum* is not between 1 and the number of *expression*s is inclusive.

The first argument of `Choose()` can be an expression. Therefore, you have to adjust the first argument so that it falls within the range of 1 to 13. If the range of values goes from 0 to 4, for example, add 1 to the first argument so that the range goes from 1 to 5.

Example

Suppose that a form contains a Price Code field. When a user enters a new product, the user should also enter a price code from 1 to 5, which corresponds to the following codes:

1 Full markup

2 5% discount

3 10% discount

4 Special order

5 Mail order

The following Choose() function assigns to a description field the correct description based on the price code (type this code all on one line):

```
Descript = Choose(Forms!Inventory![Product Code], "Full markup",
    "5% discount", "10% discount", "Special order", "Mail order")
```

Summary

This chapter described more ways you can test for data values and data types. Using the Is...() inspection functions, you can determine if a data value is a date, empty, Null, or a number so that your code can operate accordingly.

The IIf() is a shortcut form of If. Although IIf() will never replace the more readable If statement, IIf() is useful (and efficient) for coding simple decision statements that have a true part and a false part.

The VarType() function is extremely useful for functions that can work with more than one data type. By first determining the data type, a subsequent If can then select the appropriate code to execute.

Finally, the Choose() function returns a value based on an index, simulating the effect of a lookup table.

Now that you can test data and execute code based on the results of the test, you're ready to learn how to make the computer *really* work! The next chapter explains how to instruct Access Basic to repeat lines of code several times when you want to process several occurrences of data.

Review Questions

Answers to review questions are in Appendix B.

1. What is the shortcut for the If statement?

2. TRUE or FALSE: Unlike If, the IIf() returns a value.

3. TRUE or FALSE: You can use a data inspection function to see whether a variable holds a string value.

4. Describe the VarType() function.

5. Describe the difference between an empty value, a Null value, a zero value, and a null string value.

6. TRUE or FALSE: Choose() cannot return a string.

7. What happens if the first argument of Choose() is less than 1?

Review Exercises

1. Rewrite the following If statement as an IIf() function call:

```
If (total > 10000) Then
    Bonus = 50
Else
    Bonus = 5
End If
```

2. Rewrite the following If statement using a Choose() function:

```
If (ID = 1) Then
    bonus = 50
ElseIf (ID = 2) Then
    bonus = 75
ElseIf (ID = 3) Then
    bonus = 100
End If
```

3. Write a Choose() function that returns the VarType() descriptions based on a data type number used as the first argument. That is, if the first argument of Choose() is 0, add 1 to it to get 1, and return the first *expression*, Empty.

CHAPTER 18

The Do...Loop

One of the things Access cannot do without Access Basic is *loop*. A loop is a series of statements that execute repeatedly. Many times you have to repeat a calculation or print the same message several times.

Access Basic provides several statements for looping. This chapter introduces the first set of loop statements called the `Do...Loops`. There are four different kinds of `Do...Loops`.

This chapter introduces the following topics:

♦ The Do While-Loop statement

♦ The `Do-Loop While` statement

♦ The `Do Until-Loop` statement

♦ The `Do-Loop Until` statement

♦ The `Exit Do` statement

Actually, the first four statements in this list are just specific versions of the more generalized `Do-Loop` statement. The placement of the `While` and `Until` determines how the loop behaves.

Introducing Loops

When using Access without Access Basic, you can do a few things that normally require a loop in other languages. For example, Access has built-in functions to count, total, and add records together. In a way, such functions, like the `DCount()` function, perform their own loop because they loop through your records counting them.

Some desired program repetition just isn't possible without Access Basic. Suppose that you ask the user if he or she wants a report sent to the screen or to the printer by displaying the dialog box shown in Figure 18.1. If the user doesn't press either an S or a P, you probably want to tell the user that you don't recognize the answer and then ask the question again. As a matter of fact, you have to keep asking the same question over and over until the user answers with something that you are expecting. The loop of statements, therefore, contains the InputBox() to ask the question, an If statement to check the answer, and a MsgBox to issue an error message so the user knows what is going on.

Figure 18.1

The user should answer by pressing either S or P.

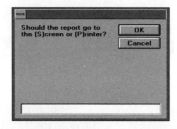

Guarding against Endless Loops

An infinite (or endless) loop never ends.

You often write procedures that loop because your procedures are processing sets of data values many times. As you add loops to your programs, guard against writing *endless loops*, which never end. A never-ending procedure is no more useful to you than one that does not work correctly in the first place. With an endless loop, your users are never able to regain control of the machine.

> **Tip:** Before you go further, you should learn what to do if you happen to write a procedure with an endless loop. In Access Basic (as with most dialects of BASIC), you can stop a procedure in mid-execution by pressing the Ctrl+Break key combination. Therefore, if you accidentally get into a loop that does not end, press Ctrl+Break. The procedure then stops, and you return to the editing screen.

The General *Do-Loop* Statement

One of the most common ways to perform a loop in Access Basic is to use the Do-Loop statement. The Do-Loop has several formats, and in this chapter you explore each of them. Your choice of formats has more to do with your own preference and style than with programming requirements. Because the many formats can get confusing, this section first presents all the Do-Loop formats for your perusal, and the following sections explain each one. The formats of the Do-Loop statement are as follows:

```
Do While condition
    Block of one or more Access Basic statements
Loop
```

```
Do
    Block of one or more Access Basic statements
Loop While condition
```

```
Do Until condition
    Block of one or more Access Basic statements
Loop
```

```
Do
    Block of one or more Access Basic statements
Loop Until condition
```

Tip: Indent the inner statements of loops so that you can spot the statements easily inside the loop.

The *condition* is a comparison, Is...() function, or any other Access Basic language element that returns a true or false result. As with the If statement's comparison, any nonzero value is true, and a zero value is always false. Therefore, the *condition* might be nothing more than a numeric variable or control.

Figure 18.2 gives you an overview of Do-Loop's action within a procedure. The arrow shows you how the Do-Loop repeats a section of the procedure. Until this chapter, all procedures that you've seen have flowed sequentially from top to bottom without any repetition.

Figure 18.2

A glimpse of a
Do-Loop's action.

These statements
repeat until the
condition being
tested becomes
true.

```
Function Birthday()
    Dim age As Variant
    ' Access Basic statements go here
    ' The loop is next
    Do

        MsgBox "It's your birthday!"
        age = inputBox(How old are you?")

    Loop Until IsNumeric(age)
    ' Rest of procedure goes here
End function
```

> **Note:** The While keyword causes Access Basic to repeat the loop as long as (*while*) the *condition* is true. The *Until* keyword causes Access Basic to repeat the loop as long as the *condition* is false (*until* the *condition* becomes true).

The *Do While-Loop*

All loops supply ways to control the statements executing through conditional tests. The loops' conditional tests use the same comparison operators you saw earlier with the If statement (refer to Chapter 16 for a review of the comparison operators).

If you look at the formats for the Do loops, you see that the *condition* resides at either the top of the loop or at the bottom. The placement of the conditional test determines how the Do loop terminates its repetition. Remember to guard against endless loops. You must have some way of quitting every loop you put in your programs. The *condition* is the way to end the loop. Basically, the While *condition* keeps the loop repeating as long as the relation is true, but as soon as the relation becomes false, Access Basic quits repeating the loop and finishes the procedure following the Loop statement.

Example

Here is an example of a Do While-Loop that tests its relation at the top of the loop:

```
Dim Count As Integer
Count = 1
Do While (Count <= 10)          ' Count up from 1
    Debug.Print "Counting at"; Count   ' Print in the immediate window
    Count = Count + 1
Loop
Debug.Print "All done now."
```

If you run a procedure with this code, you see the following output appear in the immediate window:

```
Counting at 1
Counting at 2
Counting at 3
Counting at 4
Counting at 5
Counting at 6
```

```
Counting at 7
Counting at 8
Counting at 9
Counting at 10
All done now.
```

Count is the variable being tested. As long as the value of Count is less than or equal to 10, the body of the loop executes. The body of the loop executes over and over until the value of Count is greater than 10. The only way the loop stops executing (and thereby not becoming an endless loop) is that the body of the loop *must* change Count.

The statement Count = Count + 1 is called a *counter* statement, not because the variable is named Count but because the same variable appears on both sides of the equal sign. When you see the same variable name on both sides of an equal sign, the variable is being changed. One is being added to Count every time your computer executes the statement Count = Count + 1. (Remember that the assignment statement evaluates whatever is to the right of the equal sign first and then stores that value into the variable on the left.) Every time the body of the loop executes, Count is changed. Eventually, Count will be more than 10, and the loop will stop looping.

> **Tip:** A counter statement can also count down by subtracting one from a counter variable each time through a loop; for example, Count = Count - 1.

Count begins at 1. The Do While-Loop continues until Count is more than 10. Once Count is more than 10, the loop stops. Because the loop tests the condition at the top of the loop, as soon as Count becomes 11, the loop stops and any code that follows the Loop statement continues then. The loop you saw earlier prints the message 10 times. On the eleventh *iteration* (another name for loop), the condition becomes false and the loop then ends.

Example

One simple but common application of the Do While-Loop is ensuring that the user enters a proper answer to what your program asks. The section of a program that follows is such a loop. Until the user enters a yes or no answer, the program keeps prompting for a correct answer. The UCase$() function converts the user's answer to uppercase to help the relational test.

```
Dim Ans As String
' Section of a procedure that asks a yes or no question
Ans = InputBox("Do you want to continue (yes or no)")
Do While (UCase$(Ans) <> "YES" And UCase$(Ans$) <> "NO")
```

```
MsgBox "You didn't answer yes or no", 48
   Beep   ' Ring the bell
   Ans = InputBox("Do you want to continue (yes or no)")
Loop
```

Note: In this example the program requires two `InputBox()` functions to ask the user for input so that it can print the error message inside the loop.

The *Do-Loop While*

The conditional test determines how a *Do loop* behaves.

The primary difference between the `Do While-Loop` and the `Do-Loop While` is the placement of the conditional test.

Note: Throughout this chapter the placement of the hyphens (-) in the loop names indicates where the body of each loop goes. For example, the `Do-Loop While` describes the loop defined with this format:

```
Do
   Block of one or more Access Basic statements
Loop While condition
```

Example

Here is the same code as shown in the previous example with its conditional `While` test at the bottom of the loop:

```
Dim Count As Integer
Count = 1
Do
  Debug.Print "Counting at"; Count ' Prints in the immediate window
  Count = Count + 1
Loop While (Count <= 10)
Debug.Print "All done now."
```

The body of this loop continues as long as `Count` is less than or equal to 10. The conditional test is located at the *bottom* of the loop. Therefore, once `Count` is more than 10, the body of the loop stops looping.

> **Tip:** The difference between the conditional test at the top or bottom boils down to only one real difference: The body of the first loop, the `Do While-Loop` (with the test at the top), may *never* execute because the test might be false before the loop ever executes. The body of the second loop, the `Do-Loop While` (with the test at the bottom), always executes *at least once*. Access Basic has no idea that the conditional test is false until it performs at least one iteration of the loop.

The *Do Until-Loop*

In each of the two previous `Do` loops you learned that the condition being tested is proceeded by a `While`. As you can see, the loop continues executing *while* the condition is true. If you replace the `While` with `Until`, the loop continues *until* the condition is true. The choice of loop that you use depends on the type of statements that you feel most comfortable with. You can write any loop with any of the four `Do` loops that you've seen.

Example

Here is a `Do-Loop While` you probably understand now:

```
Do
    Debug.Print "A"     ' Immediate window
    ans = InputBox("Again?")
Loop While (ans = "Y")
```

Following is the same code using a `Do-Loop Until`:

```
Do
    Debug.Print "A"     ' Immediate window
    ans = InputBox("Again?"))
Loop Until (ans = "N")
```

The test being compared in each set of loops is the opposite, even though the output is identical. The first loop prints a letter *A* while a certain condition is true, and the second prints the *A* until a certain condition is true.

You also can write `Do Until-Loops` that test at the top, such as this one:

```
Do Until (ans = "N")
    Debug.Print "A"
    ans = Inputbox("Again?")
Loop
```

Example

The next procedure asks the user for a number. A `Do-Loop Until` (which tests the relation at the bottom of the loop) beeps at the user that number of times.

```
' Beep at the user however many times the user wants
Dim times As Integer
Dim Count
Times = InputBox("How many times do you want to hear a beep")
Count = 0   ' Initialize a count variable
Do
    Beep
    Count = Count + 1
Loop Until (Count = Times)
MsgBox "That's all the beeps for now!"
```

> **Note:** The `Beep` statement rings the computer's bell.

If You Need to Exit Early...

The `Exit Do` statement provides a way for you to quit any of the `Do...Loops` earlier than their normal conclusion. Generally, you use an `Exit Do` in the body of an `If` statement. Therefore, you can write a loop that is controlled by the `Do` condition, but if an extraordinary circumstance arises, such as the user entering an unexpected value inside the loop, the `Exit Do` statement forces Access Basic to terminate the loop immediately and continue with the rest of the procedure, no matter how the `Do` condition tests.

Summary

After you learn to write looping control statements, you can repeat sections of code over and over. Without loops, you have to write the same code back-to-back, and even if you do that, some loops iterate (a fancy term for *repeat*) several thousand times depending on the amount of data being manipulated.

Throughout this section of the book, you learned about several loop constructions. The first presented in this chapter are the `Do...Loops`, of which there are four kinds. They center around the `While` and the `Until` keywords. The location of the conditional test determines how the loops behave; if the test is at the top of the loop, the loop may never execute because the condition might be false to begin with. If the test is at the bottom of the loop, the loop always executes at least one time.

The While keyword forces the loop to continue while a certain condition is true. The condition might use a comparison operator or a function or method that returns a true or false result. A zero always produces a false result, and a nonzero value produces true, so the conditional test may be a variable or control value.

The Until keyword causes the loop to continue until a certain condition is true. Although you can structure any loop to work with either a While or Until keyword, you will find that certain loops are easier to write with one or the other keyword, depending on the conditional test you are making.

In the next chapter you read about another kind of loop. The For-Next loop encloses a loop that repeats for a specific number of times. All the Do...Loop loops that you saw in this chapter looped while or until a certain comparison is true.

Review Questions

Answers to review questions are in Appendix B.

1. What is a loop?

2. What is the difference between the four Do loops?

3. Describe the following statement:

```
Counter = Counter + 1
```

4. What causes an endless loop?

5. How can you terminate an endless loop if you accidentally execute one (what is the keystroke)?

6. How many times does the following MsgBox statement execute?

```
n = 10
Do While (n > 0)
    n = n - 2
    MsgBox "**"
Loop
```

7. Why should you execute the Edit method before editing a dynaset's record?

8. How many times does the following MsgBox statement execute?

```
n = 0
Do While (n > 0)
    n = n + 3
    MsgBox "**"
Loop
```

9. How many times does the following MsgBox statement execute?

```
n = 10
Do
    n = n + 3
    MsgBox "**"
Loop Until (n > 20)
```

10. What, if anything, is wrong with the following loop?

```
n = 10
Do
    MsgBox "**"
Loop Until (n > 100)
```

Review Exercises

1. Write a Do loop that prints the message "Happy Birthday" ten times.

2. Describe how you change the EliminateNulls procedure so that the numbers that replace the Null values begin at 1.

3. Ask the user (with InputBox) for his or her age. Then write a Do loop that prints "Happy Birthday" once for each year in the age. Beep each time through the loop as well.

CHAPTER 19

For-Next Loops

In addition to the `Do...Loops` statements you learned in the preceding chapter, Access Basic also offers `For-Next` loops, which are perfect for repeating sections of your programs a fixed number of times. Whereas the `Do...Loops` provide loops that iterate while or until a certain condition is true, the `For-Next` loops iterate for a fixed number of times.

A `For-Next` loop always begins with a `For` statement and ends with a `Next` statement. In a way, the `For` and `Next` statements wrap around the body of the loop, just as the `Do` and `Loop` statements wrap around the loops you saw in Chapter 18. You should indent the body of a `For-Next` loop so that you can spot the contents of the loop easily.

This chapter introduces the following topics:

♦ The `For-Next` statement

♦ Changing the loop's control values

♦ Counting up and down with `For-Next` loops

♦ Nesting `For-Next` loops

♦ The `Exit For` statement

Tip: In reality, you can write virtually any loop using any of the four `Do...Loops` or the `For-Next` loop. The type of loop you choose depends as much on style and personal preference as anything. Nevertheless, you may find that the `For-Next` loops generally are easier to code when you need a loop that loops a certain number of times rather than one that loops based on a condition.

Introducing *For* and *Next*

You don't see *For* without *Next*.

The For and Next statements always appear in pairs. If your program has one or more For statements, it also should have a Next statement somewhere. The For and Next statements enclose one or more Access Basic statements that form the loop; the statements between For and Next repeat continuously a certain number of times. You, as the programmer, control the number of times the loop repeats.

The format of the For-Next loop is as follows:

```
For Counter = Start To End [Step Increment]
   One or more Access Basic statements go here
Next [Counter] [, Counter...]
```

The *Counter* is a numeric variable you supply. It helps control the body of the loop (the statements between For and Next). The *Counter* variable is initialized to the value of *Start* before the first iteration of the loop. The *Start* value typically is 1 but can be any numeric value (or variable) you specify. Every time the body of the loop repeats, the *Counter* variable changes (either increments or decrements) by the value of the *Increment*. If you do not specify a Step value, the For statement assumes an *Increment* of 1.

The value of *End* is a number (or variable) that controls the end of the looping process. When *Counter* is equal to or greater than *End*, Access Basic does not repeat the loop but continues at the statement following Next.

The Next statement is the way that Access Basic has to end the loop—the signal to Access Basic that the body of the For-Next loop is finished. If the *Counter* variable is less than the *End* variable, Access Basic increments the *Counter* variable by the value of *Increment*, and the body of the loop repeats again.

Note: Although the *Counter* variable after Next is optional, most programmers specify one. The *Counter* variable is the same one used at the top of the loop in the For statement.

Example

The following example uses the immediate execution window to show you how the For-Next loop really works. This procedure uses the *Ctr* variable to control the loop.

```
Function forNext ()
   Dim Ctr As Integer      ' A local variable
   For Ctr = 1 To 10       ' Ctr starts off with 1 and ends with 10
      Debug.Print Ctr
   Next Ctr                 ' End of the loop
End Function
```

> **Note:** The Debug object refers to the immediate execution window.

To see this procedure execute, attach the forNext() function procedure to an After Update control on any form, such as the Customer's form in the Northwind Traders sample database. (Do not save the form after you make this addition because you're adding the procedure just to see how it operates. Put the form back in its original contents before you added the extra control.) Open the immediate execution window with **View Immediate Window** before compiling the program. Open the Customer's form and edit the field to which you've attached the forNext() function. The procedure executes as soon as you edit the contents of the field.

The loop counts from 1 to 10, printing the numbers each time the count increments once more. Before looking at the procedure any further, look at the program and then its immediate execution window output shown in Figure 19.1. The results speak for themselves, illustrating the For-Next loop very well.

Figure 19.1

After running the *For-Next* loop.

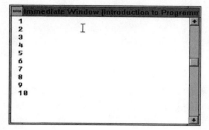

When the loop first begins, the Ctr variable is assigned a 1—the *Start* value of the loop. Each time through the loop, Ctr is one more than the previous loop. You can see the stepping up of Ctr in the immediate window's display in Figure 19.1.

Following is a procedure that contains a Do...Loop that works just like the previous For-Next loop. Although both loops do the same thing, the For-Next loop provides easier syntax and requires less work on your part when a counter variable is involved.

```
Function whileFor ()
' This procedure simulates the previous one
  Dim Ctr As Integer      ' A local variable
  Ctr = 1     ' You must initialize the variable
  Do
    Debug.Print Ctr
    Ctr = Ctr + 1        ' You must add 1 to Ctr
  Loop Until Ctr > 10  ' You must provide for the loop's exit
End Function
```

> **Caution:** Don't confuse the loops with the `If` statement. The `Do...Loop` and `For-Next` statements are loops, and the `If` statement is not a loop. The body of an `If` statement executes at most one time, whereas the body of a loop can execute many times.

Example

Any time you need to repeat something a fixed number of times, use a `For-Next` loop. The number of times a `For-Next` loop iterates can be determined by a variable. The following function procedure beeps as many times as the value in `ringNum` determines.

```
Function BeepIt (ringNum As Integer)
' Function that beeps a certain number of times
Dim Ctr As Integer    ' For-Next counter variable
  For Ctr = 1 To ringNum
     Beep    ' Ring the bell
  Next Ctr
End Function
```

> **Note:** A For-Next loop may never execute. If the preceding procedure passed a 0 or a negative value, for example, the loop would never execute because the ending value would be less than the start value of 1.

Example

For assumes a *Step* value of 1.

Access Basic assumes a `Step` value of 1 if you do not specify `Step`. You can make the `For` loop increment the counter variable by any value. The following procedure prints the even numbers from 1 to 10. It then prints the odd numbers from 1 to 10. To print, specify a `Step` value of 2. This specification ensures that 2 is added to the counter variable each time the loop executes, rather than the default of 1 as in the previous example. To run this procedure after compiling it, add it to an After Update control on a form, open the immediate window, and edit the control as done previously.

> **Tip:** Enlarge the immediate window to see the full output after running this procedure.

```
Function oddEven ()
' Prints the first few odd and even numbers
  Dim Num As Integer
  Debug.Print "Even numbers below 10" ' Use immediate window
  For Num = 2 To 9 Step 2   ' Start at 2, the first even number
    Debug.Print Num
  Next Num        ' End of first loop

  Debug.Print    ' Prints a blank line
  Debug.Print "Odd numbers below 10"
  For Num = 1 To 10 Step 2
    Debug.Print Num
  Next Num
End Function
```

The first section's start value is 2, not 1. If it were 1, the number 1 would print first, as it does in the odd number section. This program contains two loops. The body of each one consists of the single Print statements. The first Print statement is not part of either loop. If it were, the screen title would print before each number printed.

For-Next loops change by the *Step* value.

The Step value determines just how much Num increments each time through the loops. The first For statement is saying, "For each iteration through the loop, with Num starting at 2, step through the loop adding 2 to Num each time." The second For statement is saying, "For each iteration through the loop, with Num starting at 1, step through the loop adding 1 to Num each time." Figure 19.2 shows the output from this procedure.

Figure 19.2

Using a *Step* value other than 1.

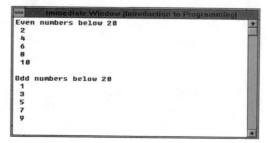

Example

1 2

The count variable can count down rather than up if you specify a Step value with a negative amount. With a negative Step value, the initial value assigned in the For statement must be greater than the ending value so that the loop can count down.

Following is a procedure that counts down from 10 to 1 and then prints Blast off! at the end of the loop. To accomplish the countdown, you must use a large beginning value (10) and a negative Step value (–1). The For statement requests that Cnt loop from 10 to 1. Each time through the loop a –1 is added to Cnt, causing the backward counting.

```
Function countDown ()
' A procedure that counts down
  For Cnt = 10 To 1 Step -1
    Debug.Print Cnt
  Next Cnt
  Debug.Print "Blast Off!"
End Function
```

If you run this program, you see the following output in the immediate execution window:

```
10
9
8
7
6
5
4
3
2
1
Blast Off!
```

The Optional *Next* Variable

The *Next* variable is optional.

The variable name, after Next, is optional; you don't need to specify it. Access realizes that every single For statement in your program requires a Next statement. Therefore, whenever Access encounters a Next without a variable, it already knows Next is the conclusion to the loop started with the last For statement.

> **Tip:** Even though the Next variable is optional, good programmers recommend that you always specify one. Access does not require the variable name, but it makes your program clearer to those (or yourself) who have to make changes to it later.

Example

To illustrate the fact that Access does not require a variable after Next, following is a counting loop that counts down from 10 to 1 and then prints a message. Access knows to match each Next with its preceding For counter variable, even though the variable name does not appear after Next.

```
For Ctr = 10 To 1 Step -1
    Debug.Print Ctr
Next              ' No variable name specified
```

If the last line of this code read

```
Next Ctr
```

the result would have been equivalent.

Example

The following example helps show you the time saved by a For-Next loop.

```
For i = 1 To 10
  Debug.Print i*2
Next
```

This For-Next loop serves to shortcut the following ten statements:

```
Debug.Print 1*2
Debug.Print 2*2
Debug.Print 3*2
Debug.Print 4*2
Debug.Print 5*2
Debug.Print 6*2
Debug.Print 7*2
Debug.Print 8*2
Debug.Print 9*2
Debug.Print 10*2
```

Nesting Loops

A nested loop is a loop within a loop.

Any Access statement can go inside the body of a For-Next loop—even another For-Next loop! When you put a loop within a loop, you are creating *nested loops*. The clock in a sporting event works like a nested loop. You might think this example is stretching an analogy a little far, but it truly works. A clock in a football game counts down from 15 minutes to 0. It counts down 4 times. The first countdown is a loop going from 15 to 0 (for each minute), and that loop is nested within another loop counting from 1 to 4 (for each of the four quarters).

Any time your program needs to repeat a loop more than one time, use a nested loop. Figure 19.3 shows an outline of nested loops. You can think of the inside loop as looping "faster" than the outside loop. The For loop counting from 1 to 10 is the inside loop. It loops fastest because the variable In goes from 1 to 10 before the outside loop, the variable Out, finishes its first iteration. Because the outside loop does not repeat until the Next Out statement, the inside For loop has a chance to finish in its entirety. When the outside loop finally does iterate a second time, the inside loop starts all over again.

Figure 19.3

An outline of nested loops.

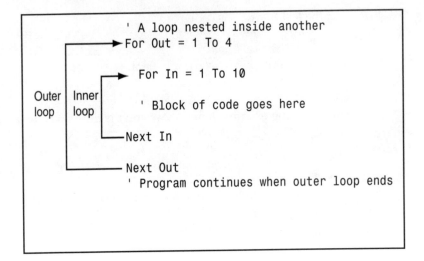

```
' A loop nested inside another
For Out = 1 To 4

    For In = 1 To 10

        ' Block of code goes here

    Next In

Next Out
    ' Program continues when outer loop ends
```

Outer loop   Inner loop

Note: The block of code inside the innermost loop of Figure 19.3 executes a total of 40 times. The outside loop iterates 4 times, and the inner loop executes 10 times for each of the outer loop's counts.

Figure 19.4 shows two loops within an outside loop. Both these loops execute in their entirety before the outside loop finishes its first iteration. When the outside loop starts its second iteration, the two inside loops repeat over again.

Figure 19.4

An outline of two loops nested inside another.

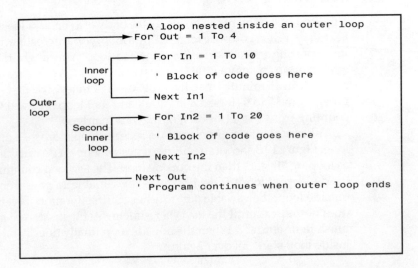

```
' A loop nested inside an outer loop
For Out = 1 To 4

    For In = 1 To 10

        ' Block of code goes here

    Next In1

    For In2 = 1 To 20

        ' Block of code goes here

    Next In2

Next Out
    ' Program continues when outer loop ends
```

Outer loop   Inner loop   Second inner loop

Note: The block of code inside the innermost loop of Figure 19.3 executes a total of 40 times. The outside loop iterates 4 times, and the inner loop executes 10 times for each of the outer loop's counts.

Notice the order of the Next variables in Figures 19.3 and 19.4. The inside loop always finishes, and, therefore, its Next must come before the outside loop's Next variable. If no variables are listed after each Next, the loops still are correct and work properly.

Figure 19.5 shows an incorrect order of Next statements. The "outside" loop finishes before the "inside" loop. This example does not fit the description of nested loops, and you get an error if you try to finish an outside loop before the inside loop finishes.

Figure 19.5

Two incorrectly
nested loops.

```
' The outer loop finished (with Next) before the inner loop

For Out = 1 To 4
    For In1 = 1 To 10

      ' Block of code goes here

      Next Out ◄──────────────Too early
  Next In ◄──────────────Too late
```

Tip: To sum up nested loops, follow this rule of thumb: In nested loops, the order of the Next variables should be the opposite of the For variables. This arrangement gives the inside loop (or loops) a chance to complete before the outside loop's next iteration.

Caution: The indention of Next statements has no effect on the order they execute. Indention serves only to make programs more readable to you and other programmers.

Nested loops become especially important later when you use them for array and matrix processing.

Example

The following procedure contains a loop within a loop—a nested loop. The inside loop counts and prints from 1 to 4. The outside loop counts from 1 to 3. Therefore, the inside loop repeats, in its entirety, 4 times; the procedure prints the values 1 to 4 and does so 3 times.

```
Function nested1 ()
' Print the numbers from 1 to 4 three times using a nested loop
  Dim Times, Num As Integer
  For Times = 1 To 3          ' Outside loop
    For Num = 1 To 4          ' Inside loop
      Debug.Print Num
    Next Num
  Next Times
End Function
```

Following is the procedure's output, which appears in the immediate execution window:

```
1
2
3
4
1
2
3
4
1
2
3
4
```

Example

If the inside loop's control variable is based on the outside loop's variable, you see effects such as that shown in the following program:

```
Function nested2 ()
' An inside loop controlled by the outer loop's variable
  Dim Outer, In As Integer
  For Outer = 5 To 1 Step -1
    For In = 1 To Outer
      Debug.Print In;              ' The ; forces number next to the
      ➡previous one
    Next In
```

```
    Debug.Print     ' This forces cursor to next line
    Next Outer
End Function
```

Here is the output from this program:

```
1 2 3 4 5
1 2 3 4
1 2 3
1 2
1
```

Table 19.1 traces the two variables Outer and In through this program's execution. Sometimes you have to "play computer" when you're learning a new concept such as nested loops. By stepping through the program a line at a time as if you were the computer, writing down each variable's contents, you produce this table.

Table 19.1. Tracing the program's output.

Variable	Values	
Outer	In	
5	1	
5	2	
5	3	
5	4	
5	5	
4	1	
4	2	
4	3	
4	4	
3	1	
3	2	
3	3	
2	1	
2	2	
1	1	

The *Exit For* Statement

The For-Next loop was designed to execute a loop a specified number of times. However, in rare instances, the For-Next loop should quit before the For's counter variable has reached its end value. You can use the Exit For statement to quit a For loop early.

The format of Exit For is as follows:

```
Exit For
```

Although Exit For can go on a line by itself, generally it does not. You place the Exit For statement in the body of a For loop. Exit For almost always follows the true condition of an If test. If the Exit For is on a line by itself, the loop always quits early, defeating the purpose of the For-Next statements.

Example

The following procedure shows what can happen when Access encounters an unconditional Exit For statement; that is, one not proceeded by an If statement.

```
Function earlyExit ()
' A For-Next loop defeated by the EXIT For statement
  Dim Num As Integer
  Debug.Print "Here are the numbers from 1 to 20"
  For num = 1 To 20
    Debug.Print Num
    Exit For       ' Will exit the For loop immediately
  Next Num         ' Never gets looked at
  Debug.Print "That's all, folks!"
End Function
```

You can tell from the following output that Exit For forces an early exit from the loop that normally loops 20 times. The Exit For immediately terminates the For loop before it goes through one cycle. The For-Next loop might as well not be in this program.

```
Here are the numbers from 1 to 20
 1
That's all, folks!
```

Example

The following procedure is an improved version of the preceding example. It asks the user if he or she wants to see another number. If so, the For-Next loop continues its next iteration. If not, the Exit For statement terminates the For-Next loop.

```
Function earlyExit ()
' A For-Next loop running at the user's request
  Dim Num As Integer, ans As String
  Debug.Print "Here are the numbers from 1 to 20"
  For Num = 1 To 20
    Debug.Print Num
    ans = InputBox("Do you want to see another (Y/N)")
    If (ans = "N") Then Exit For    ' Exits loop if user wishes
  Next Num          ' Never executes!
  Debug.Print "That's all, folks!"
End Function
```

If you run this procedure after you open the immediate execution window, the For-Next loop iterates 20 times, as long as you answer the InputBox() function with a **y** or **Y**. However, if you indicate that you want to exit early from the loop by answering the InputBox() with an **n** or **N**, the Exit For terminates the loop. (At most, however, the loop loops a maximum of 20 times due to the For-Next counter variable.)

Note: If you nest one loop inside another, the Exit For terminates the "most active" loop, that is, the innermost loop in which the Exit For resides.

Tip: The *conditional* Exit For (an If followed by an Exit For) is good for missing data. When you start processing data files or large amounts of user data entry, you may expect 100 input numbers and only get 95; you can use an Exit For to terminate the For-Next loop before it cycles through its 96th iteration.

Using Loops with Forms and Reports

Use *For-Next* to step through *Forms* and *Reports* objects.

Now that you've learned the mechanics of loops using simple variables and the immediate execution window, you're ready to see some database examples of loops.

The Forms and Reports predefined objects (as opposed to objects you create such as tables and your table's forms and reports) change as you open and close forms and reports in your database. The Forms object contains the name of every open form, and the Reports object contains the name of every open report. A predefined object named Form (without the *s*) defines the current form's or report's subform. The Forms and Reports objects do not contain subforms, so you must get to subforms using the Form object.

Example

Before accessing the Forms and Reports objects, you should realize that Access enables you to refer to all the forms and reports within Forms and Reports without knowing the names of the individual forms and reports that are open. If you have three forms named AcPayForm, AcRecForm, and AcReviewForm open, for example, the predefined object Forms contains these three forms. Each form is numbered, starting at zero, and you can refer to the forms by number rather than by name. The number, called a *subscript*, goes after the Forms predefined object.

Table 19.2 shows you how you can refer to the three forms by using the subscript.

Table 19.2. Referring to three forms by their subscripts.

Form Name	Forms Subscript Notation
AcPayForm	Forms(0)
AcRecForm	Forms(1)
AcReviewForm	Forms(2)

> **Tip:** You now know three ways to refer to an individual form or report: by name, by a variable that holds the name, and by a subscript. All the following can refer to the AcPayForm, assuming that the variable myFormVar is a string variable that holds the name AcPayForm:
>
> ```
> Forms![AcPayForm]
> Forms(myFormVar)
> Forms(0)
> ```
>
> You also can use the parentheses notation to refer to the form by name, as follows:
>
> ```
> Forms!("AcPayForm")
> ```

Subscripts for Controls

You also may refer to individual controls, such as fields, inside your forms and reports by a subscript number rather than by name. Therefore, your programs can step through all the fields in a report without having to access the fields' individual names.

Example

Suppose that a form named Store contains these five controls: three control fields named StoreNum, StoreName, and StoreLoc, and two list box controls named StoreEmps and StoreMgrs. Your Access procedures can refer to each of the controls by a subscript number, starting at 0, as shown in Table 19.3.

Table 19.3. Referring to five form controls by their subscripts.

Control Name	Forms Subscript Notation
StoreNum	Forms!Store(0)
StoreName	Forms!Store(1)
StoreLoc	Forms!Store(2)
StoreEmps	Forms!Store(3)
StoreMgrs	Forms!Store(4)

Caution: Don't confuse the subscripts when used with open forms and reports and when used with an individual form or report. If a predefined object—**Forms**, **Reports**, or **Form**—precedes the subscript, the subscript refers to a particular form, report, or subform. If the name of a form or report appears before the subscript, the subscript refers to a control on that form or report.

The Forms and Reports *Count* Property

The Count property is available to you when you need to work with the Forms and Reports predefined objects. Count simplifies your programming so that you don't have to know how many individual form and report names are in the current database or the number of controls in either. By using Count, you can write generalized procedures that work on all the forms and reports currently open and on all the controls in each one.

The Count property always returns an integer.

Example

The following code declares two integer variables—c1 and c2—and then stores the number of open forms in c1 and the number of open reports in c2.

```
Dim c1 As Integer, c2 As Integer
c1 = Forms.Count    ' Save the number of open forms
c2 = Reports.Count   ' Save the number of open reports
```

If you want to know the number of controls on a specific form or report, you can use the Count property as well. The following code declares two integer variables—ct1 and ct2—and stores the number of controls on a form named MyForm in ct1 and the number of controls on a report named MyReport in ct2.

```
Dim ct1 As Integer, ct2 As Integer
ct1 = MyForm.Count    ' Save the number of controls on the form
ct2 = MyReport.Count  ' Save the number of controls on the report
```

Example

The IsLoaded() function shown in this example appears in the Utility Functions module of the Northwind Traders database. The function is passed the name of a form, and the function returns True or False depending on whether the form name matches any of the form names currently open at the time.

> **Note:** In Access, True and False are keywords that represent true and false values which you can use in expressions and with which you can perform comparison and conditional tests. You always can use -1 or 0 in place of True and False, respectively, but the keywords serve to document code better than numbers.

As you can see from the code, a For-Next loop is the perfect tool for stepping through all the open forms in the current database. Always remember to start the controlling loop with a beginning value of 0, as done here, because 0 is the subscript of the first form.

The initial assignment of False to the IsLoaded function return value is returned only if the For loop does not assign the function return a True value. The Count property is used to determine the number of forms currently open, and then 1 is subtracted to get a final form subscript because the subscripts begin at 0.

If, at any time during the stepping through of the forms, a form's name matches that of the argument passed to the function, the function ends early with an Exit Function statement, and True is passed back to the calling code. If the argument does not match any of the open form names, the initial False value is returned to the calling code.

```
Function IsLoaded (MyFormName)
' Accepts: a form name
' Purpose: determines if a form is loaded
' Returns: True if specified the form is loaded;
'          False if the specified form is not loaded.
    Dim i As Integer

    IsLoaded = False
    For i = 0 To Forms.Count - 1
        If Forms(i).FormName = MyFormName Then
            IsLoaded = True
```

```
            Exit Function
                ' Quit function once form has been found.
        End If
    Next
End Function
```

> **Note:** The FormName property identifies the name of a report or form so that the comparison can be made.

Summary

The For-Next loop gives you the capability to control a loop when you know how many iterations are supposed to be performed. Although you can write Do...Loops to behave exactly like For-Next loops (and the reverse is true as well), the For-Next loops reduce the amount of coding you have to do when you iterate through loops using control variables that count up or down.

By changing the value of the Step option, you can force the For-Next loop to count up or down by any increment or decrement you want. If you don't specify a Step value, the For-Next loop assumes a Step value of 1.

For-Next loops can be nested so that an outer loop can control one or more inner loops. Any statement can appear in the body of a For-Next loop, including the Do...Loops you read about in Chapter 18.

Toward the end of this chapter, you learned about combining For-Next loops with subscripted form and report names and controls. Using the For-Loop, you can work with forms and reports without having to refer to each of them by name.

In the next chapter you see how to make several decisions using a single statement. Select Case enables you to make data comparisons in a much cleaner way than nested If statements allow.

Review Questions

Answers to review questions are in Appendix B.

1. How many times does this code beep?

```
For c = 1 To 5
   Beep
Next c
```

2. TRUE or FALSE: If a program has at least one For statement, there is always a Next statement somewhere later in the program.

3. What is the value of the first subscript when working with predefined objects?

4. List the three predefined objects.

5. Why should the Exit For statement follow an If rather than appearing by itself?

6. How many times does the Beep occur in this set of nested loops?

```
For i = 1 To 5
  For j = 1 To 6
    Beep
  Next j
Next i
```

7. TRUE or FALSE: If you don't specify a Next variable, you get an error.

8. What happens if you don't specify a Step value?

9. TRUE or FALSE: A For-Next loop may never execute depending on the start and ending values.

10. What, if anything, is wrong with the following nested loop?

```
For out = 1 To 3
  For in1 = 1 To 10
    Debug.Print in1
  Next out
Next in1
```

11. Which is better—a Do...Loop or a For-Next loop—if you want to keep printing a report as long as the user answers affirmative to your request?

12. What does the Count property do?

Review Exercises

1. Use an InputBox() function to ask the user for his or her age. Using a For-Next loop, beep once for every year the user has lived and print a congratulatory message (using MsgBox) at the end of the procedure.

2. Write a procedure that prints your name three times, then beeps four times, and then prints That's all folks! five times. Use three For-Next loops.

3. Write a procedure that prints to the immediate execution window the names of every open form and report in the current database.

4. Write a procedure that computes and prints the total number of controls and all open forms and reports in the current database.

CHAPTER 20

Select Case

You probably should not rely on the block If-Then-ElseIf to take care of too many conditions because more than three or four nested If statements tend to add confusion (you get into messy logic such as: If this is true, then if this is true, then do something, else if this is true do something, else if this is true do something, and so on). The Select Case statement described in this chapter handles multiple If selections better than a long set of If-Then-ElseIf statements.

There are three forms of the Select Case statement. Select Case is one of the longest statements in Access Basic. Despite that foreboding length, Select Case is one of the easiest statements to master. Select Case exists to make your programming decisions easier, not harder.

This chapter introduces the following topics:

♦ The Select Case statement

♦ Replacing nested If statements with Select Case

♦ Conditional Select Case choices

♦ Ranges of Select Case choices

The Select Case statement is the last control statement left for you to learn in the Access Basic language. After you master Select Case, you'll know the structure of the language.

Introducing *Select Case*

Select Case chooses among several conditions.

Select Case improves upon the block If-Then-Else by streamlining the nested "If within an If" construction. The format of the primary Select Case is as follows:

```
Select Case Expression
Case expressionMatch
    Block of one or more Access Basic statements
[Case expressionMatch
    Block of one or more Access Basic statements...]
[Case Else
    Block of one or more Access Basic statements]
End Select
```

As the brackets indicate, you can have two or more sets of Case expressions and code following a Select Case statement. Your application determines the number of Case expressions that follow the Select Case line. The *expression*s can be either text or numeric expressions (with constants or variables). The expressions are not conditional True or False expressions but expressions that equate to integer or character values.

The *Block of one or more Access Basic statements* is similar to the block of statements you saw for the block If; you can type one or more statements following each other to make up that block. The Case Else line is optional; not all Select Case statements require it. You must put the End Select line at the end of every Case Select statement, however. Otherwise, Access Basic does not know where the last block of Case statements ends.

Using Select Case is easier than its format might lead you to believe. If Select Case *expression* is the same as any of the Case *expression*s, that matching Case code executes. If none of the Case *expression*s match the Select Case *expression*, the Case Else code executes. If you do not supply a Case Else, the next statement in the program executes. You can use a Select Case anywhere that you can use a block If-Then-Else, and Select Case is the easier of the two to read.

Example

In Chapter 17 you learned about the VarType() function, which determines the data type of its argument by returning a numeric value. Here is the function procedure used (without explanation this time) to teach you VarType():

```
Function PrntType(aVar)   ' Variant if you don't specify otherwise
    If VarType(aVar) = 0 Then
        MsgBox "The argument is Empty"
    ElseIf VarType(aVar) = 1 then
        MsgBox "The argument is Null"
    ElseIf VarType(aVar) = 2 then
        MsgBox "The argument is Integer"
```

```
  ElseIf VarType(aVar) = 3 then
     MsgBox "The argument is Long"
  ElseIf VarType(aVar) = 4 then

     MsgBox "The argument is Single"
  ElseIf VarType(aVar) = 5 then
     MsgBox "The argument is Double"
  ElseIf VarType(aVar) = 6 then
     MsgBox "The argument is Currency"
  ElseIf VarType(aVar) = 7 then
     MsgBox "The argument is Date"
  ElseIf VarType(aVar) = 8 then
     MsgBox "The argument is String"
  End If
End Function
```

Although nothing is wrong with this procedure as coded, nested `If-ElseIf` statements can be confusing. `Select Case` statements do the same thing but are easier to follow. Following is an equivalent function that uses `Select Case`:

```
Function PrntType(aVar)  ' Variant if you don't specify otherwise
  Select Case VarType(aVar)  ' VarType() returns an integer
    Case 0
      MsgBox "The argument is Empty"
    Case 1
      MsgBox "The argument is Null"
    Case 2
      MsgBox "The argument is Integer"
    Case 3
      MsgBox "The argument is Long"
    Case 4
      MsgBox "The argument is Single"
    Case 5
      MsgBox "The argument is Double"
    Case 6
      MsgBox "The argument is Currency"
    Case 7
      MsgBox "The argument is Date"
    Case 8
      MsgBox "The argument is String"
  End Select
End Function
```

The long `Select Case` statement, with indented `Case` statements, cleans up the code when your program must select from among many choices. The expression at the end of the `Select Case` line, in this case `VarType(aVar)`, determines which of the subsequent `Case` statements execute. Although only one statement follows each `Case` statement in this example, several statements can execute for a `Case`, and other procedures may be called as well.

> **Note:** The `VarType()` function always returns a value from 1 to 8. If none of the `Case` values match the expression, use a `Case Else` statement. A `Case Else` executes if none of the other `Case` values match the `Select Case` expression.

Example

Optionally, you can insert a colon (:) after each `Case` if you like. Doing so does not change the `Select Case` statement. The following are equivalent:

```
Select Case VarType(aVar)  ' VarType() returns an integer
  Case 0
    MsgBox "The argument is Empty"
  Case 1
    MsgBox "The argument is Null"
  Case 2
    MsgBox "The argument is Integer"
End Select
```

and

```
Select Case VarType(aVar)  ' VarType() returns an integer
  Case 0:
    MsgBox "The argument is Empty"
  Case 1:
    MsgBox "The argument is Null"
  Case 2:
    MsgBox "The argument is Integer"
End Select
```

The colon helps maintain consistency with other versions of BASIC such as QBasic.

Example

The `Select Case` is great for handling user selections. The following procedure is a math tutorial, which asks for two numbers and then asks the user which type of math to perform with the numbers.

```
Function mathPractice ()
' Procedure to practice math accuracy
  Dim num1, num2 As Integer
  Dim op, ans As String
  num1 = InputBox("Please type a number")
  num2 = InputBox("Please type a second number")
  ' Find out what the user wants to do with the numbers
  op = InputBox("Do you want +, -, *, or / ?")
  ' Perform the math
  Select Case (op)
    Case "+"
      ans = Str$(num1 + num2)  ' Make answer a string
      MsgBox Str$(num1) & " plus" & Str$(num2) & " is" & ans
    Case "-"
      ans = Str$(num1 - num2)  ' Make answer a string
      MsgBox Str$(num1) & " minus" & Str$(num2) & " is" & ans
    Case "*"
      ans = Str$(num1 * num2)  ' Make answer a string
      MsgBox Str$(num1) & " times" & Str$(num2) & " is" & ans
    Case "/"
      ans = Str$(num1 / num2)  ' Make answer a string
      MsgBox Str$(num1) & " into" & Str$(num2) & " is" & ans
    Case Else
      Beep
      MsgBox "You didn't enter a correct operator.", 48
  End Select
End Function
```

This Select Case statement demonstrates that string expressions work as well in Select Case statements as integer expressions.

Caution: Never use a floating-point expression for a Select Case match because it is extremely difficult to store and match exact floating-point quantities. Stick to integer and string expressions for Select Case.

Str$() converts numbers to strings.

The Str$() expression used in this example is probably new to you here. The MsgBox statement requires a string expression, but MsgBox is used here to display the result of a mathematical expression. Therefore, the answer to the expression, stored in ans, is converted to a string with Str$() before being concatenated to other strings in the MsgBox message.

> **Note:** If the user enters an operator other than +, -, *, or /, the `Case Else` takes over and displays an error box.

Example

The following `ListMondays()` function appeared in Version 1.1 of Access. Even though you might now be using Version 2.0, this example code provides a lot of power and insight into the `Select Case` statement. The function lists the next four Mondays following the current date. The function is used from within a list or combo box so that the Mondays can be displayed or scrolled through. Depending on the code passed to the function, the `Select Case` returns a different value. If 3 is passed in the code, for example, the calling procedure wants to know how many Mondays will be returned (4) so that room can be made. Generalizing `ListMondays()` enables the function to perform several dialog box tasks and enables the author of the function to modify it (such as changing the function to return eight Mondays rather than four), and the calling procedures don't have to be changed. The specifics of the `code` value are cryptic, but again, the `Select Case` use is excellent.

For this example, concentrate on the action of the `Select Case`. Notice that the final `Case` statement contains two statements, and the others have one each showing that the number of statements following a `Case` is dependent on the need of that `Case` and is not limited by Access Basic.

```
Function ListMondays (fld As Control, id, row, col, code)
' Accepts: a control, an identifier, a row, a column, a code
' Purpose: lists the next four Mondays following the current
date.
'           A list box or combo box is required to use this
➥function.
' Returns: the requested date

    Dim offset

    Select Case code
        Case 0                  ' Initialize.
            ListMondays = True
        Case 1                  ' Open.
            ListMondays = Timer ' Unique ID number for control.
        Case 3                  ' Number of rows.
            ListMondays = 4
        Case 4                  ' Number of columns.
            ListMondays = 1
```

```
        Case 5                      ' Column Width.
            ListMondays = -1     ' Use default width.

        Case 6                      ' Get data.
            offset = Abs((9 - Weekday(Now)) Mod 7)
            ListMondays = Format(Now + offset + 7 * row, "mmmm d")
    End Select

End Function
```

Conditional *Select Case* Choices

As with the If statement, the expression tested for by Select Case can be conditional. You must use the extra Is keyword in the conditional Case. Because you can
put a conditional test after one or more of the Cases, you can test for a broader range
of values with the conditional Select Case. The keyword Is is required if you use
a conditional test in a Case.

> **Note:** You cannot combine And, Or, or Not in a conditional Select Case
> statement. If you need to make a compound conditional test, you must use a
> block If-Then-ElseIf.

Example

This procedure asks the user for an age and prints an appropriate message. Without
the conditional Case testing, it would take too many individual Cases testing for
each possible age to make the Select Case usable here.

```
Function ageTest ()
' Procedure to describe legal vehicles based on age
  Dim age As Integer
  age = InputBox("How old are you?")
  Select Case age
    Case Is < 14
      MsgBox "You can only ride a bike."
    Case Is < 16
      MsgBox "You can ride a motorcycle."
    Case Else
      MsgBox "You can drive a car"
  End Select
End Function
```

The Range of *Select Case* Choices

Another option of Select Case shows that you can test for a range of values on each line of Case. You can use the To keyword in a Case statement to specify a range of values that Access Basic checks to determine which Case executes. This capability is useful when possibilities are ordered sequentially and you want to perform certain actions if one of the sets of values is chosen. The first expression (the one to the right of To) must be lower numerically—or as determined by the ANSI table if it is character data—than the second expression.

> **Tip:** Put the most likely Case selection at the top of the Case for efficiency. Access Basic then does not have to search down the list as much.

Example

Here is the same age-testing procedure as the preceding example, except that a range of ages is tested with the To keyword rather than a conditional test.

```
Function ageTest ()
' Procedure to describe legal vehicles based on age
  Dim age As Integer
  age = InputBox("How old are you?")
  Select Case age
    Case 1 To 13
      MsgBox "You can only ride a bike."
    Case 14 To 15
      MsgBox "You can ride a motorcycle."
    Case 16 To 99
      MsgBox "You can drive a car"
    Case Else
      MsgBox "You typed a bad age."
  End Select
End Function
```

This procedure ensures that anyone aged 16 or older is told that he or she can drive a car. Any ages that do not match a Case, such as 0 and negative ages, trigger an error message.

Combining *Select Case* Formats

Access Basic provides a great deal of customization for Select Case statements. You can combine any and all of the previous Select Case formats into a single Select Case statement.

Example

Here are some sample Case statements that show you how you can combine different formats:

```
Case 5, 6, 7, 10

Case 5 To 7, 10

Case "A", "a", "K" To "P", "k" To "p"

Case 1, 5, 10, Is > 100, amount To quantity
```

Example

Being able to combine different forms of Case enables you to add functionality to your selections. Here is the math Select Case presented again. This time, the user can enter an operator or the name of an operator, and the appropriate math is performed.

```
Function mathPractice ()
' Procedure to practice math accuracy
  Dim num1 As Integer, num2 As Integer
  Dim op As String, ans As String
  num1 = InputBox("Please type a number")
  num2 = InputBox("Please type a second number")
  ' Find out what the user wants to do with the numbers
  op = InputBox("Do you want +, -, *, or / ?")
  ' Convert the operator to uppercase in case a name was entered
  op = UCase$(op)
  ' Perform the math
  Select Case (op)
    Case "+", "ADD", "PLUS"
      ans = Str$(num1 + num2)  ' Make answer a string
      MsgBox Str$(num1) + " plus" + Str$(num2) + " is" + ans
    Case "-", "SUBTRACT", "MINUS"
      ans = Str$(num1 - num2)  ' Make answer a string
      MsgBox Str$(num1) + " minus" + Str$(num2) + " is" + ans
    Case "*", "MULTIPLY", "TIMES"
      ans = Str$(num1 * num2)  ' Make answer a string
      MsgBox Str$(num1) + " times" + Str$(num2) + " is" + ans
    Case "/", "DIVIDE", "INTO"
      ans = Str$(num1 / num2)  ' Make answer a string
      MsgBox Str$(num1) + " into" + Str$(num2) + " is" + ans

    Case Else
      Beep
      MsgBox "You didn't enter a correct operator.", 48
  End Select
End Function
```

The plus sign is used here to concatenate `MsgBox` strings (either & or + concatenate string values).

Example

The following `Select Case` statement calculates overtime payroll figures based on the hours worked. Such decision-based calculations are difficult to provide in Access without your using Access Basic's control statements such as `Select Case`.

```
Select Case (hours)
   Case 1 To 40
      overTime = 0.0
   Case 41 To 49
     ' Time and a half
     overHrs = (hours - 40) * 1.5
     overTime = overHrs * rate
   Case Is >= 50
     ' Double time for hrs over 50 and
     ' 1.5 for 10 hours
     overHrs = ((hours - 50) * 2) + (10 * 1.5)
     overTime = overHrs * rate
End Select
```

The `Select Case` variable `hours` was put in parentheses to make it stand out better.

Summary

Congratulations! You have now learned the powerful control statements of Access Basic, including `Select Case`. `Select Case` is a long but readable statement that selects from one of several cases based on an expression match in the `Select Case` statement.

`Select Case` has several formats. You can write the statement so that a `Case` match is made based on a single integer or string value. You also can use the `Is` keyword to select from a case based on a conditional expression. With the `To` keyword, you can select from a range of values. In addition, you can combine all the formats of `Case` into a multiple-part `Select Case` statement.

The next chapter begins the exploration into Access Basic's built-in functions, so you can access the functions already written for you.

Review Questions

Answers to review questions are in Appendix B.

1. What is an advantage of Select Case over If-ElseIf statements?

2. How many formats of Select Case are there?

3. TRUE or FALSE: A colon (:) after a Case changes the behavior of the Case statement.

4. Where does the Case Else appear? What is it used for?

5. TRUE or FALSE: The Case Else statement is optional.

6. Which keyword of Select Case—Is or To—lets the Select Case select from a range of values?

7. TRUE or FALSE: The following Case statement contains an error.

```
CASE Is 34 To 48
```

Review Exercises

1. Rewrite the following nested If-ElseIf using a Select Case:

```
If (a = 1) Then
    MsgBox "Ok"
ElseIf (a = 2) Then
    MsgBox "No way"
ElseIf (a = 3) Then
    MsgBox "There's a problem."
End If
```

2. Rewrite the following nested If-ElseIf using a Select Case:

```
If (A >= B) Then
    MsgBox "+++"
ElseIf (C = 10) Then
    MsgBox "&&&"
ElseIf (D <= 20) Then
    MsgBox "@@@"
Else MsgBox "!!!"
End If
```

3. Write a Select Case statement that asks the user for the name of the month and prints "Happy Hot Summer!" if the month is a summer month, "Stay Warm!" if the month is in winter, and "Enjoy the Weather!" if the month is a month other than a summer or winter month.

Part V

The Built-In Routines

CHAPTER 21

The Domain's D...() Functions

This chapter begins a new section that discusses the built-in functions in depth. The *domain functions,* more accurately called the *domain aggregate functions,* return statistics about domains of data.

A *domain* is just a set of records in a table or a query. After you create or load a domain, you often want to know something about that domain (the sum, the average, and so on).

This chapter introduces the following topics:

♦ The DFirst() and DLast() functions

♦ The DLookup() function

♦ The DCount() function

♦ The DSum() function

♦ The DMin() and DMax() functions

♦ The statistical domain functions: DAvg(), DStDev(), DStDevP(), DVar(), and DVarP()

The domain functions are relatively easy to understand and use after you've seen some examples.

The *DFirst()* and *DLast()* Functions

The DFirst() function simply returns a value from the first record in a domain, and DLast() returns the last. Here are the formats of the two functions:

```
DFirst(expression, domain [, criteria])

DLast(expression, domain [, criteria])
```

All three domain function arguments are string expressions.

The *expression* must be a string expression that identifies the field to search and return. The DFirst() and DLast() functions return single values (as do all functions), not records. Therefore, the *expression* tells Access Basic exactly what values you want returned. The values can be any one of the following:

◆ A table's field

◆ A form's control such as a field name

◆ A constant

◆ Any function (yours or any built-in function) except a domain function

> **Note:** The first *expression* can also be a calculation that uses data in a field, as examples later in this chapter illustrate.

The *domain* must be a string expression that describes or creates the domain. The *domain* is either a table name or a query name (or an SQL expression if you are familiar with SQL).

The *criteria* is optional, as indicated by its surrounding brackets in the function formats. If you don't specify a *criteria*, the entire domain is searched, whereas if you specify a *criteria*, only selected records from the domain are searched. Therefore, if you specify a *criteria* that somehow limits the domain search to the last five records in the domain, the first of the five records is the record used for DFirst().

Any nonnumeric (string) text used in the *criteria* must be enclosed in single quotation marks unless the text is a field name.

> **Caution:** Be careful when using DFirst() and DLast() with indexed tables. If the domain is an indexed table, the table's current index determines the order and, therefore, the first and last record in the domain. If the domain is not an indexed table, the first and last record in the domain is determined by the actual order of the records in the table.

The domain
functions can
return *Null*.

Both DFirst() and DLast() return Null if no records are in the domain or if no records result from the *criteria*.

Example

The following DFirst() function call stores the first customer's fax number in the variable named cFax:

```
cFax = DFirst("[Fax]", "Customers")
```

Figure 21.1 shows you the parts of this expression and function call. The variable cFax must be defined as a String or Variant data type because the Customers table's Fax field is defined as a Text data type.

Figure 21.1

Looking at the parts of a *DFirst()* function call.

Field from the Customers table

```
cFax = DFirst("[Fax]", "Customers")
```

Variable to hold the first record's fax number after DFirst() finishes

Table to search

Example

The following statement stores the last record's fax number in cFax:

```
cFax = DLast("[Fax]", "Customers")
```

You also can store either the field name (Fax) or the table name (Customers) in string variables and use the variable names in place of the string constants.

Example

You can use any of the domain functions wherever their return values are appropriate. The previous examples' function calls return text values, so you can call them from wherever text values are appropriate. For example, the following MsgBox statement prints the first fax number:

```
MsgBox "The fax number is " & DFirst("[Fax]", "Customers")
```

Remember that & between strings indicates that the strings are concatenated into a single string. If the first fax number in the table is (801) 555-6851, you see the message box shown in Figure 21.2 when this MsgBox statement executes.

Figure 21.2

Calling *DFirst()* from within the *MsgBox* statement.

Example

The following statement limits the domain searched to only those customers whose state is Washington. Several customers have the state WA in the Region field of the Customers table. The last customer's ID from the limited domain is stored in lastCustID.

```
lastCustID = DLast("[Customer ID]", "Customers", "[Region]='WA'")
```

Note: This statement in the Northwind Traders database stores WHITC in the lastCustID variable because WHITC is the last customer from Washington state's ID.

Notice the single quotation marks around the state name. As you learned in the section before these examples, you must enclose all string constants in single quotation marks within a domain's criteria.

Example

Criteria can consist of any conditional expression (such as those that follow If statements). You also can combine several criteria expressions together with logical operators such as OR and AND. You can add the following criteria expression to the previous example to limit the search to the states of Washington or California:

```
"[Region]='WA' OR [Region]='CA'"
```

Note: The *criteria* is actually an SQL WHERE clause without the WHERE (notice the uppercase OR keyword). If you are unfamiliar with SQL, you still can limit criteria by specifying conditional expressions for the criteria, as shown here.

Calculating with Fields

In the DFirst() and DLast() functions, as well as any of the other domain functions, you can calculate with the field used as the first expression in the domain function. If you want to return more than one text field concatenated, or return a sum of two or more numeric fields (such as the total of a 30-day balance, 60-day balance, and 90-day balance from a selected customer), you can insert an expression inside the quotation marks for the domain functions' first argument.

Example

Suppose that you want to return both the voice phone number and the fax number of the first customer in the table. The string concatenation operator (&) does just that. The first of the following statements stores the voice phone number and the fax number in the Phones variable, and the next statement prints the two numbers in a message box.

```
Phones = DFirst("[Phone]& ' and ' & [Fax]", "Customers")
MsgBox "The numbers are " & Phones
```

The *DLookup()* Function

You use the DLookup() function to find a specific value—not just the first or last as you do with DFirst() and DLast()—within a domain. Often, you have the value of a field (such as a customer ID) and want to find another field's value from the matching record (such as that customer's phone number).

The DLookup() function follows a similar format as DFirst() and DLast() (as do all the domain functions). Here is the format of DLookup():

```
DLookup(expression, domain [, criteria])
```

Example

The following statement stores the phone number of Customer ID DOLLC into the phone variable:

```
phone = DLookup("[Phone]", "[Customers]", "[Customer ID] =
➥'DOLLC'")
```

Example

If any expression inside a domain function is very long, you may want to build the expression in one or more statements that precede the domain function call and store the expression in a string variable. The following statements first concatenate a long expression into a single string variable (stWhere$) before using the variable in a DLookup() function.

```
stWhere$ = "((OrderID=" + Format$(nOrderID%) + ") AND "
stWhere$ = stWhere$ + "(ProductID='" + stProductID$ + "'))"
nQtyNotShipped% = DLookup("Qty", "OrderLines", stWhere$)
```

The *DCount()* Function

DCount() counts the number of records in a given domain. You can use DCount() to find counts such as how many customers live in a given state, how many orders are over a certain dollar amount, and how many Null values are in a certain field.

The DCount() function follows a similar format as DFirst() and DLast() (as do all the domain functions). Here is the format of DCount():

```
DCount(expression, domain [, criteria])
```

Caution: DCount() does not normally count fields with Null values, but if you specify the * (asterisk) wildcard character for the *expression*, DCount() includes the Null values in the count.

Example

The following expression counts the total number of customers in the Customers table and stores the result in the numCust variable:

```
numCust = DCount("[Customer ID]", "Customers")
```

Note: If any Null records are in the Customers table (none are in the sample Northwind Traders database), the Null records are not included in the count.

Example

The following expression counts how many products in the Products table cost more than $20:

```
highProducts = DCount("[Unit Price]", "Products", "[Unit Price] >
➡20")
```

In the sample Northwind Traders database, 37 products have a unit price over $20.

Example

If you want to count the total number of records in a table, including Null records, use the asterisk wildcard. The following expression stores the total number of order records in the sample Orders table, including those that are Null:

```
totalOrders = DCount("*", "Orders")
```

Example

If you want to base a count on a Yes/No field, you can specify an expression that equates to Yes, True, No, or False. The following DCount() expression stores the number of discontinued products in the variable named discontd:

```
discontd=DCount("[Discontinued]","Products","[Discontinued]=True")
```

Example

By subtracting the total number of records found (including Null records) from the total number that don't have Null values, you can determine the number of Null records. The following statements first count the total number of records including those that are Null and store the value in recNull. The total number of records without Null values are then stored in recNoNull. The difference, the total number of Null records, then is stored in totalNullRecs.

```
recNull = DCount("*", "Orders")
recNoNull = DCount("[Shipped Date]", "Orders")
totalNullRecs = recNull - recNoNull
```

The Northwind Traders database has 21 Null Shipped Date field values in the Orders table.

The *DSum()* Function

The DSum() function returns the sum of values in the domain specified. Although DSum() totals numeric fields, you can specify any fields for the *criteria* selection for the domain.

The DSum() function follows a similar format as DFirst() and DLast() (as do all the domain functions). Here is the format of DSum():

```
DSum(expression, domain [, criteria])
```

Caution: You cannot use DSum() to total nonnumeric values. DSum() totals only numeric values.

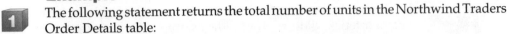

Example

The following statement returns the total number of units in the Northwind Traders Order Details table:

```
totalUnits = DSum("[Quantity]", "Order Details")
```

Example

The Order Details table has a Unit Price field and a Quantity field. If you want to know the total dollar amount of all the orders in the table, you can request that the DSum() function return the sum of the Unit Price *times* the Quantity fields, as shown here:

```
totalDol = DSum("[Unit Price] * [Quantity]", "Order Details")
```

The value computed is very large because there are several records in the Order Details table.

The *DMin()* and *DMax()* Functions

Whereas DFirst() and DLast() return the first and last values in a given domain, the DMin() and DMax() functions return the lowest and highest values in a table.

The DMin() and DMax() functions follow similar formats to the DFirst() and DLast() functions (as do all the domain functions). Here are the formats of DMin() and DMax():

```
DMin(expression, domain [, criteria])
```

and

```
DMax(expression, domain [, criteria])
```

Example

The following statements find the lowest and highest prices in the Products table:

```
lowPrice = DMin("[Unit Price]", "Products")
highPrice = DMax("[Unit Price]", "Products")
```

> **Caution:** The DMin() and DMax() functions work only with numeric field values, not text.

Statistics with *DAvg()*, *DStDev()*, *DStDevP()*, *DVar()*, and *DVarP()*

The statistical domain functions save you programming time by calculating useful statistics on your numerical data. Table 21.1 lists the purpose of each function.

Table 21.1. The statistical domain functions.

Function Name	Description
DAvg()	The arithmetic mean of the domain's values
DStDev()	The estimated standard deviation for a population sample
DStDevP()	The estimated standard deviation for a population
DVar()	The estimated variance for a population sample
DVarP()	The estimated variance for a population

These statistical domain functions follow the same formats as the previous domain functions. For example, here is the format for the DAvg() function (the others follow the same format):

```
DAvg(expression, domain [, criteria])
```

Records that contain Null values are not included in the statistical calculations.

Note: If the resulting domain contains fewer than two records, the statistical domain functions return Null results.

Example

The following statements return each of the statistical values based on the Unit Price in the Northwind Traders Products table.

```
avgPrice = DAvg("[Unit Price]", "Products")
stdDevPrice = DStDev("[Unit Price]", "Products")
stdDevPPrice = DStDevP("[Unit Price]", "Products")
varPrice = DVar("[Unit Price]", "Products")
varPPrice = DVarP("[Unit Price]", "Products")
```

Summary

You now have the tools in your tool belt to perform powerful domain-searching and statistical functions. The domain functions supply built-in calculations and searching of values so that you don't have to do as much programming. Although several non-domain built-in functions are similar to the domain functions presented here (such as Max() and Avg()), the domain functions give you more control over the records being used.

The DFirst() and DLast() domain functions return the first and last records in a domain. DLookup() finds a specific value in the domain. The remaining domain functions—DMin(), DMax(), DStDev(), DStDevP(), DVar(), and DVapP()—return statistical values based on the data within the domain.

In the next chapter you learn about many of Access Basic's built-in numeric functions, which perform useful conversions and calculations on numeric data.

Review Questions

Answers to review questions are in Appendix B.

1. What is a domain?

2. TRUE or FALSE: The expressions in the domain functions require string arguments.

3. Which of the three arguments to the domain functions is optional?

4. When do the standard deviation and variance functions return Null values?

5. Why do you use a wildcard character (*) with the DCount() function?

6. How do DFirst() and DLast() differ from DMin() and DMax()?

7. What is the difference between DStdDev() and DStDEvP()?

8. How can you perform a calculation on the field being used in the domain functions?

Review Exercises

1. Write a statement that finds the total number of records in the Northwind Traders Products table.

2. Write a statement that finds the total number of records in the Products table whose Category ID field contains BEVR.

3. Write a statement that finds the total number of records in the Products table whose Category ID field contains *either* BEVR or MEAT.

4. Write a single statement that finds the average number of units on order *and* in stock, from the Products table, for those products with a Category ID of BEVR.

CHAPTER 22

Numeric Functions

Access Basic includes many built-in numeric functions that convert and calculate with your database data. Although some of the built-in functions are highly technical, many of them are used daily by Access Basic programmers who do not use much math in their programs. Most of the built-in functions reduce your programming time. Instead of having to "reinvent the wheel" every time you need Access Basic to perform a numeric or string operation, you can use one of the many built-in functions to do the job for you.

This chapter introduces the following topics:

♦ The integer conversion functions: Fix() and Int()

♦ The data type conversion functions: CCur(), CDbl(), CInt(), CLng(), CSng(), and CVar()

♦ The sign functions: Abs() and Sgn()

♦ The math functions: Exp(), Log(), and Sqr()

♦ The trigonometric functions: Atn(), Cos(), Sin(), and Tan()

♦ The randomizing tools: Randomize and Rnd()

After you learn about the numeric functions in this chapter, you explore some string functions that work with your text data in the next chapter.

Before Looking at Functions

The numeric functions return values and take arguments.

As with built-in functions and functions that you write, all the functions in this chapter return a value of some kind, and most of them require arguments. Not all functions, such as some calls to Rnd(), require arguments, however, and those that do not should not have the parentheses following their name when you call them.

> **Note:** In all the math functions that receive arguments, you can use variables or expressions for the function arguments.

The Integer Conversion Functions

The Int() and Fix() functions work with integers. Here are their formats:

```
Int(numericValue)
Fix(numericValue)
```

One of the most common integer functions is Int(), which returns the integer value of the number you pass in the parentheses. If you pass a single-precision or double-precision number to Int(), the function converts it to an integer.

Fix() truncates to integers.

Fix() returns the *truncated* whole number value of the argument. Truncation means that the fractional part of the argument is taken off the number. Therefore, Fix() always returns an integer value.

The data type of these functions' values differs depending on the data type of their argument. Int() and Fix() both return the same data type as their argument except in two cases: if their argument is a string that can be converted to a number, the functions return double-precision; and if the functions are passed Null values, they return Null values as well.

> **Caution:** If you pass either Int() or Fix() a nonnumeric argument (such as strings that cannot be converted to numbers by the functions), you get a Type mismatch error.

For practical purposes, you can assume that Int() and Fix() return integer-like values (whole numbers) even though they may return those whole numbers in a higher precision format, such as single-precision or double-precision.

The primary difference between Int() and Fix() appears when you pass them negative arguments, as shown in the following examples.

Example

The following statement stores an 8 (the function's return value) in `iAns`:

```
iAns = Int(8.93)
```

Int() does not round.

`Int()` returns a value that is equal to or less than the argument in the parentheses. `Int()` never rounds numbers up.

Example

Both of the following pieces of code store 8s in variables:

```
num = 8.93          ' Pass Int() a variable
iAns = Int(num)       ' Stores 8 in iAns
num = 8
iAns = Int(num + 0.93)  ' Stores 8 in iAns
```

Example

`Int()` also works for negative arguments. The following line of code stores –8 in `iAns`:

```
iAns = Int(-7.6)
```

The –8, as opposed to –7, may surprise you until you learn the complete definition of `Int()`. `Int()` returns the highest integer that is less than or equal to the argument in parentheses. The highest integer less than or equal to –7.6 is –8.

Example

The following statement stores 8 in `iAns`:

```
iAns = Fix(8.93)
```

For positive numbers, `Fix()` and `Int()` work identically.

Example

For negative numbers, `Fix()` and `Int()` return very different return values. `Fix()` simply drops the fractional part of the number—whether it is positive or negative—from the argument.

```
iAns1 = Fix(-8.93)
iAns2 = Fix(-8.02)
```

Therefore, the preceding lines store –8 in both `iAns1` and in `iAns2`, whereas `Int()` would store –9 in both examples because `Int()` does not truncate but returns the closest integer less than or equal to the argument.

The Data Type Conversion Functions

The data type conversion functions, denoted by their initial letter *C* for *convert*, are listed in Table 22.1 with their descriptions. Each function converts its argument from one data type to another.

Table 22.1. The data type conversion functions.

Function Name	Description
CCur()	Converts its argument to the Currency data type
CDbl()	Converts its argument to the Double data type
CInt()	Converts its argument to the Integer data type
CLng()	Converts its argument to the Long data type
CSng()	Converts its argument to the Single data type
CVar()	Converts its argument to the Variant data type

Note: In the next chapter you read about a similar conversion function to String.

Caution: You must be able to convert the argument to the target data type. You cannot convert the number 123456789 to Integer with CInt(), for example, because an Integer data type cannot hold an integer that large. Null arguments cause each of the conversion functions to produce an Invalid use of Null error message.

Example

CInt() does round.

Unlike Int() and Fix(), CInt() returns the closest *rounded* integer to the value of the argument. Look at the remarks to the right of each of the following statements to see what is stored in each variable.

```
cA1 = CInt(8.1)        ' Stores an 8 in cA1
cA2 = CInt(8.5)        ' Stores an 8 in cA2
cA3 = CInt(8.5001)     ' Stores a 9 in cA3
cA4 = CInt(9.5)        ' Stores a 10 in cA4
```

Notice how CInt() (for *convert integer*) handles the rounding. For positive numbers, if the fractional portion of the argument is exactly equal to one-half (.5), CInt() rounds to the nearest *even* integer.

Example

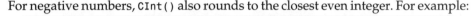

For negative numbers, CInt() also rounds to the closest even integer. For example:

```
cA1 = CInt(-8.1)      ' Stores a -8 in cA1
cA2 = CInt(-8.5)      ' Stores a -8 in cA2
cA3 = CInt(-8.5001)   ' Stores a -9 in cA3
cA4 = CInt(-9.5)      ' Stores a 10 in cA4
```

Example

Use the CLng() (for *convert long integer*) if you need to round numbers outside CInt()'s extremes. For example,

```
lA1 = CLng(-44034.1)  ' Stores -44034 in lA1
lA2 = CLng(985465.6)  ' Stores 985466 in lA2
```

> **Note:** CLng() rounds integers within the range of –2,147,483,648 to 2,147,483,647.

Example

The remaining conversion functions probably offer no real problems to you. They convert their arguments to appropriate data types. The following code declares a variable of four different data types and then converts each argument to those data types. Remember that you also can pass these functions expressions that produce numeric results so that you can control the data types of your calculated results before storing them in a field or variable.

```
Dim vCur As Currency
Dim vDbl As Double
Dim vSng As Single
Dim vVar As Variant
vCur = CCur(123)      ' Converts 123 to currency data type
vDbl = CDbl(123)      ' Converts 123 to double-precision data
type
vSng = CSng(123)      ' Converts 123 to single-precision data
type
vVar = CVar(123)      ' Converts 123 to the variant data type
```

The Sign Functions

The Abs() and Sgn() functions often work with the sign of a number instead of the value itself. The Abs() function returns the *absolute value* of its argument, and Sgn() returns a –1 if its argument is negative, 0 if the argument is zero, and 1 if its argument is positive.

Example

Absolute value always returns the positive value of its argument. At first, you may not see a need for Abs(). The absolute value of 10 is 10, and the absolute value of –10 also is 10. You may find some good uses for absolute value, however, especially in distance and age/weight differences (the distance between two cities is always positive no matter how you find the difference).

Suppose that you want to know how many years' difference in two employees' ages. The number of years between their ages is the absolute value of the difference between the ages. The following statement stores the difference in ages between Emp1Age and Emp2Age:

```
ageDiff = Abs(emp1Age - emp2Age)
```

Example

The Sgn() function (called the *sign function*) determines the sign of its argument. You can use Sgn() to determine whether a balance is more than 0 or whether a temperature is below 0, for example.

Banks charge interest for negative balances and pay interest on positive balances. When you add interest to a negative balance, the balance gets *more* negative. When you add interest to a positive balance, the balance gets more positive. Zero balances neither pay nor receive interest. The following assignment statement updates a customer's balance with an interest calculation. The Sgn() function ensures that the proper interest (negative or positive) is added to the balance. No interest is added if the balance is zero because Sgn() produces zero.

```
balance = balance + (Sgn(balance) * .12)
```

The Math Functions

You don't have to be an expert in math to use many of the mathematical functions that come with Access Basic. Often, even in business applications, the following functions come in handy:

```
Exp()
Log()
Sqr()
```

Exp() returns the natural logarithm base, Log() returns the logarithm of a number, and Sqr() computes the square root of its argument.

Example

If you don't understand the purpose of Exp() or Log(), that's okay. You may program in Access Basic for years and never need them.

Exp() returns the base of natural logarithm (*e*) raised to a specified power. The argument to Exp() can be any constant, variable, or expression less than or equal to 709.782712893. *e* is the mathematical expression for the value 2.718282. The following program shows Exp():

```
For num = 1 To 5
    Debug.Print Exp(num)
Next num
```

This code produces the following output in the immediate execution window:

```
2.718282
7.389056
20.08554
54.59815
148.4132
```

Notice the first number—*e* raised to the first power does indeed equal itself.

Example

Log() returns the natural logarithm of its argument. The argument to Log() can be any positive constant, variable, or expression. The following program shows the Log() function in use:

```
For num = 1 To 5
    Debug.Print Log(num)
Next num
```

This code produces the following output in the immediate execution window:

```
0
.6931472
1.098612
1.386294
1.609438
```

Example

The argument to *Sqr()* must be positive.

Sqr()'s argument can be any positive numeric data type. (Square root is not defined for negative numbers.) If you use a negative value as an argument to Sqr(), you get an Illegal function call error message. The section of code

```
aVar1 = Sqr(4)
aVar2 = Sqr(64)
aVar3 = Sqr(4096)
```

stores 2, 8, and 64 in the three respective variables.

The Trigonometric Functions

The trigonometric functions are probably the least-used functions in Access Basic. This is not to belittle the work of scientific and mathematical programmers who need them; thank goodness Access Basic supplies these functions! Otherwise, programmers would have to write their own versions.

The Atn() function returns the arctangent of the argument in radians. The argument is assumed to be an expression representing an angle of a right triangle. The result of Atn() always falls between $-pi/2$ and $+pi/2$. Cos() always returns the cosine of the angle, expressed in radians, of the argument. Sin() returns the sine of the angle, expressed in radians, of the argument. Tan() returns the tangent of the angle, expressed in radians, of the argument.

> **Tip:** If you need to pass an angle expressed in degrees to these functions, convert the angle to radians by multiplying it by (pi/180). (Pi is approximately 3.141592654.)

The Randomizing Tools

Two randomizing tools are available in Access Basic. You never use the Randomize statement by itself. If a module includes Randomize, you find the Rnd() function later in the procedure. Here is the format of the Randomize statement:

```
Randomize [number]
```

The format of the Rnd() function is as follows:

```
Rnd[(number)]
```

Notice that neither the Randomize statement nor the Rnd() function requires values after them. The purpose of Rnd() is to generate a random number between 0 (inclusive) to 1 (1 is never generated by Rnd()). You can use the random number function for games, such as simulating dice rolls or card draws.

If you run a procedure with four Rnd() numbers printed, each number is different (random) if you include no *number* argument. If, however, you specify 0 as the argument to Rnd(), such as x = Rnd(0), the four numbers are the same number. If you specify a number greater than 0 as the argument to Rnd(), a different random number is produced (the same as leaving off the argument altogether). An argument less than zero, such as x = Rnd(-3), always produces the same random number *if* you specify the same negative argument, and a different random number if the negative argument is always different.

All these Rnd() options become confusing. Here's the bottom line: If you want a different random number generated with Rnd() every time it executes within a procedure, do not specify an argument. If you want the same set of random numbers produced from a series of Rnd() function calls (such as a scientific simulation that you want to repeat several times), specify the same negative argument.

No matter which argument you use with Rnd(), Rnd() always produces the *same* set of values between procedure runs unless you provide a Randomize statement before the first Rnd(). In other words, if you run a procedure 20 times, the *same* set of random numbers results no matter what argument (or lack of argument) you use with the Rnd() function calls. The Randomize statement *reseeds* the random-number generator, a fancy term meaning that Randomize ensures that Rnd() produces a new set of random values each time you run a program.

If you don't specify a *number* after Randomize, the value of Timer (see Chapter 24) is used. (Timer returns the number of seconds since midnight.) Because the value of Timer changes every second, the Randomize statement ensures that a new seed value is used for the next occurrence of Rnd().

> **Tip:** If you want truly random values every time Rnd() appears, even between program runs, put the Randomize statement (with no arguments) at the top of the first procedure in the module and leave off all arguments to Rnd() in subsequent Rnd() calls.

Example

The following procedure always produces the same three random numbers every time you run it (assuming no Randomize statement has executed yet within the module):

```
Function randIt()
   Debug.Print Rnd          ' A random number
   Debug.Print Rnd(0)       ' The same random number
   Debug.Print Rnd(0)       ' The same random number
End Function
```

Example

If you put a Randomize statement anywhere in the module so that it executes before the three Rnd() statements shown in the preceding example (as done in the following code), you still get the *same* three random numbers due to Rnd()'s zero argument. But at least these numbers differ from program run to program run.

```
Function randIt()
   Randomize                ' Ensures that next Rnd() is random
   Debug.Print Rnd          ' A random number
   Debug.Print Rnd(0)       ' The same random number
   Debug.Print Rnd(0)       ' The same random number
End Function
```

Example

If you want three different random numbers always generated (as you usually do), do not specify an argument after Rnd(), as in the following:

```
Function randIt()
   Randomize                ' Ensures that next Rnd() is random
   Debug.Print Rnd          ' A random number
   Debug.Print Rnd          ' A different random number
   Debug.Print Rnd          ' A different random number
End Function
```

Example

You rarely want a random number from 0 to 1, as produced by Rnd(). Using the following simple formula, however, you can generate a random number from low to high (assuming those two variables have been initialized):

```
Int((high - low + 1) * Rnd + low)
```

Suppose that you want to offer a special discount to a different customer each month. If your customer numbers fall between 1000 and 6456 (meaning that you have a total of 5,457 customers), you can do something like the following:

```
low = 1000      ' Lowest customer number
high = 6456     ' Highest customer number
specialCustNum = Int((high - low + 1) * Rnd + low)
```

Example

You can even write games with Access Basic!

With the following procedure, you actually can use Access Basic to write a number-guessing game. The computer generates a random number from 1 to 100 and then uses control statements to offer the user hints until the user correctly guesses the number.

```
Function Guessing ()
' Number-guessing game
  Dim rNum, userNum As Integer
  Dim title As String
  Randomize     ' Ensure that the number is always different
  rNum = Int(100 * Rnd + 1)  ' Generates a number from 1 to 100
  userNum = InputBox("Welcome to a game! Guess a number...",
  ➥title)
  ' Keep looping until the user guesses correctly
  Do While (userNum <> rNum)
    If (userNum < rNum) Then
      userNum = InputBox("Too low, try again...", title)
    Else
      userNum = InputBox("Too high, try again...", title)
    End If
  Loop
  Beep
  MsgBox "Congratulations! You guessed my number!", 64
End Function
```

Summary

As you have seen in this chapter, Access Basic supplies many built-in numeric functions. These functions save you work; you don't have to take the time to write the code yourself, but rather, you can call on these functions to do the work for you. You may not use all these functions, but some prove useful as you program in Access Basic.

Most of the built-in functions require parentheses after their names. The parentheses are where you pass to the function the data (the *arguments*) to work on.

Several numeric functions work with integers. These functions primarily round noninteger data to integer results. Other numeric functions exist to convert data to different data types for you. Several math and trigonometric functions are available in Access Basic if you ever need them.

Finally, the random statement and function pair generate random numbers for you. You have several ways to generate random numbers depending on your application's needs. You might have to replicate a series of random numbers, or you might want the same series every time a procedure runs.

Whereas this chapter taught many of Access Basic's built-in numeric functions, the next chapter explains how to use Access Basic's string functions. Much of the data in your database tables is string data, but the string data is not always in the format that you need. The string functions manipulate and change strings according to your needs.

Review Questions

Answers to review questions are in Appendix B.

1. What are the two integer functions?

2. What happens if an argument is too big to be converted with a data type conversion function?

3. What value does the following function call return?

```
CVar(Null)
```

4. How do `Int()` and `Fix()` differ?

5. Why do you usually need the `Randomize` statement when you use `Rnd()`?

6. TRUE or FALSE: If the following statement appeared in the first procedure executed within a module, the next `Rnd` statement would produce a different result virtually every time the module is run.

```
Randomize Timer
```

7. Why do the following function calls return different results?

```
Int(-9.5)    Fix(-9.5)      CInt(-9.5)
```

8. TRUE or FALSE: Both of these sets of code produce the same result:

```
x = Sgn(Balance)
```

and

```
If (Balance < 0) Then
   x = -1
ElseIf (Balance = 0) Then
   x = 0
Else
   x = 1
End If
```

Review Exercises

1. Write a `For-Next` loop that passes the following series of numbers to `Int()`, `Fix()`, and `CInt()`:

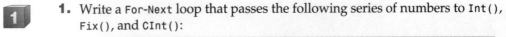
```
        -2.0    -1.5    -1.0    -0.5    0    0.5    1.0
1.5     2.0
```

Use a `Step` value of `0.5` and print each result in the immediate execution window with a `Debug.Print` statement like this:

```
Debug.Print Int(val), Fix(val), CInt(val)
```

Study the results to learn how each function differs from one another.

2. Create a form with a different field for each data type. Write a module that contains a function (trigger the function from the form's On Current property) to ask the user (with `InputBox()`) for a number from 1 to 10. Get the number in a string variable. Convert the number to each of the numeric and `Variant` data types and display each of the generated numbers in each field in the form.

3. Change the number-guessing module to add a counter that begins at 1 and increments every time the user guesses incorrectly. In the ending message box, print the number of times the user guessed. Use the `Str$()` function to convert the number to a string and concatenate the string to the message as done in the second-to-last example of Chapter 20.

CHAPTER 23

String Functions

In the preceding chapter you learned the numeric functions, but in this chapter you learn the built-in functions that work with strings. Some functions described here convert between strings and numbers.

Access Basic (as well as most of the dialects of the BASIC language) provides better string-handling capabilities than most programming languages, including those considered to be more powerful than BASIC. The string functions described here are the primary reason for the string power of Access Basic. Your database field data is often comprised of string data. You may need to test various string values and change string values, and you'll find those tasks easy after you learn the string functions.

This chapter introduces the following topics:

- The `Len()` length function
- The string conversion functions: `CStr()`, `Str$()`, and `Val()`
- The ANSI string functions: `Chr$()`, `Asc()`, and `String$()`
- The substring functions: `Left$()`, `Right$()`, and `Mid$()`
- The `Mid$()` statement
- Searching with `InStr()`
- Comparing with `StrComp()`
- Justifying string data with `LSet` and `RSet`
- Trimming strings with `LTrim$()`, `RTrim$()`, and `Trim$()`
- Making a case with `LCase$()` and `UCase$()`

After you learn the string functions in this chapter, you explore some date and time functions that help you work with time- and date-stamped data in the next chapter.

> **Note:** Actually, some of the material taught in this chapter are statements and not functions. However, the statements taught here work hand in hand with string functions (such as the `Mid$()` function and the `Mid$()` statement), and this chapter is the most logical chapter in which to group this material together.

The *Len()* Length Functions

Len() returns the storage length of its argument.

The Len() function is one of the few functions that can take either a numeric variable or a string for its argument. Len() returns the number of memory bytes needed to hold its argument. Here are the formats of Len():

```
Len(stringExpression)
```

and

```
Len(numericVariable)
```

Notice that `Len()` accepts any string value (variable, constant, or expression) but only numeric variables, not numeric constants or expressions, work as `Len()` arguments.

Example

Programmers need to know the internal size each variable takes if there are going to be many variables (several hundred or more) used in the same program. If you're getting ready to store 200 single-precision variables and you want to see how much memory the data takes, you can code the following:

```
Dim testIt As Single
testIt = 0      ' A sample single-precision variable
storage = (Len(testIt) * 200.0)
```

This code stores the amount of memory needed to hold 200 single-precision values.

Example

The Len() function is good to use when you want to know the length of a string. Len() returns the length (number of characters) of the string variable, string constant, or string expression inside its parentheses. The following Print statement produces a 6 as its output:

```
Debug.Print Len("abcdef")
```

> **Tip:** If the string contains Null, Len() returns a value of 0. If the string contains an empty string (""), Len() returns 0. Testing for an empty string lets you test to see if a user entered data in response to an InputBox() function or a field value.

The String-Conversion Functions

Several conversion functions work with string data. In the earlier chapters of this book, you saw Str$(), a string-conversion function that converts its number to a string so that you can print the number with a MsgBox statement.

Table 23.1 describes each of the string-conversion functions used in the following examples.

Table 23.1. The string-conversion functions.

Function Name	Description
CStr()	Changes its argument to a string
Str$()	Converts its numeric argument to a string. If you omit the dollar sign, the argument is converted to a Variant data type.
Val()	Converts its string argument to a number, assuming that a string-like number is passed

> **Caution:** Although they are easier to use, neither CStr() nor Str$() are as powerful as Format$(), which you learn about in Chapter 24. Format$() can do all the work of CStr() and Str$() and more.

Example

Both `CStr()` and `Str$()` convert their arguments to string values. The only difference is that `CStr()` does *not* add a leading blank before positive numbers converted to strings; `Str$()` does.

```
Function convStr ()
  Dim s1, s2 As String
  s1 = CStr(12345)
  s2 = Str$(12345)
  MsgBox "***" & s1 & "***"
  MsgBox "***" & s2 & "***"
End Function
```

Figure 23.1 shows the first message box printed, and Figure 23.2 shows the second. Notice that no blank appears before the first string because the `CStr()` function was used, not `Str$()`.

Figure 23.1

Displaying the
string created with
CStr().

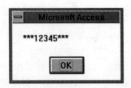

Figure 23.2

Displaying the
string created with
Str$().

Note: If you use `Str()` in place of `Str$()`, the results are the same, but the resulting value is of the `Variant` data type and not `String`.

The ANSI Functions

Appendix A lists the ANSI table used with the ANSI functions. You use the `Chr$()` function and the `Asc()` function to convert strings to and from their numeric ANSI values. Also, `String$()` uses the ANSI table to generate lists of characters.

By putting a number inside the `Chr$()` parentheses, you can produce the character that corresponds to that number in the ANSI table. Using `Chr$()`, you can generate characters for variables and controls that do not appear on your computer's keyboard but that do appear in the ANSI table.

> **Note:** If you omit the dollar sign from Chr$(), Chr() returns its argument as a Variant data type.

The Asc() function is the mirror-image function from Chr$(). Whereas Chr$() takes a numeric argument and returns a string character, Asc() requires a numeric argument and converts that argument to its corresponding ANSI table number.

> **Note:** If you've heard of the ASCII table, you probably know that it is similar in almost every respect to the ANSI table except for some obscure characters that appear in the ANSI table.

String$() replicates the second argument.

The String$() function also uses the ANSI table to do its job. You generally use this function to create strings for output and storage. The String$() function requires two arguments: an integer followed by a second argument; the second argument can be a character, a character string, or another integer. Depending on the values that you pass, String$() has two formats. The formats of String$() are as follows:

```
String[$](number, ANSIcode)
```

and

```
String[$](number, string)
```

If you omit the dollar sign, String() returns a Variant data type. Otherwise, String$() returns a string.

Example

When you enclose an ANSI number inside the Chr$() parentheses (its argument), Access Basic substitutes the character that matches the ANSI value. Therefore, an A is stored in aVar in the following assignment statement because the ANSI value of A is 65:

```
aVar = Chr$(65)     ' Stores an A in aVar
```

Example

Of course, it makes more sense to store an A directly in the aVar variable in the preceding example's statement. What, however, if you want to ask a Spanish question inside a message box? Spanish questions always begin with an upside-down question mark, and no upside-down question mark appears on your keyboard. Therefore, you can resort to using Chr$() as follows:

```
Dim myQuest As String
myQuest = Chr$(191) & "Se" & Chr$(241) & "or, como esta?"
MsgBox myQuest
```

Figure 23.3 shows the message box displayed from this code.

Figure 23.3

Displaying
characters not on
the keyboard.

Example

Asc() returns the ANSI number of the character argument you give it. The argument must be a string of one or more characters. If you pass Asc() a string of more than one character, it returns the ANSI number of the first character in the string. For example, the statement

```
Debug.Print Asc("A"), Asc("B"), Asc("C")
```

produces the following output in the immediate execution window:

```
65              66              67
```

Look at the ANSI table to see that these three numbers are the ANSI values for A, B, and C.

Example

You also can use string variables as arguments.

```
letter1 = "A"
letter2 = "B"
letter3 = "C"
Debug.Print Asc(letter1), Asc(letter2), Asc(letter3)
```

This code produces the same output as the preceding example.

Example

If you pass a string with more than one character to Asc(), Asc() returns the ANSI value of only the first character. Therefore, the statement

```
aStrVar = Asc("Hello")
```

stores 72 (the ANSI value of H) in the aStrVar variable. This method of testing is better for input than you've seen so far in the book.

Now look at the following example:

```
ans = InputBox("Do you want to see the name")
If ((Asc(ans) = 89) Or (Asc(ans) = 121)) Then
    MsgBox "The name is " + aName
End If
```

The user can answer the prompt with y, Y, Yes, or YES. The If-Then test works for any of those input values because 89 is the ANSI value for Y, and 121 is the ANSI value of y.

Example

The best way to learn the String$() function is to see it used. Consider the following statement:

```
Debug.Print String$(15, "a")
```

This statement prints the lowercase letter a 15 times, as follows:

```
aaaaaaaaaaaaaaa
```

Example

If you use a string of characters (or a string variable) as the second argument, String$() replicates only the first character of the string. If the second argument is an ANSI number (from 0 to 255), String$() replicates the matching ANSI character. The following section of code illustrates this point:

```
Debug.Print String$(60, 43)
```

The preceding line produces the following row of 60 plus signs:

```
++++++++++++++++++++++++++++++++++++++++++++++++++++++++++++
```

The Substring Functions

You can access parts of a string.

In Chapter 3 you learned about the Right$() function when you were looking at macros. Right$() returns characters from the right side of a string. Right$()'s cousin function, Left(), returns characters from the left side of a string. The strings can be variables, text controls, or constants enclosed in quotation marks. The Mid$() function takes up where Right$() and Left$() fail: Mid$() enables you to pick characters from the middle of a string.

> **Note:** Actually, Mid$() can do the same thing as Right$() and Left$(), but Mid$() takes an extra argument. Also, Right$() and Left$() are easier to use if you need characters from only one side of a string.

Here are the formats of the substring functions:

```
Left$(string value, numeric value)

Right$(string value, numeric value)

Mid$(string value, [start position, ] length )
```

Both Left$() and Right$() require two arguments: a string variable, constant, or an expression followed by an integer constant or a variable. The integer determines how many characters are stripped from the left or right of the string and returned.

Example

The following section of code explains Left$():

```
a$ = "abcdefg"
partSt1 = Left$(a$, 1)     ' Stores a
partSt2 = Left$(a$, 3)     ' Stores abc
partSt3 = Left$(a$, 7)     ' Stores abcdefg
partSt3 = Left$(a$, 20)    ' Stores abcdefg
```

Notice from the last statement that if you try to return more characters from the left of the string than exist, Left$() returns the entire string and not an error message.

Example

Right$() works in the same manner as Left$(), except that it returns the rightmost characters from a string, as shown here:

```
a$ = "abcdefg"
partSt1 = Right$(a$, 1)     ' Stores g
partSt2 = Right$(a$, 3)     ' Stores efg
partSt3 = Right$(a$, 7)     ' Stores abcdefg
partSt3 = Right$(a$, 20)    ' Stores abcdefg
```

Example

The Mid$() function accomplishes what Left$() and Right$() cannot: Mid$() returns characters from the *middle* of a string. Mid$() uses three arguments: a string followed by two integers. The first integer determines where Mid$() begins stripping characters from the string (the position, starting at 1), and the second integer determines how many characters from that position to return. If you do not specify two integers, Mid$() uses 1 as the starting position.

Mid$() can pull any number of characters from anywhere in the string. The following example shows how the Mid$() function works:

```
a$ = "QBasic FORTRAN COBOL C Pascal"
lang1 = Mid$(a$, 1, 6)     ' Stores QBasic
lang2 = Mid$(a$, 8, 7)     ' Stores FORTRAN
lang3 = Mid$(a$, 16, 5)    ' Stores COBOL
lang4 = Mid$(a$, 22, 1)    ' Stores C
lang5 = Mid$(a$, 24, 6)    ' Stores Pascal
```

Example

Mid$() does not require a *length* argument. If you don't specify the length, Access Basic returns all the characters to the right of the starting position. If the length is longer than the rest of the string, Access Basic ignores the *length* argument.

```
city = "Venice"
partial = Mid$(city, 2)        ' Stores enice

city = "Venice"
partial = Mid$(city, 2, 100)   ' Also stores enice
```

Example

The following Reverse() function includes several of the string functions described in this chapter. The goal of the following function is to reverse a certain number of characters within a string.

```
Function Reverse (s, ByVal n As Integer)
' Accepts: a string, an integer indicating the number of
'          characters to reverse
' Purpose: reverses the specified number of characters in the
'          specified string
' Returns: the modified string

' Reverses the first n characters in s.

    Dim Temp As String, i As Integer

    If n > Len(s) Then n = Len(s)
    For i = n To 1 Step -1
        Temp = Temp + Mid(s, i, 1)
    Next
    Reverse = Temp + Right(s, Len(s) - n)

End Function
```

> **Tip:** As always, the Reverse() function should be well documented in the remarks at the top of the function. In your own functions, add remarks that describe the function's purpose, its received arguments, and its return argument.

Suppose that the Reverse() function were called with the following statement:

```
newStr = Reverse ("Access Basic", 6)
```

If all goes well, the string named newStr will hold the characters sseccA Basic (the first 6 characters are reversed).

Here is how the function works. The first statement, `Dim`, declares two local variables, the first of which, a string variable named `Temp`, holds the reversed string as it is being built. The second variable, `i`, is used in the `For` loop.

The `If` statement makes sure that the integer passed to `Reverse()` is not larger than the length of the string passed. It is impossible to reverse *more* characters than exist in the string. If more characters are passed, the `If` ensures that the entire string is reversed by changing the length to reverse to the exact length of the string via the `Len()` function.

The `For` loop then counts down, from the position to reverse (stored in `n`) to 1. Using the `Mid$()` function, Access Basic concatenates one character from the string, at position `n`, to the new string being built. As `n` reaches 1, the reversed characters are sent to the new string. Once all the characters that need to be reversed are reversed, the rightmost portion of the passed string is concatenated *as is* to the reversed characters.

Figure 23.4 shows the action of the function assuming that the first six letters in `Access Basic` are to be reversed.

Figure 23.4

The action of *Reverse()*.

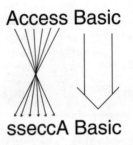

Access Basic

sseccA Basic

The *Mid$()* Statement

Mid$() is also a command.

`Mid$()` is *both* a command and a function. `Mid$()` works as a command when it appears on the left side of an assignment statement's equal sign. `Mid$()` is a function when it appears anywhere else. Following is its format:

```
Mid$(string, start [, length])
```

Example

When you use `Mid$()` as a statement, `Mid$()` changes the contents of the string used inside the statement's parentheses. The following code initializes a string with three words and then changes the middle word with `Mid$()`:

```
sentence = "Rain in Spain"
' Change the middle word
Mid$(sentence, 6, 2) = "on"
' After the change
Debug.Print "After change: "; sentence  ' Prints Rain on Spain
```

Searching with *InStr()*

InStr() is different from the other string functions you've seen in this chapter. InStr() is a *string search* function. You use it to find the starting location of a string inside another string. InStr() returns the character position (an integer) at which one string starts within another string.

InStr() has two formats, depending on which version you want to use. Here are the formats:

```
InStr( [start position, ] string value1, string value2)
```

and

```
InStr( startPosition, string1, string2, compare)
```

> **Caution:** Remember that InStr() returns an integer, not a string.

InStr() looks to see whether the second string expression (InStr()'s third argument) exists within the first string expression. If it does, InStr() returns the starting position of the string within the first string. InStr() assumes a beginning position of 1, unless you override it by including the option integer as InStr()'s first argument. If you give InStr() a starting value of 5, for example, InStr() ignores the first four characters of the search string. If InStr() fails to find the first string within the search string, it returns a 0.

If you elect to use the second format of InStr(), the compare value must be one from Table 23.2.

Table 23.2. *InStr()* compare options.

Compare Value	Description of the Comparison
0	Compare with case-sensitive strings (binary)
1	Compare without case sensitivity
2	Compare via the Database method using the New Database Sort Order

> **Note:** If you don't specify a compare option (using the first InStr() format), Access Basic performs a binary compare (so ABC compares differently from abc) or the compare specified by the Option Compare statement if one exists.

Example

The following lines make InStr()'s operation clear:

```
a = "QBasic FORTRAN COBOL C Pascal"
n = InStr(a, "FORTRAN")    ' Stores 8
n = InStr(1, a, "Fortran", 0)  ' Not found due to case
n = InStr(a, "COBOL")      ' Stores 16
n = InStr(a, "C")          ' Also stores 16!
n = InStr(a, "PL/I")       ' PL/I not found, 0 stored
n = InStr(16, a, "FORTRAN")   ' 0 stored FORTRAN doesn't
                              ' exist past column 16
n = InStr(5, a, "PL/I")    ' 0 stored
n = InStr(a, "")           ' NULL is returned
n = InStr(5, a, "")        ' or start value
```

The fourth assignment does not return 22 (the position of the C denoting the C language) because the C is also in COBOL. InStr() returns only the first occurrence of the string.

Comparing with *StrComp()*

As its name implies, the StrComp() function compares two strings. Here is the format of the StrComp() function:

```
StrComp(string1, string2 [, compare])
```

The StrCmp() function compares the two strings to each other. The comparison method is determined by the *compare* value. The *compare* value must be one from Table 23.2, like that used by InStr().

If the first string compares less than the second string, StrCmp() returns a –1. If the strings are equal, a 0 is returned. If the second string is more than the first string, a 1 is returned.

Tip: Imagine a minus sign between StrCmp()'s first two arguments. If it were possible to subtract two strings, you'd get a negative result if the first string were less than the second. If the strings were equal, subtraction would produce zero. If the second string were less than the first, you'd get a positive result. Knowing this helps you remember the -1, 0, and +1 result of StrCmp().

Example

The following statements store -1, 0, and +1 in the variables a, b, and c:

```
a = StrComp("ABC", "XYZ")
b = StrComp("NOP", "NOP")
c = StrComp("XYZ", "ABC")
```

Justifying Strings with *LSet* and *RSet*

LSet and RSet are not functions, but this chapter is a good place to introduce these two statements because of their similarity to string functions. Here are the formats of LSet and RSet:

```
LSet string1 = string2

RSet string1 = string2
```

Before you learn LSet and RSet, you should understand how to declare fixed-length strings. Until now, all strings have been variable-length. That is, you could store a small string into a string variable and then replace that small string with a larger string. The string lengths could vary.

By adding an extra option to the Dim statement, you can declare the size of a string at the time you declare the string. After you declare the size, you cannot store a string larger than the size of the string variable.

Use *Dim* to declare fixed-length strings.

Add the * *number* option to the Dim statement to fix a string to a certain size. The following statement both declares a string variable, for example, and declares that its maximum size is five characters:

```
Dim fixedStr As String * 5
```

After you declare a string, you can use LSet to *left justify* one string into another string. The RSet statement *right justifies* one string into another string. When a string is left-justified or right-justified, its contents are pushed to the left or right of a string, and any leftover character positions are padded with blanks.

> **Tip:** Remember that both LSet and RSet assign new strings to old strings but do not change the length of the target string from its previous value. Ordinarily, when you assign one string to another, the target string changes length to equal the string you are assigning to it.

If you attempt to set a new string into another and the new string is longer than the target string, Access Basic *truncates* (chops off) the extra characters and copies only as many characters as there are in the target string's length.

Example

The string variable in each of the following statements is declared to have 10 characters. The length of that string value determines how many spaces have to be used to pad the strings.

```
Dim string1 As String * 10, string2 As String * 10
string1 = "1234567890"           ' 10 characters
LSet string1 = "left"            ' LSet "left" in those 10 characters
Debug.Print "¦"; string1; "¦"    ' Print lines between to see result
string2 = "1234567890"           ' 10 characters
RSet string2 = "right"           ' RSet "right" in those 10 characters
Debug.Print "¦"; string2; "¦"    ' Print between lines to see result
```

This section of code produces the following output in the immediate execution window:

```
¦left      ¦
¦     right¦
```

Trimming Strings

The LTrim$() and RTrim$() functions trim spaces from the beginning or end of a string. LTrim$() returns the argument's string without any leading spaces. RTrim$() returns the argument's string without any trailing spaces. The Trim$() function trims both leading and trailing spaces from a string.

Here are the formats ●f the string-trimming functions:

```
LTrim[$](stringExpression)

RTrim[$](stringExpression)

Trim[$](stringExpression)
```

> **Note:** If you omit the dollar signs from the function names, the functions can accept a **Variant** data type, including the Null value as an argument. If you pass **Null** to the functions, a **Null** value is returned.

LSet and RSet are statements that work almost like LTrim$() and RTrim$() functions, except that rather than trimming spaces from strings, LSet and RSet insert spaces at the beginning or end of strings.

Example

The following statements trim spaces from the beginning, end, or both sides of strings:

```
st1 = LTrim$("     Hello")  ' Stores Hello
st2 = RTrim$("Hello     ")  ' Stores Hello
st3 = Trim$("    Hello   ") ' Stores Hello
```

Without the trimming functions, the spaces are copied into the target variables as well as the word Hello.

Example

Earlier, you learned how to use Str$() to convert a number to a string. Because Str$() always converts positive numbers to strings with a leading blank (where the imaginary plus sign appears), you can combine LTrim$() with Str$() to eliminate the leading blank. The first of the following two statements stores the leading blank in st1. The second uses LTrim$() to get rid of the blank before storing the string into st2.

```
st1 = Str$(234)          ' Stores " 234"
st2 = LTrim$(Str$(234))  ' Stores "234"
```

Changing String Case

You've already seen examples of the LCase$() and UCase$() functions. Just for a review, LCase$() returns its argument converted to lowercase, and UCase$() returns its argument converted to uppercase. If the LCase$() argument contains one or more lowercase letters or if the UCase$() argument contains one or more uppercase letters, no change is made.

You can omit the dollar sign from either function name if you want the return value to be the Variant data type.

Summary

You now have at your disposal several string functions that manipulate, change, and test string values. Many of the string function names end with the $ suffix to signal their capabilities to work with string data. Some, such as Len(), do not, however.

The Len() function serves as a bridge between the numeric and string functions. It is the only function that works with both string and numeric arguments by returning the length (the number of characters of storage) of the argument.

Many string functions return portions (such as the leftmost or rightmost characters) of strings. These functions are sometimes called the substring functions.

RSet and LSet are not functions but act a lot like Access Basic's Trim$() functions by justifying strings within a certain length. You can test to see if one string resides inside another (with InStr()), and you can tell if one string is equal to another string (with StrCmp()).

In the next chapter you learn how to use the date and time functions. In most database programming, you have to track the time and date that data is entered, printed, or updated. The date and time functions help you work with date and time values.

Review Questions

Answers to review questions are in Appendix B.

1. TRUE or FALSE: Both UCase$() and LCase$() change their arguments.

2. Which function—Str$() or CStr()—omits the leading blank from the number being converted to a string?

3. What type of return value results if you call LTrim(), RTrim(), Trim(), LCase(), or UCase() *without* a dollar sign in the names?

4. What type of return value results if you call LTrim$(), RTrim$(), Trim$(), LCase$(), or UCase$() *with* a dollar sign in the names?

5. How can you tell whether the use of Mid$() is a function or a statement?

6. What is wrong with the following statement?

```
num = Len$("George")
```

7. How do LSet and RSet differ from the LTrim() and RTrim() functions?

8. Without your looking at the ANSI table in Appendix A, what is stored in n after the following statement finishes?

```
n = Asc(Chr$(192))
```

Review Exercises

1. Assuming that the date "12-23-93" is stored in a string variable named soldDate, use the Left$(), Mid$(), and Right$() functions to store soldDate's day, month, and year into three separate integer variables. Because you are storing strings in the three integer variables, you must convert the substrings to numbers before assigning them to the integer variables.

2. Write a function that prints (in the immediate execution window) every ANSI character from 32 to 255. Use a For-Next loop.

3. Convert the following statement so that it uses the Mid$() function rather than Right$().

```
lastName$ = Right$(fullName$, 7)
```

4. Write a function that returns the reverse of whatever string is passed to it (as opposed to the one described in this chapter that reverses only the first few characters). Return the reversed string in all uppercase letters.

5. Write a function that encrypts whatever string is passed to it and returns the encrypted string. Use Asc() and Chr$() to add 1 to the ANSI value of each character before concatenating the encrypted character to the return string.

CHAPTER 24

Date and Time Functions

This chapter teaches you about several functions that are not available in most other languages. The time and date functions are critical when processing data, especially in a database environment. It might be important to record exactly when a field was edited for security or verification purposes. Also, all printed reports should have the date and time (often called *date-* and *time-stamping*) printed on the report, showing exactly when the report was produced. In a stack of like reports, the date and time stamps show when the latest report was printed.

This chapter introduces the following topics:

♦ Date and time retrieval functions: `Date()`, `Now()`, and `Time()`

♦ Date and time-setting statements: `Date` and `Time`

♦ Computing time between events with `Timer`

♦ Date arithmetic: `DateAdd()`, `DateDiff()`, and `DatePart()`

♦ Working with serial date and time values

♦ Formatting with `Format$()`

The `Format$()` function is not just for dates or times, but after you learn the date and time functions, you will know about all of the data types available with `Format$()`. This chapter is a good place to learn about this multi-talented function. You may not always want your date, time, and other data printed in its default output format. Often, you want to format your data to look the way you want it to look, and `Format$()` supplies the power to do just that.

> **Note:** As with the preceding chapter's Mid$() statement among the string functions, some of the material taught in this chapter consists of statements and not solely functions. However, the statements taught here work hand in hand with the date and time functions, and this chapter is the most logical chapter in which to group all this material together.

Retrieving the Date and Time

Access can read your system's clock.

Inside most computers are a clock and calendar that Access Basic programs can read. You may have used the Date$() and Time$() functions in your database forms and reports. The dollar sign in each name is optional.

Date() returns the system date in the Variant data type number 7 (see Chapter 17) in the following format:

```
mm-dd-yyyy
```

where mm is a month number (from 01 to 12), dd is a day number (from 01 to 31), and yyyy is a year number (from 1980 to 2099).

Time() returns the system time in the Variant data type number 7 in the following format:

```
hh:mm:ss
```

where hh is the hour (from 00 to 23), mm is the minute (from 00 to 59), and ss is the second (from 00 to 59).

> **Tip:** Check at least weekly to make sure your computer's date and time values are set properly. You can check the date and time (and optionally enter new values) by typing **date** or **time** at the DOS prompt before starting Access. You also can set the date and time from within the immediate execution window or from within a program, as shown later in this chapter.

The Date$() function uses a 24-hour clock. Therefore, all hours before 1:00:00 in the afternoon equate to a.m. time values, and all times from 1:00:00 until midnight have 12 added to them so 14:30 is 2:30 in the afternoon.

The Now() function (a dollar sign is not allowed with Now()) combines both the Date$() and Time$() functions. Now() returns a Variant data type in the following format (if you were to print the Variant return value of Now() in the immediate execution window, you'd see this format):

```
mm/dd/yy hh:mm:ss [AM][PM]
```

where the placeholder letters correspond to those of the Date$() and Time$() functions with the exception that a 12-hour clock is used and either AM or PM appears next to the time.

The most important thing to remember about all three date and time retrieval functions is that they return date and time values that are stored internally as double-precision values (with enough precision to ensure that the date and time values are stored accurately), and it is up to your program to format the values and output them in whatever format you want. The best way to format date and time values is to use Format$(), which you learn later in this chapter.

In Access Basic, the parentheses for the Date$(), Time$(), and Now() functions are not needed. You don't pass arguments to these functions, so the parentheses are optional. However, if you use these functions in macros or controls, the parentheses are required. Therefore, if you get used to using the parentheses, your date and time retrievals always work whether you're working in Access Basic or not.

Include the
parentheses for
consistency.

Example

Assuming that it is exactly 9:45 in the morning, the statement

```
currentTime = Time$()
```

stores 9:45:00 in the variable currentTime.
If the date is 2/23/94, the statement

```
currentDate = Date$()
```

stores 2/23/94 in the variable currentdate.
The statement

```
currentDateTime = Now()
```

stores 2/23/94 9:45:00 AM in the variable currentDateTime.

Example

If it is exactly 9:45 at night, this statement

```
currentTime = Time$()
```

stores 21:45:00 (subtract 12 to get the p.m. time in 12-hour format) in the variable currentTime.

Setting the Date and Time

Using the Date and Time statements, you can set the current date and time from within Access Basic. Once you set your computer's date and time, the date and time remain in effect until you change them again.

> **Caution:** If you use a DOS version earlier than 3.3, you have to use a system disk that came with your computer to set your clock for more than the computer's current power-on session or upgrade to a later version of DOS.

Neither the Date nor Time statements can have parentheses following them (the parentheses serve to distinguish between the functions and the statements).

Here are the formats of the Date and Time statements:

```
Date[$] = dateExpression
Time[$] = timeExpression
```

The Date Expression Format

If you don't specify the trailing dollar sign (Date), you must enter the *dateExpression* with pound signs surrounding the date, as follows:

```
Date = #11/21/1993#
```

If you do specify the trailing dollar sign (Date$), you can enter the *dateExpression* with either surrounding pound signs or enclosed in quotation marks, as follows:

```
Date$ = "11/21/1993"
```

or

```
Date$ = #11/21/1993#
```

Because there are several date formats, just about any way you are used to specifying the date is recognized by Access Basic. Date$ (with the dollar sign) can recognize the following date formats:

```
mm-dd-yy
mm-dd-yyyy
mm/dd/yy
mm/dd/yyyy
```

`Date` (without the dollar sign) can recognize the following formats (in addition to the formats recognized by `Date$`):

```
monthName dd, yyyy
mmm dd, yyyy    (where mmm is an abbreviated month name like Dec)
dd monthName yy
dd-mmm-yy       (where mmm is an abbreviated month name like Dec)
```

Example

The following procedure tells the user the currently set date and lets the user enter a new date. If the user presses Enter without entering a date, the previous date is kept.

```
Function enterDate ()
  Dim newDate As Variant
  MsgBox "The current date is " & Date$     ' Calls function
  newDate = InputBox("What do you want to set the date to?")
  If IsDate(newDate) Then
    Date$ = newDate
  End If    ' Don't do anything if a good date isn't entered
  MsgBox "The date is now " & Date$

End Function
```

The Time Expression Format

If you don't specify the trailing dollar sign (`Time`), you can enter the *timeExpression* as either a 12-hour clock or a 24-hour clock with quotation marks, as follows:

```
Time = "1:30 PM"
```

or

```
Time = "13:30"
```

If you do specify the trailing dollar sign (`Time$`), you can enter the *timeExpression* in any of these formats:

```
hh
hh:mm
hh:mm:ss
```

where *hh* is an hour number (from 00 to 23), *mm* is a minute number (from 00 to 59), and *ss* is a second number (from 00 to 59). You must use a 24-hour clock with *Time$*.

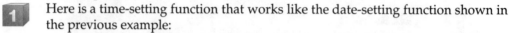

Tip: Using these `Time$` formats, you change only what you want to change. If the time zone has just turned to daylight saving time, for example, you can change just the hour.

Example

Here is a time-setting function that works like the date-setting function shown in the previous example:

```
Function enterTime ()
  Dim newTime As Variant
  MsgBox "The current time is " & Time$    ' Calls function
  newTime = InputBox("What do you want to set the time to?")
  If IsDate(newTime) Then
    Time$ = newTime
  End If   ' Don't do anything if a good time isn't entered
  MsgBox "The time is now " & Time$

End Function
```

Note: Notice that the `IsDate()` function returns true or false if a good or bad time value is passed to it.

Computing the Time between Events

The `Timer()` function returns the number of seconds since your computer's internal clock struck midnight. Here is the format of `Timer()`:

```
Timer[()]
```

As the brackets indicate, the parentheses are not required, but they are recommended. You might wonder why you'd ever need to know how many seconds have elapsed since midnight. The `Timer()` function is perfect for timing an event, as in the next example.

Example

You can ask the user a question and determine how long it took him or her to answer. First, save the value of `Timer()` before you ask the user; then subtract that value from the value of `Timer()` *after* he or she answers. The difference of the two `Timer()` values is the number of seconds the user took to answer.

Following is a procedure that does just that:

```
Function CompTime ()
' Procedure that times the user's response
  Dim Before, After, timeDiff As Variant
  Dim mathAns As Integer
  Before = Timer()    ' Save the time before asking
  mathAns = Inputbox("What is 150 + 235?")
  After = Timer()     ' Save the time after answering
  ' The difference between the time values
  ' is how many seconds the user took to answer
  timeDiff = After - Before
  MsgBox "That took you only" + str$(timeDiff) & " seconds!"
End Function
```

Example

The following procedure is a waiting procedure that pauses for a certain number of seconds as determined by the argument passed to the function. If the function is passed 10, the procedure loops for 10 seconds.

```
Function pauseSecs (secs As Long)
' Procedure that pauses for a specified time
  Dim procEntryTime As Long
  procEntryTime = Timer    ' Get the time now
  Do
    ' Nothing is really done but wait...
  Loop Until (Timer >= procEntryTime + secs)
  Beep
End Function
```

More Date Arithmetic

The Timer() function does find the number of seconds between time values, but only for those time values that fall on the same day. The DateAdd(), DateDiff(), and DatePart() functions take up where Timer() leaves off. Table 24.1 lists the three date arithmetic functions and their descriptions.

Table 24.1. The date arithmetic functions.

Function Name	Description
DateAdd()	Returns a new date after you add a value to a date

continues

Table 24.1. Continued

Function Name	Description
DateDiff()	Returns the difference between two dates
DatePart()	Returns part (an element) from a given date

All three date arithmetic functions can work with the parts of dates listed in Table 24.2. Table 24.2 contains the parts of dates these functions work with as well as their *interval values* that label each part. You use the interval values inside the date arithmetic functions to get to a piece of a date or time.

Table 24.2. The time period interval values.

Interval Value	Time Period
yyyy	Year
q	Quarter
m	Month
y	Day of year
d	Day
w	Weekday (Sunday is 1, Monday is 2, and so on for Day(), Month(), Year(), and DateDiff())
ww	Week
h	Hour
n	Minute (careful, not m)
s	Second

The *DateAdd()* Function

Despite its name, the DateAdd() function works with both dates and times (as do all the date functions) because the date passed to DateAdd() must appear in the VarType number 7 format. Following is the format of DateAdd():

```
DateAdd(interval, number, oldDate)
```

The *interval* must be a value (in string form) from Table 24.2. The *interval* you specify determines what time period is added or subtracted (a second value, minute value, or whatever). The *number* value specifies how many of the *interval* values you want to add. Make *interval* positive if you want to add to a date, and make *interval* negative if you want to subtract from a date. The *oldDate* is the date or time from which you want to work (the date or time you are adding to or subtracting from). The *oldDate* does not change. The DateAdd() function then returns the new date.

Example

Suppose that you buy something today with a credit card that has a 25-day grace period. The following statement adds 25 days to today's date and stores the result in intStarts:

```
intStarts = DateAdd("y", 25, Now())
```

The date stored in intStarts is the date 25 days from today.

> **Note:** You can use either "y", "d", or "w" for the interval if you are adding days to a date.

Example

When you work for a company, you have 10 years before you are vested in the retirement program. The following statement adds 10 years to your start date and stores the vested date in vested:

```
vested = DateAdd("yyyy", 10, hired)
```

Notice that the interval string value determines what is added to the date.

> **Tip:** For any of the date arithmetic functions, if you don't specify a year, the current year (the year set on the system's clock) is returned.

The *DateDiff()* Function

The DateDiff() function returns the difference between two dates. The difference is expressed in the *interval* that you specify. Following is the format of DateDiff():

```
DateDiff(interval, date1, date2)
```

> **Caution:** DateDiff() returns a negative value if *date2* is more than *date1*.

Example

The following statement determines how many years an employee has worked for a company:

```
beenWith = DateDiff("yyyy", hireDate, Now)
```

The *DatePart()* Function

The DatePart() function returns a part of a date (the part specified by the *interval*). With DatePart(), you can find what day, month, week, or hour (or whatever other interval you specify) that a date falls on. Here is the format of DatePart():

```
DatePart(interval, date)
```

Example

The following statement stores the day number that an employee started working:

```
DatePart("w", hireDate)
```

Working with Serial Date and Time Values

All date and time functions work with serial values.

Although you may not know about *serial values,* the date and time functions you have been reading about work with serial values. A serial value is the internal representation of a date or time, stored in a VarType 7 (the Date data type) or a Variant data type. These values actually are stored as double-precision values to ensure the full storage of date and time and that accurate date arithmetic can be performed.

The functions explained in this section—DateSerial(), DateValue(), TimeSerial(), TimeValue(), Day(), Month(), and Year()— convert their arguments to a serial date, which really means that they take their arguments and convert those arguments to the internal date format.

Following is the format of the DateSerial() function:

```
DateSerial(year, month, day)
```

where *year* is an integer year number (either 00 to 99 for 1900 to 1999 or a four-digit year number) or expression, *month* is an integer month number (1 to 12) or expression, and *day* is an integer day number (1 to 31) or expression. If you include an expression for any of the integer arguments, you specify the number of years, months, or days from or since a value. To clarify the serial argument expressions, you use the following two DateSerial() function calls, which return the same value:

```
d = DateSerial(1990, 10, 6)
```

and

```
d = DateSerial(1980+10, 12-2, 1+5)
```

The DateSerial() functions ensure that your date arguments don't go out of bounds. For example, 1992 was a leap year, so February of 1992 had 29 days. However, the following DateSerial() function call appears to produce an invalid date because February, even in leap years, cannot have 30 days:

```
d = DateSerial(1992, 2, 29+1)
```

Nothing is wrong with this function call because DateSerial() adjusts the date evaluated so that d holds March 1, 1992, one day following the last day of February.

> **Note:** You probably will not deal with constant values such as 29+1 in your expressions. Your DateSerial() function calls will hold expressions with variables and field values from which you need to produce dates.

The DateValue() function is similar to DateSerial() except that the DateValue() function accepts a string argument, as the following format shows:

```
DateValue(stringDateExpression)
```

The *stringDateExpression* must be a string that Access Basic recognizes as a date (such as those for the Date$ statement described earlier in this chapter). If you ask the user to enter a date a value at a time (asking for the year, then the month, and then the day), you can use DateValue() to convert those values to an internal serial date. If you ask the user to enter a full date (that you capture into a string variable) such as **October 19, 1994**, DateValue() converts that string to the internal serial format needed for dates.

The TimeSerial() and TimeValue() functions work the same as their date counterparts. If you have three individual values for a time of day, TimeSerial() converts those values to an internal time format (the Variant or VarType 7). Here is the format of TimeSerial():

```
TimeSerial(hour, minute, second)
```

The `TimeSerial()` function accepts expressions for any of its arguments and adjusts those expressions as needed, just as the `DateSerial()` function does.

If you have a string with a time value (maybe the user entered the time), the `TimeValue()` function converts that string to a time value with this format:

```
TimeValue(stringTimeExpression)
```

The `Day()`, `Month()`, and `Year()` functions each convert their date arguments (of `Variant` or the `VarType` 7 data type) to a day number, month number, or year number. These three functions are simple: here are their formats:

```
Day(dateArgument)
Month(dateArgument)
Year(dateArgument)
```

In addition, the `Weekday()` function returns the number of the day of the week (see Table 24.2) for the date argument passed to it.

Example

Pass today's date (found with `Now()`) to the `Day()`, `Month()`, and `Year()` functions as shown here:

```
d = Day(Now())
m = Month(Now())
y = Year(Now())
```

the current date's day of week number (see Table 24.2), month number, and year are stored in the three variables.

Example

The following function contains an interesting use of the `DateSerial()` function:

```
Function DueDate (anyDate)
' Accepts: a Date value
' Purpose: Calculates the first non-weekend day of the month
'          following the specified date
' Returns: the calculated date

    Dim Result

    If Not IsNull(anyDate) Then
        Result = DateSerial(Year(anyDate), Month(anyDate) + 1, 1)
        If Weekday(Result) = 1 Then      ' Sunday, so add one day.
            DueDate = Result + 1
```

```
        ElseIf Weekday(Result) = 7 Then                    ' Saturday,
so add two days.
            DueDate = Result + 2
        Else
            DueDate = Result
        End If
    Else
        Result = Null
    End If

End Function
```

When this function is called, it is passed a date value stored in the Variant or VarType 7 Date data type. As the remarks tell, the function computes the number of the first weekday (2 for Monday through 6 for Friday) of the next month (the first business day of the month following the argument).

Notice that the DateSerial() function is passed the date broken into three parts. The Year() and Month() functions are used (and a 1 is used as the day to trigger the beginning of the month) so that 1 can be added to the month number. In effect, the statement

```
Result = DateSerial(Year(anyDate), Month(anyDate) + 1, 1)
```

breaks the date into three parts, increments the month, and then assembles the new date with the new month number and stores the new date into the variable named Result.

The If-Then test uses the Weekday() function to see if the first day of the next month falls on a Saturday or Sunday and adjusts accordingly. The result is then returned to the calling routine. (If Null is returned, a Null value was passed for an argument.)

The *Format()* Function

Format() changes the look of its argument.

One of the most powerful and complex functions, Format(), returns its argument in a different format from how the argument was passed. Here is the format of the Format() function:

```
Format[$](expression [, format])
```

If you don't specify a trailing dollar sign, Format() returns a Variant data type; otherwise, Format$() returns a string. The *expression* can be any numeric or string expression. If you don't specify a *format* (rarely left out), Format$() works just like Str$() (and Format() without the dollar sign works just like Str()), except that no leading blank is left for positive numbers.

The optional (but almost always specified) *format* parameter specifies how you want the argument to *look* when Format() finishes its job. You can format all kinds of data (numbers, strings, dates, and times) to look differently. For example, you might want to print check amounts with commas and a dollar sign.

Describing the Format()'s *format* argument makes the function seem more difficult than it really is. The *format* is a string variable or expression that contains one or more of the *display-format* characters shown in Tables 24.3 through 24.5. The table that you use depends on the kind of data (string, numeric, or date) that you want to format. Display-format characters describe the pattern that you want the data to look like. The tables are long, but after looking at a few examples, you will learn how to use the display-format characters.

Table 24.3. The string display-format characters with their descriptions.

Symbol	Description
@	A character appears in the output at the @ position. If there is no character at the @'s position in the string, a blank appears. The @ is filled (if there is more than one) from right to left.
&	This character is just like @, except nothing appears (instead of a blank) if no character at the &'s position appears in the string being printed.
!	The exclamation point forces all placeholder characters (the @ and &) to fill from left to right instead of from right to left.
<	The less-than character forces all characters being formatted in the string to appear in lowercase.
>	The greater-than character forces all characters being formatted in the string to appear in uppercase.

Table 24.4. The numeric display-format characters with their descriptions.

Symbol	*Description*
Null string	This string displays the number without any formatting.
0	A digit appears in the output at the 0 position if a digit appears in the number being formatted. If no digit is at the 0's position in the number being formatted, a 0 appears. If there are not as many zeros in the number being formatted as there are zeros in the format field, leading or trailing zeros print. If the number contains more numeric positions, the 0 forces all digits to the right of the decimal point to round to the display-format's pattern and all digits to the left print as is. You mostly use this display-format character to print leading or trailing zeros when you want them.
#	The pound-sign character works like the 0 placeholder, except nothing appears if the number being formatted does not have as many digits as the display-format has #s.
.	The period character specifies how many digits (by its placement within 0 or #s) are to appear to the left and right of a decimal point.
%	The number being formatted is multiplied by 100, and the percent sign (%) is printed at its position inside the display-format string.
,	If a comma appears in the midst of 0s or #s, the thousands are easier to read because the comma groups every three places in the number (unless the number is below 1,000). If you put two commas together, you request that the number be divided by 1,000 (to scale down the number).
E-, E+, e-, e+	The number is formatted into scientific notation if the format also contains at least one 0 or #.

continues

Table 24.4. Continued

Symbol	Description
:	The colon causes colons to appear between a time's hour, minute, and second values.
/	The slash ensures that slashes are printed between a date's day, month, and year values.
-, +, $, (space)	All these characters appear as is in their position within the formatted string.
\	Whatever character follows the backslash appears at its position in the formatted string.

Table 24.5. The date display-format characters with their descriptions.

Symbol	Description
c	Displays either the date—just like the ddddd symbol if only a date is present in the value being formatted—or the time—just like the ttttt symbol if only a time is present in the value being formatted; displays both the date (ddddd) and time (ttttt) if both values are present
d	Displays the day number from 1 to 31
dd	Displays the day number with a leading zero from 01 to 31
ddd	Displays an abbreviated 300-character day from Sun to Sat
dddd	Displays the full day name from Sunday to Saturday
ddddd	Displays the date (month, day, year) according to your settings in the International section of your Control Panel's Short Date format (usually m/d/yy)

Symbol	Description
dddddd	Displays the date (month, day, year) according to your settings in the International section of your Control Panel's Long Date format (usually mmmm dd, yyyy)
w	Displays the day of week number (1 for Sunday, 2 for Monday, and so on)
ww	Displays the year's week number from 1 to 54
m	Displays the month number from 1 to 12. The m also means minute if it follows an h or hh.
mm	Displays the month number with a leading zero from 01 to 12. The mm also means minute if it follows an h or hh.
mmm	Displays the abbreviated month name from Jan to Dec
mmmm	Displays the full month name from January to December
q	Displays the quarter of the year
y	Displays the number of the day of the year from 1 to 366
yy	Displays the two-digit year from 00 to 99
yyyy	Displays the full year number from 1000 to 9999
h	Displays the hour number from 0 to 23
hh	Displays the hour as a two-digit number from 00 to 23
n	Displays the minute number from 0 to 59
nn	Displays the minute number with a leading zero from 00 to 59
s	Displays the second number from 0 to 59
ss	Displays the second number with a leading zero from 00 to 59
ttttt	Displays the time (hour, minute, second) according to your settings in the International section of your Control Panel's Time format (usually h:nn:ss)

continues

Table 24.5. Continued

Symbol	Description
AM/PM	Uses the 12-hour clock time and displays either AM or PM as needed
am/pm	Uses the 12-hour clock time and displays either am or pm as needed (notice lowercase am and pm)
A/P	Uses the 12-hour clock time and displays either A or P as needed
a/p	Uses the 12-hour clock time and displays either a or p as needed (notice lowercase a and p)
AMPM	Uses the 12-hour clock to display the string assigned to the s1159 and s2359 variables (usually these strings are assigned AM or PM unless they are changed) in your system's WIN.INI file

Example

Here are a few statements that demonstrate the string display-format characters. The remarks to the right of each statement explain that the target variable (the variable on the left of the equal sign) is receiving formatted data.

```
s$ = Format$("AbcDef", ">")     ' ABCDEF is assigned
s$ = Format$("AbcDef", "<")     ' abcdef is assigned
s$ = Format$("A", "@@@")          ' A is assigned (2 spaces precede)
s$ = Format$("A", "!!!")          ' A is assigned
s$ = Format$("2325551212", "(@@@) @@@-@@@@")      ' (232) 555-1212
```

As the last statement shows, you can put string data into the format you prefer. If the data to be formatted, such as the phone number in the last line, is a string variable from a table's text field, the Format$() statement works just the same.

Example

Suppose it is possible to leave out the area code of the phone number that you want to print. Format$() fills from right to left, so this statement

```
s$ = Format$("5551212", "(@@@) @@@-@@@@")
```

stores the following in s$:

```
(   ) 555-1212
```

If you had included the area code, it would have printed inside the parentheses. Only use the ! when you want the fill to take place from the other direction (when data at the *end* of the string being formatted might be missing). The statement

```
s$ = Format$("5551212", "!(@@@) @@@-@@@@")
```

incorrectly stores the following in s$:

```
(555) 121-2
```

Example

The following statements demonstrate how numeric formatting works. The remark to the right of each statement describes how the data is formatted.

```
s$ = Format$(9146, "¦######¦")   ' ¦9146¦ is stored
s$ = Format$(9146, "¦000000¦")   ' ¦009146¦ is stored
s$ = Format$(2652.2, "00000.00") ' 02652.20 is stored
s$ = Format$(2652.2, "#####.##") ' 2652.2 is stored
s$ = Format$(2652.212, "#####.##") ' 2652.21 is stored
' Rounds if needed:
s$ = Format$(2652.216, "#####.##") ' 2652.22 is stored
s$ = Format$(45, "+###")  ' Stores a +45
s$ = Format$(45, "-###")  ' Stores a -45
s$ = Format$(45, "###-")  ' Stores a 45-
s$ = Format$(2445, "$####.##")   ' Stores a $2445.
s$ = Format$(2445, "$####.00")   ' Stores a $2445.00
s$ = Format$(2445, "_#_###.##_#_#") ' Stores _2_445._ _
s$ = Format$(2445, "00Hi00")  ' Stores 24Hi45
```

Example

The following statements demonstrate how date and time formatting works. The remark to the right of each statement describes how the data is formatted.

```
Dim d As Variant
d = Now()   ' Assume the date and time is
            ' May 21, 1994 2:30 PM
nd$ = Format$(d, "c") ' Stores 12/25/94 2:30:02 PM
nd$ = Format$(d, "w") ' Stores 1 (for Sunday)
nd$ = Format$(d, "ww")' Stores 53
```

```
nd$ = Format$(d, "dddd") ' Stores Sunday
nd$ = Format$(d, "q") ' Stores 4
nd$ = Format$(d, "hh") ' Stores 14
nd$ = Format$(d, "h AM/PM") ' Stores 2 PM
nd$ = Format$(d, "hh AM/PM") ' Stores 02 PM
nd$ = Format$(d, "d-mmmm h:nn:ss")
                            'Stores  25-December 14:30:02
```

Summary

Apparently, Microsoft thought well ahead when designing Access so that you have available to you every date and time function you'll ever need. This chapter focused on the date and time functions and the related statements that enable you to retrieve and set the date and the time.

The functions and statements described in this chapter almost all work with an internal Variant or VarType 7 Date data type. Access Basic recognizes most formats of dates, and whether you spell out a month name when entering a date is up to you because Access can interpret the date.

The last part of this chapter explained how to format your data so that it appears on-screen the way you want. Formatting does not change the data itself, but the Format$() function changes the way your data looks to the user.

After a tour into the financial functions in the next chapter, you'll be finished with the built-in functions.

Review Questions

Answers to review questions are in Appendix B.

1. TRUE or FALSE: The following statement sets the current time to a new value:

   ```
   Time() = "11:21:15"
   ```

2. What is the difference between the Now() function and the Time() function?

3. TRUE or FALSE: The Format$() returns its argument but usually makes the argument look different from its original format.

4. What is the difference (or is there any) between Date() and Date$()?

5. What is the difference between the TimeValue() function and the TimeSerial() function?

6. Which display-format symbol right justifies a string within a fixed number of spaces?

7. What is stored in the variable named s$ by the following statement?

```
s$ = Format$("74135", "&&&&&-&&&&") ' Too short ZIPcode?
```

8. What is stored in the variable named s$ by the following statement?

```
s$ = Format$(d, "h am/pm")
```

9. What is stored in the variable named s$ by the following statement?

```
s$ = Format$(12345.67, "000000.00")
```

10. What is stored in the variable named s$ by the following statement?

```
s$ = Format$(12345.67, "######.###")
```

Review Exercises

1. Write a statement that stores the number of days from today until New Year's Eve.

2. Write a statement that prints the quarter number that an employee started working (assume that the hire date is stored in the variable named HireDate).

3. Turn the following statement into a stand-alone function that accepts a hireDate and prints the name of the day of the week the employee was hired. Use a Select Case for the day name.

```
DatePart("w", hireDate)
```

4. Write a procedure that requests an employee number from the user (with InputBox()) and from the Employees table prints the name of the day that the employee began working.

CHAPTER 25

Financial Functions

Several Access Basic functions are useful for financial calculations. You may not have a need for these functions at this time or at any time in the future. If you're sure that you will not need them, you can safely skip this chapter and turn to the next chapter, which introduces arrays.

Some of the material here may be useful for banking transactions and investment analysis. If you write Access applications that deal with money, you should at least skim this chapter to see what Access can do for you. You can find many of the financial functions in Access in spreadsheet applications such as Microsoft Excel and Lotus 1-2-3, but you don't often find these functions in programming languages (although you do occasionally).

This chapter introduces the following topics:

♦ Depreciation with SLN(), DDB(), and SYD()

♦ Annuity calculations with IPmt(), PPmt(), NPer(), Pmt(), and Rate()

The theory behind these functions is not fully explained in this chapter, just as the theory behind trigonometry was not explained when you learned about the trigonometric functions in Chapter 22. Nevertheless, a preliminary discussion of financial terms is presented to help clarify the way many of the functions work.

Note: Three financial functions—Npv(), Irr(), and Mirr()—are presented in the next chapter. You need an understanding of arrays before you can understand these three functions.

Depreciation

Depreciation is the deducting of costs over time.

Access includes several built-in functions that help you compute *depreciation*. There are several ways to depreciate an item, and the method that a company chooses depends on which method serves it best. Access includes three functions that depreciate three different ways, and the following sections explain each depreciation method.

> **Caution:** The asset's expected life must be more than one year in all the depreciation calculations.

Straight-Line Depreciation with *SLN()*

The easiest method of depreciation is the *straight-line* method. The cost of the item is written off equally over its lifetime. Suppose that an asset costs $12,000, has an estimated life of 10 years, and will be worth $2,000 at the end of its lifetime. The straight-line depreciation on such an item is $1,000 a year. (If you write off $1,000 a year for 10 years, you're left with $2,000, which equates to the salvage value.)

Here is the format of the straight-line depreciation function:

```
SLN(originalCost, salvageAmount, estimatedLifeYrs)
```

Example

The following procedure asks the user for the three needed values of SLN() and then prints the yearly depreciation amount.

```
Function slDepr ()
  Dim cost As Currency, salvage As Currency, life As Integer
  Dim slAmount As Currency
  Dim slAmountSt As String  ' For formatted printing
  cost = InputBox("How much did the asset cost?")
  salvage = InputBox("How much will the asset be salvaged for?")
  ' The estimated life must be expressed in years
  life = InputBox("How many years is the asset expected to
  ➥last?")
  slAmount = SLN(cost, salvage, life)
  slAmountSt = Format$(slAmount, "$##,##0.00")     ' Format depr.
  ➥as string
  MsgBox "The annual depreciation is " & slAmountSt$
End Function
```

Double-Declining Balance with *DDB()*

Some companies want to write off their assets faster than the straight-line depreciation method provides. The government allows businesses to write off their assets faster than the SLN() method. The *double-declining balance* method writes off the majority of assets in their earliest years. The earlier write-off allows the company to show less of a profit (on the tax records) than the straight-line depreciation method allows. If a company expects to make a lot of money quickly from an asset purchase, the company probably prefers the faster depreciation.

Here is the format of the DDB() function:

```
DDB(originalCost, salvageAmount, estimatedLife, period)
```

The calculation used for the DDB() method is as follows:

```
periodAmt=((originalCost-totalDeprToThisPeriod)*2)/estimatedLife
```

The depreciation for each year is different using DDB() than using SLN(). Therefore, the extra argument, *period*, tells the DDB() function for which of the years you want the depreciation method calculated.

> **Tip:** You can calculate depreciation for any time period (months, weeks, quarters) using DDB() as long as both the *estimatedLife* and the *period* are both expressed in the same time periods.

Example

The following procedure asks the user for the four needed values of DDB() and then prints the period's depreciation amount.

```
Function DDBdepr ()
  Dim cost As Currency, salvage As Currency
  Dim life As Integer, periods As Integer
  Dim ddbAmount As Currency
  Dim ddbAmountSt As String  ' For formatted printing
  cost = InputBox("How much did the asset cost?")
  salvage = InputBox("How much will the asset be salvaged for?")
  life = InputBox("How many periods is the asset expected to
  ➡last?")
  periods = InputBox("For which period do you want deprecia
  ➡tion?")
  ddbAmount = DDB(cost, salvage, life, periods)
  ddbAmountSt = Format$(ddbAmount, "$##,##0.00")    ' Format
  ➡depr. as string
  MsgBox "The period's depreciation is " & ddbAmountSt$
End Function
```

Sum-of-Years' Digits with *SYD()*

The *sum-of-years' digits* method of depreciation is yet another method recognized by the government for which you can accelerate depreciation. The depreciation method is based on a mathematical series of numbers where the next number in the series is the sum of the previous two numbers.

Here is the format of the SYD() function:

```
SYD(originalCost, salvageAmount, estimatedLife, period)
```

As with the DDB() function, the depreciation amount for each year varies, so SYD() returns the depreciation for the period that you request. Also, if you want to compute depreciation for a period other than a year, make sure that the time periods for both the *estimatedLife* and the *period* arguments match.

Example

The following procedure asks the user for the four needed values of SYD() and then prints the period's depreciation amount.

```
Function sydDepr ()
  Dim cost As Currency, salvage As Currency
  Dim life As Integer, periods As Integer
  Dim sydAmount As Currency
  Dim sydAmountSt As String  ' For formatted printing
  cost = InputBox("How much did the asset cost?")
  salvage = InputBox("How much will the asset be salvaged for?")
  life = InputBox("How many periods is the asset expected to
  ➡last?")
  periods = InputBox("For which period do you want deprecia
  ➡tion?")
  sydAmount = SYD(cost, salvage, life, periods)
  sydAmountSt = Format$(sydAmount, "$##,##0.00")        ' Format
  ➡depr. as string
  MsgBox "The period's depreciation is " & sydAmountSt$
End Function
```

Annuity Calculations

An annuity consists of equal payments.

An annuity is an equal payment made over a series of years (or any uniform time period). If you deposit $2,000 each year into a retirement account, you are funding an annuity. If you make equal payments to repay a loan, your lender is receiving annuity-like payments.

You often need to calculate various annuity-related values. The values often are based on a *present-value* or *future-value* calculation. Consider the following questions:

♦ How much will I have in my retirement account in 15 years?

♦ How much do I have to put in an account today to pay me $15,000 a year for 20 years?

The first question is concerned with future value, and the second is concerned with present value. The basic premise of all financial calculations is that money has value because of the interest that it earns.

If you are given a choice of receiving $1 today or $1 a year from now, always choose to get $1 today. You can invest that $1 and have *more* than $1 at the end of a year (assuming that you are a prudent investor).

If you're given a choice of receiving $1.00 today or $1.05 a year from now, the choice is not as easy as the preceding one. If you cannot earn the 5 percent needed to have $1.05 at the end of the year, you probably would rather have $1.05 a year from now than $1.00 today. If you could invest the $1.00 and have *more* than $1.05 a year from now, however, you'd probably rather have the $1.00 today.

> **Note:** Functions presented in the next section deal directly with future and present value, but this review is helpful for the annuity calculations as well.

Calculating the Interest Payment

IPmt() calculates the amount of interest.

As you repay a loan, a part of that payment goes to interest each month. The IPmt() function computes the amount of each payment that goes toward the interest. Because a different amount of interest applies to each payment, you must tell the IPmt() function for which period you want the interest calculated (in the same manner that you specified in which depreciation period you were interested).

> **Note:** The amount of interest calculated for each payment depends on when you make the payments. If your payments are due at the beginning of the month, the interest is different from the calculation if your payments are due at the end of the month. (The latter requires more interest due to the larger number of days before each payment.)

The format of IPmt() seems foreboding, but every required argument makes sense when you consider what information the IPmt() function needs to do its job.

Here is the format of the IPmt() function:

```
IPmt(rate, period, numPeriods, prsntVal, fuVal, whenDue)
```

Table 25.1 lists each of the IPmt() arguments and a description of each.

Table 25.1. The *IPmt()* arguments.

Argument	Description
rate	The interest rate per period. The period must coincide with the period between each payment (a month, quarter, year, or whatever), so you have to divide the yearly interest rate by the number of time periods with the year.
period	The period for which you want interest calculated. (The number must fall between 1 and the total number of periods, numPeriods.)
numPeriods	Number of periods in the entire annuity. If you're paying monthly for 30 years, the number of payments is 360 (12 * 30 years).
presntVal	The present value of the annuity (such as the amount of money you borrowed)
fuVal	The future value of the entire annuity (zero if you are paying back a loan because you owe nothing at the end of the loan period)
whenDue	0 if payments are due at the end of the month and 1 if payments are due at the beginning

Example

The following procedure calculates the amount of interest you pay in the first year and last year of a loan. A vast amount of your mortgage payment goes to interest the first year and only a small amount goes to interest the last year.

```
Function intYrs ()
' Calculates the amount of interest you pay in a loan's
' first year and last year. Assumes monthly payments.
  Const DUE = 1   ' Assumes payments are due on the 1st
  Const FV = 0    ' Assumes loan will be completely paid off
```

```
Dim firstYr As Currency, lastYr As Currency
Dim intFmt As String
Dim ctr As Integer    ' For loop counting variable
Dim preVal As Currency, intRate As Single
Dim nPeriods As Integer
preVal = InputBox("How much did you borrow?")
intRate = InputBox("What is the annual interest rate (i.e.
➥.11)?")
intRate = intRate / 12    ' Convert interest to monthly interest
nPeriods = InputBox("How many years in the loan?")
nPeriods = nPeriods * 12 ' Convert periods to monthly periods

' Compute the amount of interest the first year
For ctr = 1 To 12
  ' Negate present value because you are borrowing, not invest-
➥ing
 firstYr = firstYr + IPmt(intRate, ctr, nPeriods, -preVal, FV,
➥DUE)
Next ctr

' Compute the amount of interest the last year
For ctr = nPeriods To (nPeriods - 12) Step -1
lastYr = lastYr + IPmt(intRate, ctr, nPeriods, -preVal, FV,
➥DUE)
Next ctr

' Print results
intFmt = "$###,##0.00"   ' For printing purposes
MsgBox "Your first year's interest is " & Format$(firstYr,
➥intFmt)
MsgBox "Your last year's interest is " & Format$(lastYr,
➥intFmt)
End Function
```

Tip: This kind of procedure is perfect for Access Basic. You probably don't want to store every month's interest rate in a table. Using Access Basic and these financial functions, you can print whatever month's interest your user wants to see without taking up table space.

Calculating the Principal

PPmt() calculates the principal of a loan.

Whereas IPmt() calculates the amount of interest in a loan payment, PPmt() calculates the amount of *principal* in a loan payment. The format of PPmt() is exactly like that of IPmt(). Here is the format:

```
PPmt(rate, period, numPeriods, prsntVal, fuVal, whenDue)
```

Example

The following procedure calculates the amount of principal you pay off in the first year and last year of a loan. This example shows that a vast amount of your mortgage payment goes to interest the first year, and only a small amount goes to principal until later in the life of the loan.

```
Function compPrin ()
' Calculates the amount of principal you pay off in a loan's
' first year and last year. Assumes monthly payments.
  Const DUE = 1    ' Assumes payments are due on the 1st
  Const FV = 0     ' Assumes loan will be completely paid off
  Dim firstYr As Currency, lastYr As Currency
  Dim prinFmt As String
  Dim ctr As Integer    ' For loop counting variable
  Dim preVal As Currency, intRate As Single
  Dim nPeriods As Integer
  preVal = InputBox("How much did you borrow?")
  intRate = InputBox("What is the annual interest rate (i.e.
    ➥.11)?")
  intRate = intRate / 12    ' Convert interest to monthly interest
  nPeriods = InputBox("How many years in the loan?")
  nPeriods = nPeriods * 12 ' Convert periods to monthly periods

  ' Compute the amount of principal the first year
  For ctr = 1 To 12
    ' Negate present value because you are borrowing, not invest-
      ➥ing
    firstYr = firstYr + PPmt(intRate, ctr, nPeriods, -preVal, FV,
    DUE)
  Next ctr

  ' Compute the amount of principal the last year
  For ctr = nPeriods To (nPeriods - 12) Step -1
    lastYr = lastYr + PPmt(intRate, ctr, nPeriods, -preVal, FV,
    ➥DUE)
```

```
    Next ctr

    ' Print results
    prinFmt = "$###,##0.00"  ' For printing purposes
    MsgBox "Your first year's principal is " & Format$(firstYr,
    ➥prinFmt)
    MsgBox "Your last year's principal is " & Format$(lastYr,
    ➥prinFmt)
End Function
```

Calculating the Periods Required

NPer() calculates the number of periods.

Suppose that you want to buy a car, but you can pay only a fixed amount each month for the car payment. The NPer() function is similar to IPmt(), except that NPer() returns the number of payment periods needed to pay off a loan that is fixed at a certain interest rate. If you look at NPer() from another direction, NPer() tells you how many months you must invest a fixed dollar amount at a fixed interest rate to achieve an ending goal of $1,000,000, for example.

The format of NPer() is similar to that of IPmt(), except that you know the interest rate with NPer() but don't know how many payments are required. Here is the format:

```
NPer(rate, payment, prsntVal, fuVal, whenDue)
```

The only new argument to NPer() is *payment*, which is the payment you can afford to make.

Example

The following procedure tells you how many months you must invest $200 to retire with $500,000.

```
Function compPeriods ()
' Calculates the number of periods you must invest $200
' to get a total of $500,000 at a specified interest rate.
  Const DUE = 1    ' Assumes payments are made monthly on the 1st
  Const FV = 500000    ' Desired investment goal
  Const PMT = 200
  Const PV = 0     ' Nothing invested so far
  Dim nPeriods As Integer
  Dim intRate As Single
  intRate = InputBox("What is the annual interest rate (i.e.
  ➥.11)?")
  intRate = intRate / 12  ' Convert interest to monthly interest
```

```
' PMT is negative because you are paying, not receiving
nPeriods = NPer(intRate, -PMT, PV, FV, DUE)     ' Calculate
➥payments
' Print results
MsgBox "You must invest $200 for" & Str$(nPeriods) & " peri-
➥ods."
End Function
```

Calculating the Payments

Pmt() calculates a payment amount.

The Pmt() function returns yet another piece of annuity calculations. The Pmt() is a function most useful to borrowers who want to know their monthly payment for a loan they receive. The format of Pmt() is similar to that of IPmt(), except that you don't know the payment amount because the payment is what IPmt() calculates for you. Here is the format:

```
Pmt(rate, numPeriods, prsntVal, fuVal, whenDue)
```

Example

The following procedure calculates the monthly payment required to pay a loan whose monthly payments are due on the first.

```
Function compPmt ()
' Calculates the monthly payment of a loan you might make.
  Const DUE = 1    ' Assumes payments are made monthly on the 1st
  Const FV = 0     ' Loan will be paid off in full
  Dim nPeriods As Integer
  Dim intRate As Single
  Dim presVal As Currency
  Dim payment As Currency
  presVal = InputBox("How much are you borrowing?")
  intRate = InputBox("What is the annual interest rate (i.e.
    ➥.11)?")
  intRate = intRate / 12    ' Convert interest to monthly interest
  nPeriods = InputBox("How many years is the loan for?")
  nPeriods = nPeriods * 12 ' Calculate number of monthly payments
  ' Calculate payments
  ' presVal is negative because you are paying, not receiving
  payment = Pmt(intRate, nPeriods, -presVal, FV, DUE)
  ' Print results
  MsgBox "You must pay " & Format$(payment, "$##,##0.00") & " a
    ➥month."
End Function
```

Calculating the Interest Rate

Rate() calculates interest.

The Rate() function calculates the rate of interest you are paying when paying off a loan at a fixed payment over time. (If you invest a fixed amount of money into an interest-bearing account, with changing interest posted throughout the life of the investment, you can use Rate() to compute the actual interest you earned.) Here is the format of Rate():

```
Rate(numPeriods, payment, prsntVal, fuVal, whenDue, guess)
```

The guess value is a starting point that you give Rate() to start calculating interest. Rate() uses an iteration method to calculate interest, and you have to give the function a starting interest rate (.10 is always good) to begin its iteration. If Rate() cannot calculate the proper interest rate (Rate() somehow knows when it has found the correct interest) after 20 tries, the Rate() function fails by returning an invalid function call error.

Example

The following example computes the interest rate on a loan.

```
Function compRate ()
   ' Calculates the interest on a loan.
   Const DUE = 1    ' Assumes payments are made monthly on the 1st
   Const FV = 0      ' Loan will be paid off in full
   Dim nPeriods As Integer
   Dim intRate As Single
   Dim presVal As Currency
   Dim payment As Currency
   presVal = InputBox("How much are you borrowing?")
   nPeriods = InputBox("How many years is the loan for?")
   nPeriods = nPeriods * 12 ' Calculate number of monthly payments
   payment = InputBox("What is the monthly payment amount?")
   ' Calculate rate
   ' payment is negative because you are paying, not receiving
   intRate = Rate(nPeriods, -payment, presVal, FV, DUE, .085)
   ' Print results
   MsgBox "You are paying " & Format$(intRate, "#0.0%") & "
   ➥interest."
End Function
```

Future and Present Value

Money gains value over time.

To make a choice between two financial transactions, many financial people compute the *present value* (today's value) of both investments. When you compute the present value of both investments, you are computing all of that investment's deposits and interest over its lifetime and discounting that money back into today's dollars. Once you have the two investments' present values, you have an even playing field and can choose whichever investment's present value is worth the most. (Likewise, you can compute two or more investments' *future values* and compare those to see which is greater as well.)

Computing Present Value with *PV()*

The PV() function computes an investment's (or loan's, depending on how you adjust the signs of the arguments) present value. Most of the arguments to PV() are similar to the ones you've seen in the earlier sections of this chapter. Here is the format of PV():

```
PV(rate, numPeriods, payment, prsntVal, fuVal, whenDue)
```

The *rate* is the interest rate per period (not per year unless you make annual payments or deposits), and *numPeriods* is the total number of payments (not years unless you make annual payments or deposits). *payment* is each period's payment or deposit, *fuVal* is the amount of the loan (0) or investment (the goal you hope to have at the end of your investment) at the end of the time periods, and *whenDue* must be 0 or 1 to indicate if the payments are due at the end of the month or at the beginning.

Example

The following procedure computes the present value for a loan. The PV() function requires that each payment be made in equal payments and that the interest rate remain constant over the life of the payments.

```
Function compPV ()
' Calculates the present value of a series of payments
    Const DUE = 0    ' Assumes payments are due on the 1st
    Const FV = 0     ' Assumes loan will be completely paid off
    Dim intRate As Single
    Dim preVal As Currency
    Dim nPeriods As Integer
    Dim pmt As Currency
    Dim fvFor As String
    pmt = InputBox("How much is each payment?")
    intRate = InputBox("What is the annual interest rate?")
```

```
    intRate = intRate / 12    ' Convert interest to monthly interest
    nPeriods = InputBox("How many years in the loan?")
    nPeriods = nPeriods * 12 ' Convert periods to monthly periods
    preVal = PV(intRate, nPeriods, -pmt, FV, DUE)
    fvFor = "$###,##0.00"  ' For printing purposes
    MsgBox "Your loan is worth " & Format$(preVal, fvFor) & "
    ➡today."
End Function
```

Computing Future Value with *FV()*

The FV() function computes an investment's (or loan's, depending on how you adjust the signs of the arguments) future value. Most of the arguments to the FV() function are similar to the ones you've seen in the earlier sections of this chapter.

Here is the format of FV():

```
FV(rate, numPeriods, payment, presentVal, whenDue)
```

Example

The following example prints the future value of a stream of equal payments (the amount of money you will have at the end of the investment cycle).

```
Function compFV ()
' Calculates the future value of a series of payments
    Const DUE = 1    ' Assumes payments are due on the 1st
    Const PV = 0
    Dim intRate As Single
    Dim futVal As Currency
    Dim nPeriods As Integer
    Dim pmt As Currency
    Dim fvFor As String
    pmt = InputBox("How much is each payment?")
    intRate = InputBox("What is the annual interest rate?")
    intRate = intRate / 12    ' Convert interest to monthly interest
    nPeriods = InputBox("How many years in the loan?")
    nPeriods = nPeriods * 12 ' Convert periods to monthly periods
    futVal = -FV(intRate, nPeriods, pmt, PV, DUE)
    fvFor = "$###,##0.00"  ' For printing purposes
    MsgBox "Your loan is worth " & Format$(futVal, fvFor) & " at
    ➡the end."
End Function
```

Summary

Making financial decisions with Access Basic is easy thanks to the built-in financial functions. Although you may need an introduction to the world of finance before you fully understand all of these functions, the examples you've seen here are an attempt to show you some real-world needs for these functions.

You might want to know an interest rate that you are earning on an investment, the number of time periods in a loan, or the present or future value of a stream of money.

Many times, an investment does not fall into the category of *annuities*. You often deposit different amounts at different times, and you sometimes pay a loan early. After you learn about arrays in the next chapter, you see three ways to compute time value of money problems with unequal money flows.

Review Questions

Answers to review questions are in Appendix B.

1. What is depreciation?

2. Name the three kinds of depreciation supported by Access Basic.

3. What is time value of money?

4. Why is accelerated depreciation better for many companies than straight-line depreciation?

5. What is the difference between present value and future value?

6. Why does Pmt() only return a single value although a loan might have several hundred payments over its lifetime?

7. Suppose you are offered $500 today or $540 next year. Do you have enough information, based on the dollar amounts alone, to decide which gift is the best deal for you?

8. What is the present value of a loan made to you for $5,000?

9. What is the future value of a loan made for $5,000 at the end of its life (after you make the final payment)?

Review Exercises

1. Suppose a company buys a kite-making machine that costs $140,000, has a salvage value of $20,000, and has a life of 10 years. What yearly depreciation amount does SLN() return?

2. Write a procedure that calculates the double-declining balance of deprecia-tion. Use a For-Next loop to step through every year, printing the depreciation for *each* year instead of for just one period, as done in this chapter's example.

3. Suppose you are planning to buy a house in the next two years but don't know how far interest rates will rise or fall. Write a procedure that prints the payments for the purchase of an $80,000 house, bought for 30 years (monthly payments), using a For-Next loop that varies the interest rate from 8 percent to 12 percent in increments of one-half percent.

Part VI

Data Structures

CHAPTER 26

Introduction to Arrays

Now it's time for you to learn how to store many occurrences of data in your Access Basic programs. Most of the programs you've seen so far have worked with very little data. Up to this point, you were learning about variables and controlling statements; lots of data would have hindered your learning how to program, especially if you were unfamiliar with programming languages before learning Access Basic.

This chapter is the first of two that teach about *arrays*. An array is not much more than a list of variables. You see in this chapter how the naming conventions for variables differ a little (but not much) from the naming conventions for regular nonarray variables.

With arrays, you can store *many* occurrences of data. With nonarray variables, each piece of data has a different name, and it is difficult to track many occurrences of data. Before you learn how to read and process table data with Access Basic, you must have a way to store the many data items that you read from a table into your programs. Arrays provide the containers for several data values such as those you get when reading from a table into your program.

This chapter introduces the following topics:

♦ The difference between arrays and regular nonarray variables

♦ Declaring arrays

♦ Using array subscripts

♦ Working with arrays of data values from forms, reports, and tables

♦ Using arrays with some financial functions

Conquering arrays is your next step toward understanding advanced uses of Access Basic. This chapter's examples are some of the longest programs you have seen in the book. Arrays are not difficult, but their power lends them to advanced programming.

Arrays and Nonarray Variables

Arrays may hold many data values.

An array is a list of more than one variable with the *same name*. Not every list of variables is an array. The following list of four variables does *not* count as an array:

```
Sales      bonus92      firstName ctr
```

This list of four variables does not define an array because each variable has a different name. You may wonder how more than one variable can have the same name; this convention seems to violate the rules of variables. If two variables have the same name, how does Access Basic know which one you want when you use its name?

Array variables are distinguished from each other by a *subscript*. A subscript is a number, inside parentheses, that differentiates one *element* of an array from another. Elements are the individual variables in an array. Before you get too much further into definitions, read the following illustration for help.

Good Array Candidates

Suppose that you want to process 35 people's names and monthly dues from your local neighborhood association. The dues are different for each person. All this data fits nicely in an Access Basic table, but suppose that you also want to hold, at one time, all the data in variables so you can perform calculations and print various statistics about the members using Access Basic.

Without arrays, you find yourself having to store each of the 35 names in 35 different variables and each of their dues in 35 different variables, and doing so makes for a complex and lengthy program! To enter the data, you have to store the data in variables with names such as the following:

```
familyName1  familyDues1  familyName2  familyDues2
familyName3  familyDues3  familyName4  familyDues4
```

The list continues until you use different variable names for all the 35 names and dues.

Every time you use Access Basic to print a list of members, calculate average dues, or use this data in any other way, you have to scan sets of 35 different variable names. The steps required in this procedure are why arrays were developed; it is too cumbersome for similar data to have different variable names. The time and typing required to process more than a handful of variables with different names is too much. Not only that, imagine if the neighborhood grew to 500 residents!

With arrays, you can store similar data, such as the neighborhood data, in a single variable. In effect, each of the data values has the same name. You distinguish the values (*elements* in the array) from each other by a numeric subscript. For example, rather than a different variable name (`familyName1`, `familyDues1`, `familyName2`, `familyDues2`, and so on), give the similar data the same variable name (`familyName` and `familyDues`) and differentiate them with subscripts as shown in Table 26.1.

Table 26.1. Using arrays to store similar data.

Old Names	Array Names
familyName1, familyDues1	familyName(1), familyDues(1)
familyName2, familyDues2	familyName(2), familyDues(2)
familyName3, familyDues3	familyName(3), familyDues(3)
familyName35, familyDues35	familyName(35), familyDues(35)

One name simplifies a list of data.

"Where is the improvement?" you might ask. The column of array names has a major advantage over the old variable names. The number inside parentheses is the *subscript number* of the array. Subscript numbers are never part of an array name; they are always enclosed in parentheses and serve to distinguish one array element from another.

How many arrays are listed in Table 26.1? If you said two, you are correct. There are 35 elements in each of the two arrays. How many nonarray variables are there in Table 26.1? There are 70 (35 family name variables and 35 dues variables). The difference is very important when you consider how you process them.

> **Tip:** Because the subscript number (the only thing that differentiates one array element from another) is not part of the array name, you can use a **For-Next** loop or any other counter variable to input, process, and output any and all elements of arrays.

To input every single family name and their dues into the two arrays using a loop, for instance, you do not need 70 statements as you do when each variable has a different name. You need only four statements, as shown here:

```
For sub = 1 To 35
  familyName(sub) = InputBox("What is the family member's name?")
  familyDues(sub) = InputBox("What are their dues")
Next sub
```

This code offers a major advantage over using nonarray variables. Notice that the For-Next loop keeps incrementing sub throughout the data input of all 70 values. The first time through the loop, the user enters a value into familyName(1) and in familyDues(1) (because sub is equal to 1). The loop then increments sub to 2, and the input process starts over again for the next two variables. These four lines of code are much easier to write and maintain than a set of 70 individual InputBox() function calls, and the For-Next loop does exactly the same thing. You cannot use the For-Next loop to process a bunch of differently named variables, even if they have numbers in their names, as they do with familyName1, familyDues1, and so on.

Any time you are working with a list of data with similar meanings, an array works best. Arrays make your input, process, and output routines much easier to write. Most importantly to Access Basic, you can read table data into large arrays if needed and work with the data in memory.

> **Note:** There are two kinds of arrays: *static arrays* and *dynamic arrays.* This book discusses static arrays, which are fixed in size and cannot be changed at runtime. (Dynamic array sizes can be changed.)

Not all of your Access Basic data is stored in arrays. You still use variables (like those you've seen throughout this book) for loop control and user input. When you have multiple occurrences of data that you must track within Access Basic, such as fields from a table that you read into memory, an array is the perfect holder for that data.

Using *Global, Dim,* and *Static* to Set Up Arrays

As you do with nonarray variables, you tell Access Basic that you are going to use an array; you have to declare the array, just as you have to declare other variables. You use the Global, Dim, or Static statements to declare arrays; your choice of statements depends on the kind of array you need.

Declare with a Global statement to create a global array that can be used throughout the entire database (across modules). The Global statement must appear in the declarations section.

If you use a Dim statement in the declarations section, you create a module-level array that can be used throughout the module.

If you want to create an array that is local to a particular procedure, use the Static statement. (You can use Dim if the entire procedure is a Static procedure.)

For declaring arrays, the format of the Global, Dim, and Static statements differs only in the keyword of the command and its placement in the module. Here are the formats of the three statements:

```
Global arName (subs) [As type] [, arName (subs) [As type]]...

Dim arName (subs) [As type] [, arName (subs) [As type]]...

Static arName (subs) [As type] [, arName (subs) [As type]]...
```

You name arrays (arName) just as you do regular variables. You can create an array of any data type, so *type* can be Integer, Single, or any of the data types with which you are familiar. The *subs* portion of the commands describes the number of elements and how you refer to those array elements. In the preceding statement formats, *subs* can take on the following format:

```
[low To] high
```

> **Note:** You can have more than one set of subscripts, as you learn in the next chapter.

Variant arrays can hold different data types.

Unlike other programming languages, Access's Variant data type enables you to specify arrays that hold several different kinds of data. All elements of non-Variant arrays must have the same data type.

> **Tip:** If you've never worked with arrays, these array declaration statements may seem foreboding, but the next few examples should clear things up.

Example

Declaring an array is easiest when you specify only the upper subscript bound. All array subscripts begin at 0 unless the following statement appears in the declarations section:

```
Option Base 1
```

The Option Base command is rather outdated and if you want to change the lower bounds of an array, you should consider using the more advanced Low To option described in following examples.

The following Static statement declares seven elements of an Integer array named Ages:

```
Static Ages(6)      ' Reserves 7 elements
```

The subscript, 6, is the upper subscript, and the lower subscript is 0 (without an `Option Base 1` appearing elsewhere that forces the beginning subscript to 1). Figure 26.1 illustrates just what is declared with this statement. An array of seven `Integer` values, all with the same name `Ages`, is reserved for use. Each variable is distinguished by its subscript number. `Ages(2)` is a completely different variable from `Ages(6)`.

Figure 26.1

The *Ages* array with seven elements.

Ages

Ages(0)
Ages(1)
Ages(2)
Ages(3)
Ages(4)
Ages(5)
Ages(6)

Note: Often, programmers ignore the zero subscript. Assuming that the statement `Static Ages(6)` reserves only six array elements (when it really reserves seven) keeps things simpler than dealing with the zero subscript.

Example

Based on the previous discussion, you can declare the `familyName` and `familyDues` arrays as follows:

```
Static familyName(35) As String   ' Reserves 36 names
Static familyDues(35) As Single   ' Reserves 36 dues
```

Actually, the subscript 35 is the upper bound, and the subscript 0 is the lower bound (automatically). Therefore, these statements each dimension 36 elements in each array. The previous discussion mentioned 35 members in the neighborhood association, so the 0 subscript is not used.

Tip: Remember this nice thing about arrays: If 500 members are in the association, the two `Static` statements are just as easy to write; you just use a different subscript (500). If, however, the variables are nonarray variables, you need an additional 465 `Dim` statements to reserve the storage. Whew!

Because `Static` was used here, the arrays have procedure-level scope. Only the code within the procedure that contains these two statements can use the two arrays unless the procedure passes the arrays to other procedures.

Example

Sometimes, specifying the lower and upper bounds of the array subscripts makes sense. As you've seen, if you specify `Option Base 1`, the lower array subscript is 1. If you specify `Option Base 0` or nothing at all, the lower array subscript bounds are zero. By using the expanded array declaration statements, however, with the `To` keyword, you can specify the upper and lower bounds of your array subscripts.

Tip: You may find that your data fits within different subscripts than those that default (such as starting at 0 or 1). Suppose that you are storing customer information, and your lowest customer number is 200. It therefore makes sense to begin the array subscripts at 200 and store the first customer at his or her array subscript number 200.

The following statements reserve global storage for three customer-related arrays. The first subscript is 200, and the highest subscript is 999.

```
Global custNumber(200 To 999) As Variant
Global custName(200 To 999) As String
Global custBalance(200 To 999) As Double
```

Caution: The high subscript no longer specifies the number of array elements. These three arrays have a total of 800 elements each (subscripted from 200 to 999).

Example

These `Dim` statements do the same thing as the preceding example:

```
Dim Amounts(0 To 50)    ' Subscripts 0 to 50
Dim Amounts(50)         ' Subscripts 0 to 50
```

And so do these pairs:

```
Option Base 1
Dim Balances(75)        ' Subscripts 1 to 75

Option Base 0
Dim Balances(1 To 75)  ' Subscripts 1 to 75
```

Using Arrays

You may see arrays used in calculations, just as nonarray variables are, like the following:

```
familyDues(5) = familyDues(4) * 1.5
```

To use data in an array, you have to use only the subscript of the array element you want to work with.

> **Tip:** In one respect, accessing an array value works like a set of boxes in a post office. The address of all the boxes is the same (they are all located in the same building), but mail is inserted into the appropriate box number.

The rest of this chapter uses some code examples to clarify how arrays work. The earlier examples use arrays to gather and work with user data. After you understand better how to work with arrays, the later examples in this chapter use arrays with forms.

Example

Although the following example shows array elements being filled up by InputBox(), most programs get most of their input data from files and forms. Because arrays can store very large amounts of data, you don't want to have to type that data into the variables every time you run a program. Assignment statements do not suffice either because they are not good statements to use for extremely large amounts of data and interactive programs.

Here is the full program that declares two arrays for the neighborhood association's 35 family names and their dues. It prompts for the input and then prints the data.

> **Note:** If you type in this program, you may want to change the number from 35 down to 5 or so to keep from having to type so much input.

Notice that the program can input and print all the names and dues with simple routines. The input routine uses a For-Next loop, and the printing routine uses a Do-Loop. The method you use to control the loop is not critical. The important thing to see at this point is that you can input and print a great deal of data without having to write lots of code. The array subscripts and loop controlling statements make the printing possible.

```
Function association ()
' Procedure to gather and print 35 names and dues
  Static familyName(35) As String ' Reserve the array elements
  Static familyDues(35) As Single
  Dim subsc As Integer
  ' Loop getting all of the data
  For subsc = 1 To 35
    familyName(subsc) = InputBox("What is the next family's
name")
    familyDues(subsc) = InputBox("What are their dues")
  Next subsc

  ' Prints all the input data
  subsc = 1 ' Initialize the first subscript
  Do
    Debug.Print "Family"; subsc; "is "; familyName(subsc)
    Debug.Print "Their dues are"; familyDues(subsc)
    subsc = subsc + 1
  Loop Until (subsc > 35)

End Function
```

This example illustrates *parallel arrays*. Two arrays are working side by side. Each element in each array corresponds to one in the other array. Parallel arrays work in memory like joined fields work together in tables.

Example

The neighborhood association program is fine for illustration, but it works only if there are exactly 35 families. What if the association grows? If it were to grow, you would have to change the program.

Therefore, most programs do not have a set limit size for data, as the preceding example does. Most programmers declare more than enough array elements to handle the largest array ever needed. The program then enables the user to control how many of those elements are really used.

> **Note:** After you master the fixed-length static arrays discussed here, you may want to learn about dynamic arrays, whose size can change at runtime. If you find that you need more array elements when the program runs, you can get more when using dynamic arrays.

The following program is similar to the preceding one, except that it declares 500 elements for each array. This number reserves more than enough array elements for the association. The user then inputs only the actual number (from 1 to 500 maximum). Notice that the program is very flexible, allowing a variable number of members input and printed each time it is run. It does, however, need an eventual limit, but that limit is only reached when there are 500 members.

> **Caution:** Declare enough array space for your estimated needs, but don't declare more array space than you can possibly use. For every extra array element that you reserve but don't use, memory is wasted.

```
Function varyNumb ()
' Procedure to gather and print 35 names and dues
  Static familyName(500) As String\  ' Reserve enough array
  ➥elements
  Static familyDues(500) As Single
  Dim subsc As Integer, numFam As Integer
  numFam = 1

  ' The following loop asks for family names and dues until the
  '  user presses Enter without typing a name.' Whenever a
  '   ➥zero-length
  ' string is entered (just an Enter keypress), the Do-Loop exits
  ' early with sub holding the number input to that point.
  Do
    familyName(numFam) = InputBox("What is next family's name?")
      If (familyName(numFam) = "") Then Exit Do ' This triggers
      ➥early exit
    familyDues(numFam) = InputBox("What are their dues?")
    numFam = numFam + 1 ' Add one to the subscript variable
  Loop Until (numFam > 500)

  ' When the last loop finishes, subsc holds one
  ' more than the actual number input

  ' Prints all the input data
```

```
    For subsc = 1 To numFam - 1
      Debug.Print "Family"; subsc; "is "; familyName(subsc)
      Debug.Print "Their dues are"; familyDues(subsc)
    Next subsc
  End Function
```

The empty Enter keypress is a good way to trigger the early exit of the loop. Just because 500 elements are reserved for each array does not mean that you have to use all 500 of them.

> **Tip:** Alternatively, if the user is familiar with the data, you can ask the user how many values he or she wants to enter. You then loop until that value is reached. Because the user is rarely familiar enough with his or her data to know how many values he or she will input, asking for the number of values to enter is not as common as this example, which enables the user to trigger the end of input when finished.

Example

You can randomly access arrays.

You do not have to access an array in the same order as it was entered. An array works like a table because you can access any element in any order, just like reading a record from file by knowing a record number. You use the subscript to "pick out" items from an array of values.

The following program requests salary data for the last twelve months. It then waits until another user types the month he or she wants to see. That month's sales then are printed, without the surrounding months getting in the way. This is how you begin to build a search program to find requested data that is stored in arrays; store the data in an array (or in a table that can be read into an array) and then wait for a request from the user to see only specific pieces of that data.

```
Function salary ()
' Store 12 months of salaries, and print selected ones
  Static sal(1 To 12) As Single ' Reserve elements for 12 salaries
  Dim subs As Integer      ' Loop subscript
  Dim num As Integer       ' User's month number
  Dim ans As String, outForm As String
  For subs = 1 To 12

  sal(subs) = InputBox("What is salary for month" & Str(subs) &
  ➥"?")
  Next subs

  ' Request the month number
  Do
```

```
        num = InputBox("For what month (1-12) do you want a salary?")
        outForm = Format$(sal(num), "$##,##0.00")
        MsgBox "The salary for month" & Str(num) & " is " & outForm
        ans = InputBox("Do you want to see another (Y/N)?")
    Loop While (ans = "Y")
End Function
```

After the user enters the 12 salaries into the array, he or she can request any or all of them one at a time, simply by supplying the month number (the number of the subscript).

Example

The following program shows some of the math operations you can perform on arrays. The program asks for a list of temperatures and keeps asking for them until the user enters **–99** to signal that there are no more temperatures. The program then computes the average temperature by adding them and dividing by the total number.

```
Function tempAvg ()
' Prompt the user for a list of temperatures and average them
    Static temp(1 To 100) As Single ' Up to 100 temps
    Dim totalTemp As Single     ' Holds totals as user enters temps
    Dim avgTemp As Single
    Dim subs As Integer      ' Subscript

    ' Prompt user for each temperature
    For subs = 1 To 100    ' Maximum limit
        temp(subs) = InputBox("What is next temperature (-99 ends)?")
        ' If user wants to stop, decrease count by 1 and exit loop
        If (temp(subs) = -99) Then
            subs = subs - 1   ' Adjust for early exit
          Exit For
        End If
        totalTemp = totalTemp + temp(subs)     ' Add to total

    Next subs
     ' Compute average
    avgTemp = totalTemp / subs
    MsgBox "The average temperature was" & Str(avgTemp)
End Function
```

Example

In Chapter 20 you learned the Select Case statement with the VarType() function. VarType() returns a number that represents the data type of its argument. Any time your programs use lists of data, you can almost always use arrays to improve upon the code.

Here is the function as you saw it in Chapter 20:

```
Function PrntType(aVar)  ' Variant if you don't specify otherwise
  Select Case VarType(aVar)  ' VarType() returns an integer
    Case 0
      MsgBox "The argument is Empty"
    Case 1
      MsgBox "The argument is Null"
    Case 2
      MsgBox "The argument is Integer"
    Case 3
      MsgBox "The argument is Long"
    Case 4
      MsgBox "The argument is Single"
    Case 5
      MsgBox "The argument is Double"
    Case 6
      MsgBox "The argument is Currency"
    Case 7
      MsgBox "The argument is Date"
    Case 8
      MsgBox "The argument is String"
  End Select
End Function
```

Here is the same function using arrays:

```
Function PrntType(aVar)  ' Variant if you don't specify otherwise
 ' Function that prints data type names using an array
  Static typeNames(7) As String  ' Will use subscripts 0 to 8
  ' Fill the array with data type names

  typeNames(0) = "Empty"
  typeNames(1) = "Null"
  typeNames(2) = "Integer"
  typeNames(3) = "Long"
  typeNames(4) = "Single"
  typeNames(5) = "Double"
  typeNames(6) = "Currency"
```

```
  typeNames(7) = "Date"
  typeNames(8) = "String"
  ' Print the data type
  MsgBox "The argument is " & typeNames(VarType(aVar))
End Function
```

> **Caution:** Shorter code does not always mean better code. Your goal should always be writing easy-to-read code, not short, tricky code that works but is hard to maintain later. Nevertheless, many times shorter code does produce easier maintenance because you have fewer lines to understand when you have to make changes later.

This procedure first stores all the data type names in a string array. The array's subscripts match those of the data types. Therefore, the VarType() function's return value can be used as the subscript to print the appropriate data type title.

Example

In Chapter 19 you learned how tables in a database and controls on a form and report can be referenced by a subscript. That chapter introduced the concept of arrays to you without your knowing about arrays. Using the Forms and Reports objects, you can refer to all the forms or reports inside a database with a subscript number. Within an individual form or report, you can refer to controls on those forms or reports with a subscript as well, just as you do with array variables.

The following procedure stores all open forms in an array called openForms and then prints the contents of that array in the immediate window:

```
Function storeForms ()
' Function that stores all form names in an array
  Dim subs As Integer
  Static openForms(10) As String
  ' Save all open forms in the array
  For subs = 0 To Forms.Count - 1
    openForms(subs) = Forms(subs).FormName
  Next subs

  ' Print the names of the open forms
  For subs = 0 To Forms.Count - 1
    Debug.Print openForms(subs)
  Next subs
End Function
```

If you have four forms open when this procedure executes, the immediate window looks like the one shown in Figure 26.2.

Figure 26.2

After saving the four open form names.

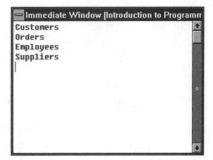

The most important things to remember about this procedure are that the open form names are stored in an array and the array's contents are printed to the immediate window.

Access provides capital budgeting functions.

Three Additional Financial Functions

In the preceding chapter you learned about several financial functions. To understand three of those functions, you must understand arrays. This section explains the Npv(), Irr(), and Mirr() financial functions. These functions are sometimes called *capital budgeting* functions. Companies must be able to budget money to purchase income-producing capital assets. These functions enable companies to determine whether a capital purchase is worth the future income that the purchase will provide.

Arrays are needed for these functions because in the real world of finance, cash flows from a capital project are rarely as even as an annuity. Instead, cash flows come randomly over a project's lifetime. Before using these functions, you have to store the estimated cash flows into arrays to simulate time period receipts from the project.

Net Present Value with *Npv()*

The *net present value* method of making capital purchase decisions is easy to understand. If you find the present value of all future income from a capital good (such as a machine that makes diskettes) and subtract from that income today's cost of the capital good, a positive result means that the machine is worth buying. A negative result means that you should not buy the machine.

In other words, suppose that a machine makes $10,000 over its lifetime in *today's* dollars. If that machine costs $9,000, then the machine will make money for you. It is vital that the future income flows be discounted back to today's dollars (finding the present value of those income flows).

Tip: Use the `Sgn()` function to test the result of `Npv()`. If `Sgn()` indicates that the net present value is negative, decline the purchase of the asset.

Here is the format of `Npv()`:

```
Npv(rate, flowArray)
```

where *rate* is the discount rate (the prevailing interest rate you can earn), and the *flowArray* represents the series of cash flows over the life of the asset.

Caution: Be sure to include your initial purchase price for the asset in the *flowArray* as a negative amount and the cash flows generated from the asset as a positive amount. The initial purchase is generally the first value in the array, unless you make a series of payments over time. The function assumes that all cash inflows are received at the end of each period. If yours do not, subtract the first cash inflow from the initial purchase in the first element.

Example

This example stores the initial purchase ($12,000) and cash flows of a capital asset into an array and prints the result of the `Npv()` function.

```
Function compNpv ()
' Function that computes net present value
  Static cashFlows(1 To 8) As Double   ' Asset's cash flows
  Dim fmt As String, ans As String
  Dim disRate As Single
  Dim netPresV As Double
  fmt = "$##,##0.00"  ' To print net present value
  disRate = .075        ' Discount rate  (7.5%)
  cashFlows(1) = -12000.51           ' Initial purchase price
  cashFlows(2) = 2422.45             ' Cash inflows come now
  cashFlows(3) = 2655.72
  cashFlows(4) = 1689.01
  cashFlows(5) = 758.99

  cashFlows(6) = 1865.36
  cashFlows(7) = 1543.03
  cashFlows(8) = 2535.72
  ' Now compute the net present value
```

```
    netPresV = Npv(disRate, cashFlows())    ' Calculates net present
    ➥value
    Select Case Sgn(netPresV)
      Case -1:
        ans = "NPV is " & Format$(netPresV, fmt) & ", don't make
        ➥purchase."
      Case 0:
        ans = "NPV is " & Format$(netPresV, fmt) & ", It's a wash."
      Case 1:
        ans = "NPV is " & Format$(netPresV, fmt) & ", make pur
        ➥chase."
    End Select
    MsgBox ans     ' Print the result
  End Function
```

Given the values shown in the procedure, you should not make the purchase.

Figure 26.3

Npv() tells you not
to purchase.

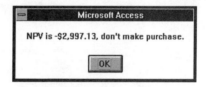

Figure 26.3 shows the message box that appears.

Example

The following procedure uses the form in Figure 26.4 to accept user's values for the
Npv() calculation. The form's name is Net Present Value, and the resulting message
box displays over the form after the values have been entered on-screen and the user
chooses the NPV button. The control for the discount rate is named DR, the control
for the initial purchase is named InitPur, and the eight cash flow fields are named
CF1 through CF8. This example assumes that an 8-period net present value is needed.
The # net to the constants 1 and 100 convert the number to a double-pension
number. This helps for internal calculations.

```
Function compNpvForm ()
' Function that computes net present value from form
  Static cashFlows(8) As Double   ' Asset's cash flows
  Dim fmt As String, ans As String
  Dim disRate As Single
  Dim netPresV As Double
  fmt = "$##,##0.00"  ' To print net present value
  disRate = forms![Net Present Value]!DR      ' Discount rate
  If (disRate > 1#) Then
    disRate = disRate / 100#      ' Adjust for decimal
```

```
End If
cashFlows(0) = -forms![Net Present Value]!InitPur      ' Note the
➥negation
cashFlows(1) = forms![Net Present Value]!CF1
cashFlows(2) = forms![Net Present Value]!CF2
cashFlows(3) = forms![Net Present Value]!CF3
cashFlows(4) = forms![Net Present Value]!CF4
cashFlows(5) = forms![Net Present Value]!CF5
cashFlows(6) = forms![Net Present Value]!CF6
cashFlows(7) = forms![Net Present Value]!CF7
cashFlows(8) = forms![Net Present Value]!CF8
' Now compute the net present value
netPresV = Npv(disRate, cashFlows())     ' Calculates net
➥present value
Select Case Sgn(netPresV)
  Case -1:
    ans = "NPV is " & Format$(netPresV, fmt) & ", don't make
    ➥purchase."
  Case 0:
    ans = "NPV is " & Format$(netPresV, fmt) & ", It's a wash."
  Case 1:
    ans = "NPV is " & Format$(netPresV, fmt) & ", make pur-
    ➥chase."
  End Select
  MsgBox ans     ' Print the result
End Function
```

Figure 26.4

Getting *Npv()* values from a form.

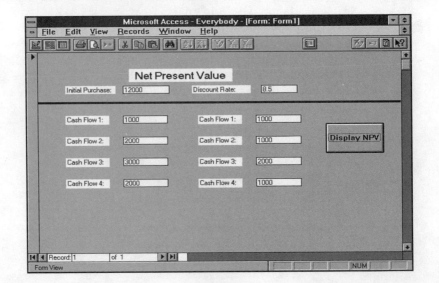

Internal Rate of Returns

Another method for determining whether a purchase is good or bad is the *internal rate of return* method. Technically, the internal rate of return is different from net present value, but both should return the same results. Simply stated, the internal rate of return is an investment's total returning interest rate, taking into effect the initial outlay for the purchase, the cash flows generated from the capital asset's purchase, and the discounting of those cash flows back to the present.

Access Basic supports two kinds of *IRR*.

There are two kinds of internal rate of return: the *regular internal* rate of return and the *modified internal* rate of return. The modified internal rate of return assumes that the interest rate at which you finance a purchase is different from the rate at which you can invest the resulting cash flows. The modified internal rate of return is more accurate.

If the project's internal rate of return rate is less than you can get elsewhere on your money, you should not make the purchase. In other words, if you can make 8 percent on your money in an investment such as a stock fund and buying a capital asset generates an internal rate of return of only 7 percent, you should not buy the asset, but you should leave your money in the stock fund.

Here are the formats for the internal rate of return functions:

```
Irr(flowArray(), guessRate)
```

and

```
Mirr(flowArray(), financeRate, investRate)
```

As with Npv(), the *flowArray()* in both functions consists of the investment and inflows generated by the asset you are considering. You must supply a best-guess interest rate with Irr() and usually .1 (10 percent) works fine. Access uses an iterative method to compute the internal rate of return, and you must supply Access with a reasonable starting value.

The *financeRate* of Mirr() is the rate at which you finance the investment you're making. The *investRate* is the rate at which you can invest the funds generated by the asset.

Example

The following example generates an internal rate of return for an asset's cash flows:

```
Function compIrr()
' Function that computes internal rate of return
   Static cashFlows(1 To 8) As Double   ' Asset's cash flows

   Dim fmt As String, ans As String
   Dim guess As Single
```

```
    Dim irrRate As Single
    fmt = "##0.0%"  ' To print IRR's result
    guess = .1      ' Initial guess
    cashFlows(1) = -10324.51        ' Initial purchase price
    cashFlows(2) = 1422.45          ' Cash inflows come now
    cashFlows(3) = 3655.72
    cashFlows(4) = 689.01
    cashFlows(5) = 1758.99
    cashFlows(6) = 3865.36
    cashFlows(7) = 5543.03
    cashFlows(8) = 3535.72
    ' Now compute the internal rate of return
    irrRate = Irr(cashFlows(), guess)
    ' Build output string with answer
    ans = "The internal rate of return is " & Format$(irrRate, fmt)
    ans = ans & ", so make purchase if yourinvestmentrate is below "
    ans = ans & "the IRR generated."
    MsgBox ans
End Function
```

Example

The following example generates a modified internal rate of return using the preceding example's cash flows and a different finance rate from the investment rate. Notice that no initial guess is needed for Mirr().

```
Function compMirr ()
' Function that computes modified internal rate of return
    Static cashFlows(1 To 8) As Double  ' Asset's cash flows
    Dim fmt As String, ans As String
    Dim finRate As Single, invRate As Single
    Dim irrRate As Single
    finRate = .08
    invRate = .05
    fmt = "##0.0%"  ' To print MIRR's result
    cashFlows(1) = -10324.51        ' Initial purchase price
    cashFlows(2) = 1422.45          ' Cash inflows come now
    cashFlows(3) = 3655.72
    cashFlows(4) = 689.01
    cashFlows(5) = 1758.99
    cashFlows(6) = 3865.36
```

```
   cashFlows(7) = 5543.03
   cashFlows(8) = 3535.72
   ' Now compute the modified internal rate of return
   irrRate = Mirr(cashFlows(), finRate, invRate)
   ' Build output string with answer
   ans = "The modified internal rate of return is "
 ans = ans & Format$(irrRate, fmt)
   ans = ans & ", so make purchase if your investment rate is
   ➡below "
   ans = ans & "the MIRR generated."
   MsgBox ans
End Function
```

Summary

This chapter covered a lot of ground. You learned about arrays, which are a more powerful way to store lists of data than using individual variable names. By stepping through arrays with subscripts, your procedures can quickly scan, print, and calculate with a list of values.

Mastering arrays gave you the knowledge to understand three additional financial functions, Npv(), Irr(), and Mirr(). These financial functions are extremely useful for making purchase decisions on capital asset goods (such as money-making machines) because they assume that cash flows over the life of the asset are not uniform (they rarely are uniform in the real world).

After you master this chapter, Chapter 27, "Multidimensional Arrays," is easy. It shows how you can keep track of arrays in a different format from the format you saw here. Not all lists of data lend themselves to multidimensional arrays, but you should be prepared for them when you do need them.

Review Questions

Answers to review questions are in Appendix B.

1. TRUE or FALSE: Arrays hold more than one variable with the same name.

2. How do Access Basic programs tell one array element (value) from another if the elements have identical names?

3. Can array elements within the same array be different types?

4. How many array elements are reserved in the following dimension statement? (Assume an `Option Base` of 0.)

```
Dim ara(78)
```

5. What is the preferred way—`Option Base` or by using the `To` keyword—to specify the beginning subscript in an array?

6. What is the difference between net present value and internal rate of return?

7. How many elements are reserved in the following `Static` statement?

```
Static staff(-18 To 4)
```

8. What is the difference between internal rate of return and modified internal rate of return?

Review Exercises

1. Write a procedure to store six of your friends' names in a single string array. Use `InputBox()` to initialize the arrays with the names. Print the names on-screen.

2. Write a simple database program to track the names of a radio station's top ten hits. After you store the array, print the songs in reverse order (to get the top ten countdown) in the immediate window.

3. Change the three financial function examples in this chapter to ask the user (using `InputBox()`) for each of the yearly cash flows and store them into the arrays as the user enters them instead of assigning values to the arrays. Also, after the financial decision is made (to purchase or not), print the total and average of the cash flows.

4. The second `Npv()` example used a form to get user input for eight time periods. Change the procedure so that it works for eight *or fewer* fields. Check each field for a value before assigning it to the `Npv()` array. (*Hint:* Zero values in the `Npv()` array do not affect the calculation.)

5. Change the second Exercise to print the hit countdown list in reverse order on a form. First, create a form with ten fields wide enough to hold song titles and then fill the form's controls with the song titles when the procedure begins.

CHAPTER 27

Multidimensional Arrays

Some data fits in lists like those you saw in Chapter 26; other data is better suited to a table of data. This chapter expands on arrays. The preceding chapter introduced *single-dimensioned* arrays, which are arrays that have only one subscript. Single-dimensioned arrays represent a list of values.

This chapter explains how to use arrays of more than one dimension, called *multidimensional arrays*. Multidimensional arrays, sometimes called *tables* or *matrices,* have rows and columns.

This chapter introduces the following topics:

♦ What multidimensional arrays are

♦ Putting data into multidimensional arrays

♦ Using nested `For-Next` loops to process multidimensional arrays

If you understand single-dimensional arrays, you should have no trouble understanding arrays with more than one dimension.

What Multidimensional Arrays Are

Multidimensional arrays have more than one subscript.

A *multidimensional array* is an array with more than one subscript. A single-dimensional array is a list of values, whereas a multidimensional array simulates a table of values or even multiple tables of values. The most commonly used table is a two-dimensional table (an array with two subscripts).

Suppose that a softball team wants to keep track of its players' hits. The team played 8 games, and there are 10 players on the team. Table 27.1 shows the team's hit record.

Table 27.1. A softball team's hit record.

Player Name	Game1	Game2	Game3	Game4	Game5	Game6	Game7	Game8
Name	1	2	3	4	5	6	7	8
Adams	2	1	0	0	2	3	3	1
Berryhill	1	0	3	2	5	1	2	2
Edwards	0	3	6	4	6	4	5	3
Grady	1	3	2	0	1	5	2	1
Howard	3	1	1	1	2	0	1	0
Powers	2	2	3	1	0	2	1	3
Smith	1	1	2	1	3	4	1	0
Townsend	0	0	0	0	0	0	1	0
Ulmer	2	2	1	1	2	1	1	2
Williams	2	3	1	0	1	2	1	1

Do you see that the softball table is a two-dimensional table? It has rows (one of the dimensions) and columns (the second dimension). Therefore, you call it a two-dimensional table with 10 rows and 8 columns. (Generally, the number of rows is specified first.)

Each row has a player's name, and each column has a game number associated with it, but these headings are not part of the data. The data consists only of 80 values (10 rows times 8 columns equals 80 data values). The data in a table, like the data in an array, always is the same type of data (in this case, every value is an integer). If the table contains names, it is a string table, and so on.

> **Note:** Access Basic supports multidimensional arrays of the `Variant` data type, so you can, in effect, declare a `Variant` array that holds more than one type of value.

Arrays can have many dimensions.

The number of dimensions (in this case two) corresponds to the dimensions in the physical world. The first dimension represents a line. The single-dimensional array is a line, or list, of values. Two dimensions represent both length and width. You write on a piece of paper in two dimensions; two dimensions represent a flat surface. Three dimensions represent width, length, and depth. You may have seen three-dimensional movies. Not only do the images have width and height, but they also (appear to) have depth.

It is difficult to visualize more than three dimensions. You can, however, think of each dimension after three as another occurrence. In other words, you can store a list of one player's season hit record in an array. The team's hit record (as shown in Table 27.1) is two-dimensional. Their league, made up of several teams' hit records, represents a three-dimensional table. Each team (the depth of the table) has rows and columns of hit data. If there is more than one league, you can consider leagues another dimension.

Access Basic gives you the capability to work with up to 60 dimensions, although real-world data rarely requires more than two or three dimensions.

Dimensioning Multidimensional Arrays

As you do with single-dimension arrays, use the Dim, Global, or Static statements to reserve storage for multidimensional arrays. Rather than put one value in the parentheses, you put a value for each dimension in the table. The basic formats for reserving multidimensional arrays are as follows:

```
Global taName (subs) [As type] [, taName (subs) [As type]]...

Dim taName (subs) [As type] [, taName (subs) [As type]]...

Static taName (subs) [As type] [, taName (subs) [As type]]...
```

The table's *subs* values can take on this general format:

```
[low To] highRow [,[low To] highColumn] [,[low To] highDepth]
[,...]
```

As with single-dimensions, actually reserving storage for tables is easier than the formats lead you to believe. To declare the team data from Table 27.1, for example, you can use the following Static statement:

```
Static Teams(1 To 10, 1 To 8) As Integer
```

This statement reserves a two-dimensional table in memory with 80 elements. Each element's subscript looks like the ones shown in Figure 27.1.

Figure 27.1

Subscripts for the softball team table.

Teams(1,1)	Teams(1,2)	Teams(1,3)	....	Teams(1,7)	Teams(1,8)
Teams(2,1)	Teams(2,2)	Teams(2,3)	....	Teams(2,7)	Teams(2,8)
Teams(3,1)	Teams(3,2)	Teams(3,3)	....	Teams(3,7)	Teams(3,8)
⋮	⋮	⋮		⋮	⋮
Teams(9,1)	Teams(9,2)	Teams(9,3)	....	Teams(9,7)	Teams(9,8)
Teams(10,1)	Teams(10,2)	Teams(10,3)	....	Teams(10,7)	Teams(10,8)

Note: If you leave off the To keyword option, the starting subscript is assumed to be 0 unless an Option Base 1 statement appears elsewhere.

Example

If you have an entire league of 15 teams to track, you add yet another subscript, as follows:

```
Static Teams(1 To 15, 1 To 10, 1 To 8) As Integer
```

where the first subscript indicates the league, the second subscript indicates the number of players in each team, and the third subscript indicates the number of games each player plays.

Example

The following statement reserves enough memory elements for a television station's shows for one week:

```
Dim shows(1 To 7, 1 To 48) As String
```

This statement reserves 7 days (the rows) of 30-minute shows (because there are 24 hours in a day, this table holds up to 48 30-minute shows).

Every element in a table is always the same type. In this case, each element is a string variable. You can initialize some of the elements with the following assignment statements, for example:

```
shows(3, 12) = "As the Hospital Turns"
shows(1, 5) = "Guessing Game Show"
shows(7, 20) = "Rasberry Iced Tea Infomercial"
```

Example

Reserving space for several multidimensional arrays quickly consumes memory space. The following statements reserve a lot of space:

```
Global ara1(10, 20) As Single
Global ara2(4, 5, 5) As Double
Global ara3(6, 10, 20, 30) As Integer
```

ara1 consumes 200 single-precision memory locations, ara2 consumes 100 double-precision memory locations, and ara3 consumes 36,000 memory locations. As you can see, the number of elements adds up quickly. Be careful that you don't reserve so many array elements that you run out of memory in which to store them.

By reading table data into multidimensional arrays and working with the data in the arrays rather than in database tables, you can speed your program's running times. Anything you can do in memory is faster than doing the same thing reading and writing to disk every time you access values. However, you have much more disk space than memory space. When you're working with large files, you have to forsake the efficiency of memory for the disk capacity.

Tables and *For-Next* Loops

As you see in some of the following examples, nested For-Next loops are good candidates for looping through every element of a multidimensional table. For example, the section of code

```
For row = 1 To 2
  For col = 1 To 3
    Debug.Print row, col
  Next col
Next row
```

produces the following output in the immediate window:

```
1          1
1          2
1          3
2          1
2          2
2          3
```

If you were to print the subscripts, in row order, for a two-row by three-column table dimensioned with the following Dim statement, you would see the subscript numbers shown by this program's nested loops.

```
Dim table(1 To 2, 1 To 3)
```

Notice that there are as many For-Next statements as there are subscripts in the Dim statement (two). The outside loop represents the first subscript (the rows), and the inside loop represents the second subscript (the columns).

You can use InputBox() statements to fill tables, although you rarely fill tables this way. Most multidimensional array data comes from forms, or more often, from tables on the disk. Regardless of what method actually stores values in multidimensional arrays, nested For-Next loops are excellent control statements to step through the subscripts. The following examples further illustrate tables and also show how nested For-Next loops work with multidimensional arrays.

Example

A computer company sells two sizes of diskettes: 3 1/2-inch and 5 1/4-inch. Each diskette comes in one of four capacities: single-sided low-density, double-sided low-density, single-sided high-density, and double-sided high-density. The diskette inventory is well suited for a two-dimensional table. The company determined that the diskettes have the following retail prices:

	Single-Sided Low-Density	Double-Sided Low-Density	Single-Sided High-Density	Double-Sided High-Density
3 1/2"	$2.30	$2.75	$3.20	$3.50
5 1/4"	$1.75	$2.10	$2.60	$2.95

The following procedure stores the price of each diskette in a table and prints the values to the immediate window using a nested For-Next loop:

```
Function disks ()
' Assigns and prints diskette prices
    Static disks(1 To 2, 1 To 4) As Single
    Dim row As Integer, col As Integer
    ' Assign each element the price
    disks(1, 1) = 2.3      ' Row 1, Column 1
    disks(1, 2) = 2.75     ' Row 1, Column 2
    disks(1, 3) = 3.2      ' Row 1, Column 3
    disks(1, 4) = 3.5      ' Row 1, Column 4
    disks(2, 1) = 1.75     ' Row 2, Column 1
    disks(2, 2) = 2.1      ' Row 2, Column 2
    disks(2, 3) = 2.6      ' Row 2, Column 3
    disks(2, 4) = 2.95     ' Row 2, Column 4
    ' Print the prices in table format
```

```
Debug.Print Tab(9); "Single-sided,  Double-sided, ";
Debug.Print "Single-sided,  Double-sided"
Debug.Print Tab(9); "Low-density    Low-density   ";
Debug.Print "High-density   High-density"
For row = 1 To 2
  If (row = 1) Then
      Debug.Print "3-1/2 inch  ";
  Else
      Debug.Print "5-1/4 inch  ";
  End If
  For col = 1 To 4
    Debug.Print Format$(disks(row, col), " #.00" & Space$(10));
Next col
    Debug.Print    ' Moves the cursor to the next line
  Next row
End Function
```

This procedure produces the output shown in Figure 27.2's immediate window after the window is resized to show the entire table.

Figure 27.2

Printing the table of diskette prices.

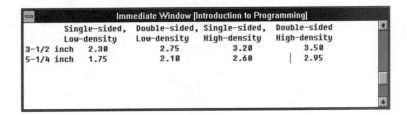

Example

The following procedure is a comprehensive program that reads the softball team hits table (see Table 27.1). Rather than assigning the values to the hits table variables, the program pulls the values from a form named Team Form. After the user clicks the Compute Stats button, the procedure runs to display the following statistics about the team:

♦ The name of the player with the most hits

♦ The name of the player with the fewest hits

♦ The game with the most hits

♦ The game with the fewest hits

This example shows the usefulness of such tables. Rather than simply printing table data, the program actually processes the table's raw data into meaningful information.

Figure 27.3 shows the `Team Form` form used to gather the hit values. Notice that the user must enter 80 values, which is a lot. In the next part of the book, you learn how to read values into tables directly from the disk rather than having the user enter them all every time the procedure runs. For now, concentrate on how the table manipulation works.

Note: The player names cannot be stored in the same table as the hit data because the names are string data and the hits are stored as integers. Therefore, a separate single-dimensioned array holds the player names. When the numbers of the rows with the most and fewest hits are determined, those two players' names are printed from the player name array using the row number.

Figure 27.3

Form for entering the 80 hit statistics.

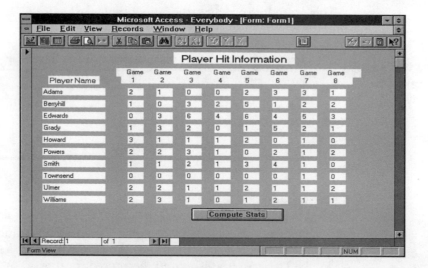

Player Hit Information

Player Name	Game 1	Game 2	Game 3	Game 4	Game 5	Game 6	Game 7	Game 8
Adams	2	1	0	0	2	3	3	1
Berryhill	1	0	3	2	5	1	2	2
Edwards	0	3	6	4	6	4	5	3
Grady	1	3	2	0	1	5	2	1
Howard	3	1	1	1	2	0	1	0
Powers	2	2	3	1	0	2	1	2
Smith	1	1	2	1	3	4	1	0
Townsend	0	0	0	0	0	0	1	0
Ulmer	2	2	1	1	2	1	1	2
Williams	2	3	1	0	1	2	1	1

Compute Stats

```
Function compStats ()
' Display hit statistics based on a form for softball team data
    Dim TF As Form
    Set TF = Forms![Team Form]      ' Assign the form variable
    Static names(1 To 10) As String            ' Player name table
    Static hits(1 To 10, 1 To 8) As Integer  ' The hit table
    Dim subsc As Integer                        ' Subscript
    Dim player As Integer, row As Integer, col As Integer
```

```
Dim highest As Integer, lowest As Integer
  Dim total As Integer       ' For intermediate calculations
  Dim highRow As Integer, lowRow As Integer
  Dim gameHigh As Integer, gameLow As Integer
  highest = 0    ' Ensure that first player's hits are more than highest
  lowest = 999  ' and less than lowest to start the ball rolling
  player = 1    ' To be used as subscripts in tables
  row = 1
  col = 1

  ' The following code just loops through the entire form and
  ' assigns all fields that begin with LN to the names() array. (All
  ' fields that begin with LN hold last names, i.e., LName1 and LName2.)
  ' The code also fills the 2-dimensional table of hits() by adjusting
  ' the row and column when needed.
  For subsc = 0 To TF.Count - 1     ' Loop through all controls
    If Left$(TF(subsc).controlname, 2) = "LN" Then
      names(player) = TF(subsc)    ' Assign to name array
  player = player + 1

    ElseIf Left$(TF(subsc).controlname, 3) = "Hit" Then
      hits(row, col) = TF(subsc)
      If row = 10 Then
        row = 1
      Else
        row = row + 1
      End If
      If col = 8 Then
        col = 1
      Else
        col = col + 1
      End If
    End If
  Next subsc      ' All tables are now filled from form

' Now compute and print statistics
  For row = 1 To 10

    total = 0   ' Initialize before each player's hit total begins
    For col = 1 To 8
      total = total + hits(row, col)
    Next col
    If (total > highest) Then
      highRow = row
      highest = total
```

```
      End If
    If (total < lowest) Then
      lowRow = row
      lowest = total
    End If
  Next row
  ' Print some results
  MsgBox names(highRow) & " had high number of hits at " &    Str$(highest)
  MsgBox names(lowRow) & " had lowest number of hits at " &    Str$(lowest)

  highest = 0  ' Ensure first game's hits are more than highest
  lowest = 999 ' and less than lowest to start things

For col = 1 To 8   ' This time, step through columns first
                   ' to add game totals
    total = 0  ' Initialize before each game's hit totals begin
    For row = 1 To 10
      total = total + hits(row, col)
    Next row
    If (total > highest) Then
      highGame = col
      highest = total
    End If
    If (total < lowest) Then
      lowGame = col
      lowest = total
    End If
  Next col
  ' Print some results
  MsgBox "Game" & Str$(highGame) & " had highest hits at" &    2Str$(highest)
  MsgBox "Game" & Str$(lowGame) & " had lowest hits at" & Str$(lowest)
End Function
```

Tip: The individual routines that compute statistics might be better planned as sub procedures rather than including one long function procedure. For example, you can put the code that finds the highest and lowest game hits in a sub procedure named findGameHits and call the procedure from the previous function by name. Any data needed by the sub procedure such as hits(), total, highest, lowest, row, and col must be passed when the function is called. Once the appropriate messages are printed, the sub procedure can return to the function procedure so that it can continue. To receive arrays, simply put the parentheses and the optional As *dataType* clause after their name in the receiving procedure.

Summary

After reading this chapter, you know how to create, initialize, and process multi-dimensional arrays. Although not all data fits in the compact format of tables, much does. Using nested For-Next loops makes stepping through a multidimensional array straightforward.

Now you're ready to move into the database interaction commands taught in the next chapter. Because you're well-grounded in Access Basic programming skills at this point, the next section explains how you can access database files from within your Access Basic programs so you can start writing procedures that manipulate the data in your tables.

Review Questions

Answers to review questions are in Appendix B.

1. Given the statement

```
Static names(5, 10) As String
```

which subscript (first or second) represents rows and which represents columns?

2. How many elements are reserved with the following statements?

```
Option Base 1
Dim ara(4, 7)
```

3. What is another name for multidimensional array?

4. How many elements are reserved with the following:

```
Static ara(4 To 5, 9 To 22)
```

5. What control statements are best for "stepping" through multidimensional arrays?

6. Given the table of integers called ara

4	1	3	5	9
10	2	12	1	6
25	43	2	91	8

what values do the following elements contain? (Assume no Option Base statement appears in the program.)

A. `ara(1, 1)`

B. `ara(1, 2)`

C. `ara(2, 3)`

7. Given the code

```
Static grades(1 To 3, 1 To 5)
For row = 1 To 3
  For col = 1 To 5
    grades(row, col) = row + col
  Next col
Next row
```

what values do the following elements contain?

A. `grades(2, 3)`

B. `grades(3, 5)`

C. `grades(1, 1)`

Review Exercises

1. Write a `Static` statement that dimensions enough string space for the names in a women's basketball league of 5 teams, 25 players, and 6 games per player.

2. Write a procedure that reserves storage for three years of sales data for five salespeople. Use assignment statements to fill the matrix with data and print the table one value per line in the immediate execution window. (*Hint:* Use columns for the years and rows for the salespeople.)

3. Modify the softball team hits example shown at the end of this chapter so that it computes and prints the average number of hits per game and the average number of hits per player.

Part VII

Handling Table I/O

CHAPTER 28

Looking into Object Variables

Access is extremely comprehensive. You can learn Access on many different levels. A beginning programming book on a regular programming language is challenging to organize. The problem with writing a book for programming in a system such as Microsoft Access is that I have to give so much time to the language that little time is left to integrate the language into the database system.

This last part of the book brings more of the database into the presence of your Access Basic programs. Bringing Access Basic programs into your database is perhaps the most important reason you wanted to learn Access Basic. Now that you have the tools of Access Basic behind you, this section of the book can shed some light on how to access your tables more clearly from within Access Basic.

This chapter introduces the following topics:

♦ Using object variables to interact with tables

♦ Declaring and assigning `Database` variables

♦ Using these recordset object variables: `Table`, `Dynaset`, and `Snapshot`

You'll soon be storing and retrieving data to and from tables as easily as you store and retrieve data using variables. This part of the book is devoted to methods and properties of the various database object variables so that you can work with table data.

Object Variables

Much of the information in this chapter refers to material first introduced in Chapter 10, "Variables and Database Objects." In Chapter 10 you learned how to declare variables of virtually any data type (such as controls, tables, and so on). You learned enough at that point to work your way through some examples that included object variables without your knowing much about them.

> **Note:** In a nutshell, an object variable is much like any other kind of variable. Object variables have names, and you can store or retrieve data with them. However, unlike `Integer`, `Single`, and the other types of regular variables, object variables represent database-like things such as databases, tables, queries, and dynasets.

> **Caution:** Object variables don't hold data in the same sense as regular variables (such as `Integer` and `Double`). Object variables often are associated with their database counterparts so that when you work with an object variable, you really are working with the database table, query, or whatever the object variable represents. Object variables are Access Basic's way of interacting with your data in the database.

Starting with Version 2.0 of Microsoft Access, you can manage *collection objects*. A collection object is a set of variables of a specific object; for example, there are forms collections that contain a set of all open forms and database collections that contain a list of all open databases. Although newcomers to Access Basic won't work with collections very often, you'll see throughout this chapter how to reference object collections.

One of the most important types of collections is called the *workspace collection*. A workspace collection is a collection of databases (which in turn can contain other objects such as recordsets), users, and groups (the last two are used in multi-user networked environments). Microsoft added the workspace collection to Access 2 to enable other programs with the *Jet Database Engine* technology to access and manipulate Access databases. The Jet Database Engine is that part of the Microsoft Access database system accessible from outside programs such as Visual Basic 3.0.

You must use an array-like notation to access elements of a collection. `Databases(0)`, for example, refers to the first opened database in the program and subsequently opened databases would be `Databases(1)`, `Databases(2)`, and so on. Using the array notation enables you to loop through collections, such as all the open forms or databases.

Database Variables

With the Database keyword, you can specify when you need a Database variable. The Dim, Static, and Global keywords declare database object variables, just as they do other kinds of variables.

Example

The following statements declare Database variables:

```
Global myDB As Database    ' Only in declarations section
Dim yourDB As Database
Static ourDB As Database
```

Nothing is unusual about the variable declarations. They work just like other variable declarations, except that they create Database variables rather than variables of the other data types, such as Integer.

Associating Database Variables

Database object variables associate to databases.

Obviously, before you can work with a table, you must have a database. Database variables must be associated (with Set) to actual databases before you can work with them.

You will associate the currently-opened database or you will need to open databases so that you can associate those newly opened databases with an object variable. As mentioned earlier, the currently opened database is known as the Databases(0) collection (the first element in the collection).

Your Workspace object contains several methods and one you'll use most often with databases is the OpenDatabase() method. Here is the format of the OpenDatabase().

```
Set Database = Workspace().OpenDatabase(databaseFile, [, exclu-
sive] [, read-only] [, source] )
```

The *Database* variable must be a Database variable you have defined. The *databaseFile* is any valid DOS file with optional disk drive and path. exclusive is a True or False (you also can use -1 and 0) value that specifies networked environment arguments. If you want access to the database and want nobody else to have any access while you have it open, pass True for the second argument (for networked environments only). If you want your access to be read-only so that you don't inadvertently change important data, pass True as the third argument as well. The *source* usually is one of these strings:

♦ dBASE III; or dBASE IV; for a Borland dBASE file

♦ Paradox 3.*x*; for a Borland Paradox file

♦ BTrieve; for a BTrieve file

♦ FoxPro 2.0 or FoxPro 3.0 for a Microsoft FoxPro database

If you omit a *source* string, Access assumes that you want to open an OBDC-compliant database file (described in Appendix D). Unless you want to open one of the aforementioned vendor's specific database files, omit the *source* string to open an Access or other OBDC-compliant database.

Example

The following code opens three database files and associates them with appropriate Database variables. Finally, the current database (the one that contains the module currently running) is assigned to a fourth Database variable named thisDB.

```
Dim payrDB As Database
Dim acctDB As Database
Dim mktgDB As Database
Dim thisDB As Database
' Associate databases to these variables
Set payrDB = Workspace.OpenDatabase("C:\PAYROLL.MDB")
Set acctDB = Workspace.OpenDatabase("D:\ACOUNTNG.MDB")
Set mktgDB = Workspace.OpenDatabase("C:\MARKETNG.MDB")
Set thisDB = Databases(0)    ' Current database
```

> **Tip:** As you can do with any DOS filenames, you can type the filenames in uppercase or lowercase letters in the OpenDatabase() method. You also can use string variables with filenames.

Example

You often will see the keyword DBEngine prefixed in front of Workspaces collection references. In the sample ORDERS database, for example, there is a module named Reattach NWIND with the following line inside the AreTablesAttached() function:

```
Set MYDB = DBEngine.Workspaces(0).Databases(0)
```

The MYDB variable (defined as a Database variable) is assigned to the user's currently opened database. If the Workspaces() collection referenced a different subscript such as 1 or 2, the associated database would be the first opened database in that particular workspace.

Example

The following function optionally is passed a database name. If the calling routine passes a database name, that database is opened; otherwise, the first database in the current workspace is associated to the db variable.

```
Function openIt(dbName As Variant)
Dim db As Database

If dbName = "" Then
   Set db = DBEngine.Workspaces(0).Databases(0)
Else
   Set db = Workspace.OpenDatabase(dbName)

End If

' Rest of function would follow that works with the database
```

The dbName is an optional argument to this function. If the calling procedure passes a value to dbName, that value determines which database is opened. However, if no value is passed in dbName, the current database is opened.

Example

In the following code, a network is being used. The first database associated to a Database variable is located on the server named \\CHILD\BOYS, and the second is on the local drive C:. The first file can be used only by the application (until code later closes the database to release the database to other users), and the second file is read-only.

```
Set boysDB = Workspace.OpenDatabase("\\CHILD\BOYS\BLUE.MDB", True)
Set girlsDB = Workspace.OpenDatabase("PINK.MDB", False, True)
```

Note: In the second Set statement, other people on the network can use the database because of the False second argument.

When you open a database with Workspace method, Access adds the newly opened database to your current database collection.

Recordset Variables

A recordset is a collection of records from a table (even attached ones, unlike table recordsets), a query, or another dynaset recordset. You can filter and sort dynaset recordset data. If the underlying table data is changed (not added to or deleted from but changed from one value to another), the dynaset recordset changes too. If, however, another user or action deletes records from the underlying table, the dynaset recordset contains Null values for those deleted records. If another user or action adds records to the underlying table, you have to re-create the dynaset recordset again to use those new records.

Recordsets
manipulate
database data.

A *recordset* literally defines a set of zero or more records. A Recordset enables you to manipulate database data. Following are the three kinds of recordset data collections:

◆ Tables

◆ Dynasets

◆ Snapshots

A table recordset type is associated with a table in an open database. A table recordset variable can be reordered, and the underlying table is reordered as well. You cannot filter or sort a `Table` variable, however. Table recordset variables are extremely dynamic, and changes that are made to the underlying table by other users or actions are immediately reflected in the table recordset variable.

A *snapshot recordset* is like a frozen picture in time of a table or query. If the underlying table changes in any way, *no* change is made to the snapshot recordset's collection of records.

As is done throughout the Access reference manuals, this chapter often refers to specific recordsets (table recordsets, dynaset recordsets, and snapshot recordsets) as *tables*, *dynasets*, and *snapshots* for ease of reading.

> **Caution:** Changing the record sets of tables and dynaset variables can change the underlying table data. Changing a snapshot recordset variable, however, does not change the underlying table in any way.

Two more tables are critical for understanding recordset variables. Table 28.1 lists the methods for `dynaset`, `table`, and snapshot recordset variables. Table 28.2 lists recordset properties that you learn about as well. (The D/S/T column indicates whether the method applies to a `dynaset`, `snapshot`, or `table recordset`.)

> **Note:** This book does not cover *all* the methods and properties listed in the tables, but the ones important for a fundamental understanding of database manipulation with Access Basic are explained in these chapters.

Table 28.1. Recordset methods.

Method Name	D/S/T	Description
AddNew	D,T	Prepares a new record so that it can be inserted.
Clone	D,S,T	Creates duplicate recordset objects.

Method Name	D/S/T	Description
Close	D,S,T	Closes an object.
Delete	D,T	Deletes the current record in a table or dynaset.
Edit	D,T	Copies the current record into a buffer area for editing.
FillCache	D,S,T	Fills all or part of an ODBC recordset.
FindFirst	D,T	Makes current the first record that satisfies a search criteria.
FindLast	D,T	Makes current the last record that satisfies a search criteria.
FindNext	D,T	Makes current the next record that satisfies a search criteria.
FindPrevious	D,T	Makes current the previous record that satisfies a search criteria.
Move	D,S,T	Updates the position of the recordset's current record.
MoveFirst	D,S,T	Makes current the first record in a recordset.
MoveLast	D,S,T	Makes current the last record in a recordset.
MoveNext	D,S,T	Makes current the next record in a recordset.
MovePrevious	D,S,T	Makes current the previous record in a recordset.
OpenRecordset	D,S,T	Creates a new recordset and adds the recordset to your Recordsets collection.
Requery	D,S	Re-executes the recordset query.
Seek	T	Makes current a record in an indexed table that satisfies a search criteria for the current index.
Update	D,T	Saves the contents of the editing buffer to a table or dynaset.

Table 28.2. Recordset Properties.

Property Name	D/S/T	Description
BOF	D,S,T	Contains True (-1) if the current record is at the beginning of the recordset.
Bookmark	D,S,T	Sets a bookmark that marks a recordset's location so that you can return to it later.
Bookmarkable	D,S,T	Contains True (-1) if recordset supports the use of Bookmarks.
CacheSize	D,S,T	Number of records in the recordset.
CacheStart	D,S,T	Bookmark of the first record to be cached.
DateCreated	T	Contains the date and time when a table was created.
EOF	D,S,T	Contains True (-1) if the current record is at the end of the recordset.
Filter	D,S	Sets a filter when you create a dynaset or snapshot.
Index	T	Sets the current index that Access uses to order records in a table and in recordsets created from that table.
LastModified	D,T	The bookmark of the most recently added or changed record.
LastUpdated	T	Contains the date and time a table was last changed.
LockEdits	D,T	Locks records during editing sessions (used in network environments).
Name	D,S,T	The user-defined name for the recordset object.
NoMatch	D,S,T	Indicates the success (with -1 or 0 for True and False) of a Find or Seek method.
PercentPosition	D,S,T	Repositions the current record based on a percentage of the recordset records.

Property Name	D/S/T	Description
RecordCount	D,S,T	Contains the number of records in a recordset.
Restartable	D,S	Describes whether or not the recordset is restartable. (Always False for tables.)
Sort	D,S	Sets the order of records in a dynaset or snapshot.
Transactions	D,T	Contains True (-1) if a series of changes to a table or dynaset can be reversed.
Type	D,S,T	Determines the type of recordset.
Updatable	D,T	Contains True (-1) if the table or dynaset can be changed. (Always false for snapshots.)
ValidationText	T	Specifies the expression that must evaluate to True (-1) if the Update method is completed.
ValidationRule	T	Same as ValidationText.

Creating Recordset Variables

The OpenRecordset method is perhaps the most important method you can use for recordsets. The OpenRecordset method creates a new recordset variable that represents either a table, dynaset, or snapshot. Here is the format of the OpenRecordset method:

```
Set rcVariable = database.OpenRecordset(source, type)
```

The *database* argument is a Database variable you've already defined and associated to a database. The *source* is a table name. The *type* can be one of the following three possible defined constants:

DB_OPEN_TABLE to open a table recordset.

DB_OPEN_DYNASET to open a dynaset recordset.

DB_OPEN_SNAPSHOT to open a snapshot recordset.

Each of the following three sections shows you how to create each kind of recordset.

Creating Table Recordset Variables

With DB_OPEN_TABLE option, you can create table recordset variables within your Access Basic programs. Before you associate a table recordset variable to a table, you must declare and associate a Database variable to a database.

Example

The following code first declares a Database variable and then defines a table recordset variable. The user is asked for the table to work with, and that table name is used to associate the table to the table recordset.

```
Dim userDB As Database
Dim userTB As Recordset
Dim userAns As String
Set userDB = DBEngine.Workspaces(0).Databases(0)    ' Associate to
                                                    ' the current
database
' Ask the user for the table to open
userAns = InputBox("Which table do you want to work with?")
' Use the OpenTable method to associate the actual table
Set userTB = userDB.OpenRecordSet(userAns, DB_OPEN_TABLE)
```

Creating Dynaset Recordset Variables

Dynaset recordset variables are as easy to declare and use as table recordset variables. The DB_OPEN_DYNASET option runs an existing select query to store the result of the query in a dynaset recordset variable. You can create a dynaset recordset variable from a table, a select query, another Dynaset variable, a snapshot, or by using the Clone method.

> **Tip:** Use a form's Records property if you want to create a dynaset from a form; you don't have to use the OpenRecordSet method.

You can omit the DB_OPEN_DYNASET option, Access Basic still will know that you want to create a dynaset recordset (the default option).

Example

The following code simply declares a Database variable and a dynaset recordset variable, opens a database, and creates a dynaset recordset from a table within the database.

```
Dim userDB As Database
Dim userDS As RecordSet
' Open the database or you cannot get the dynaset from it
Set userDB = OpenDatabase("RENTALS.MDB")
' Create the dynaset from the table
' Notice the DB_OPEN_DYNASET is not needed
Set userDS = userDB.OpenRecordSet("TENANTS")
```

In this example, TENANTS is a table from the RENTALS.MDB database. In place of TENANTS, you can store the name of a select query such as Find Out-of-Town Tenants (assuming that the query already is in place), and the resulting dynaset recordset variable contains that query's data.

Creating Snapshot Recordset Variables

Snapshots are dynasets frozen in time.

You create snapshot recordset variables by using the DB_OPEN_SNAPSHOT option. You must remember that a snapshot is a still-frame dynaset. Therefore, if the data changes in any way, the snapshot recordset variable's contents never change (unless you reassign the variable a new snapshot). The OpenRecordSet method creates the actual snapshot and associates the variable to it.

> **Tip:** At first, snapshot recordset variables seem too limiting, but many times you may want to save the *current* image of a dynaset (such as a set of records as they appear before a large update).

Example

The following example creates and associates a snapshot recordset variable:

```
Dim userDB As Database
Dim userDS As RecordSet
Dim userSS As RecordSet
Set userDB = DBEngine.Workspaces(0).Database(0)
' Create a dynaset from a query
Set userDS = userDB. OpenRecordset("Under 16 Customers",
DB_OPEN_DYNASET)
' Create a snapshot from that dynaset
' (Notice that no name is given for the dynaset)
Set userSS = userDS. OpenRecordset(DB_OPEN_SNAPSHOT)
```

Notice that no argument is used in this OpenRecordset method because userDS is not a database but a dynaset recordset object.

Cleaning Up When You're Done

Every programming language includes functions for the programmer to close a file when that file is no longer needed in the program. It always is recommended that you explicitly close files when finished with them. Access Basic is no exception.

Use the `Close` method when you're done with recordset variables. Even though the `Close` eventually happens automatically, it may be awhile and valuable resources are being used while the recordsets are still open.

> **Caution:** Closing your recordset variables in a networked environment is most critical because other users might be scrambling for resources that you still have open but no longer need.

If you close a database recordset variable associated with the current database, the database is not really closed. Also, if you close a dynaset recordset variable associated with a form, the dynaset is not closed because the form is still available. However, closing all other recordset data releases the recordset from your program and frees resources for other use.

Example

The following statement closes a table recordset variable:

```
dsTable.Close
```

Summary

After reading this chapter, you will be more familiar with the declaration and association of object variables within Access Basic. This chapter sets the groundwork for this part of the book that explores the use of Access Basic with your table data.

The recordset variables are important because when using them, Access Basic can manipulate, sort, input, and output an entire set of data. A recordset contains either table, dynaset, or snapshot data. A database must be open before you can associate recordset variables to actual data within the database.

The next chapter describes what to do once you have recordset variables and want to use Access Basic to process the data in them.

> **Note:** Microsoft completely rewrote the recordset methods described in this chapter. Older versions of Access (versions 1.0 and 1.1) supported `Table`, `Dynaset`, and `Snapshot` variables that were distinct and required their own specific methods.

Review Questions

Answers to review questions are in Appendix B.

1. What is a recordset?

2. TRUE or FALSE: The following statement declares a `Database` variable and associates a database to it.

   ```
   Dim db As Database
   ```

3. From which elements (for example, a table) can you create dynaset and snapshot recordset variables?

4. What collection element is used to associate a `Database` variable to the currently open database?

5. Why is it important to close a `Database` or recordset variable when you are finished with it?

6. TRUE or FALSE: The number of records in a dynaset recordset variable can change.

7. TRUE or FALSE: The number of records in a snapshot recordset variable can change.

Review Exercises

1. Write a function that accepts three database names as arguments. Open all three databases and associate them to Database variables. Assume that all three arguments contain data.

2. Change Exercise 1 to test the arguments. At most, only one of the arguments can be a zero-length string (meaning no database name is passed). For that empty argument, open the current database. If more than one empty argument is passed to the function, display an error message and exit the function.

3. Write the first few lines of a function that creates a `Database` variable, a table recordset variable, a dynaset recordset variable, and a snapshot recordset variable from four arguments passed to the function. Only the name of the database can be a zero-length string, and if it is, open the current database. Also write appropriate `Close` methods for each of the variables for the end of the function. (You learn more about the body of such functions in the next chapter.)

CHAPTER 29

Working with Records

Now that you can declare and associate recordset variables, it's time to use them to get to your database data and bring that data into your Access Basic programs.

Often, you want to load specific data from a table into your Access Basic programs. Other times, you may want to work with all the data in a table. Many of the action queries available in macros are highly efficient for working with all your table's data or for working with specific fields for an entire table or dynaset.

> **Tip:** Microsoft is including a copy of the Access *jet database engine* in versions of Visual Basic 3.0 and beyond. The database engine, referred to in Access as the *jet* database engine, is code that enables you to access database data from within a program just like you're doing here. There is talk that Microsoft will include the database engine in all of its products some-day. Becoming skillful in this chapter's table interaction can make you automatically proficient in many other Microsoft products in the near future!

This chapter concentrates on teaching you to select records from within Access Basic with which you want to work. This chapter presents several methods for your review, so that you have the right tools when you need them.

This chapter introduces the following topics:

♦ Using the Move... methods to move through recordsets

♦ Reordering recordset data

♦ Finding specific records with Find... and Seek

♦ Creating QueryDefs to see only what you want

♦ Changing table data from within your Access Basic programs

Reading Table Data into Variables

The position of the recordset variables determines the data read.

As you assign data from tables to recordset variables, you must keep in mind the position of the recordset variable in the table. When you declare a Dynaset variable and load data from the table into the Dynaset variable, for example, what prints if you printed a field in the Dynaset variable? The entire dynaset? One record? All the records from a query? The answer depends on many factors, but the primary consideration is the position of the recordset variable.

After you associate recordset variables to tables, you then must control a recordset position within the recordset to access different records. If you do nothing special, the first record in the recordset remains the current position, and no matter how many times you print or store data from the recordset into other variables, they always hold the first recordset record's data.

The following program performs two tasks: it shows you one way to access data from a table and store that data into a recordset variable (myTable), and it shows that the recordset's position does not change on its own.

```
Sub getContact ()
' Read three contact names from the Customers table into an array
  Dim myDB As Database, myTable As Recordset
  Set myDB = DBEngine.Workspaces(0).Databases(0)'Assumes
➡Northwind Traders
  Set myTable = myDB.OpenRecordSet("Customers", DB_OPEN_TABLE)
  ' Declare three array variables to hold data from the table
  Static ContName(1 To 3) As Variant

  ' The next 3 lines display the first 3 contacts
  ContName(1) = myTable![Contact Name]
  ContName(2) = myTable![Contact Name]
  ContName(3) = myTable![Contact Name]

  Debug.Print ContName(1)      ' All three Prints
  Debug.Print ContName(2)      ' prints the SAME
  Debug.Print ContName(3)      ' names!
End Sub
```

> **Caution:** Be sure to store recordset data in `Variant` variables unless you know for certain that no `Null` values are read. To be safe when storing recordset data into non-`Variant` variables, read the data into a `Variant` variable and then if `IsNull()` fails, you can assign that value to whatever variable you need.

This sub procedure appears to store the first three contact names (in the Northwind Traders database table called Customers) in a three-element array. However, each access of the `RecordSet` variable grabs the *same* record. When the first assignment statement stores the first record's `Contact Name` field value into `ContName(1)` as follows:

```
ContName(1) = myTable![Contact Name]
```

the *only* thing to happen is that the assignment takes place. Access does not move the `Recordset` variable's record pointer down automatically. Therefore, the following two lines

```
ContName(2) = myTable![Contact Name]
ContName(3) = myTable![Contact Name]
```

also store the first record's `Contact Name` value in the array elements.

The following three names appear in your immediate window if you attached the previous code to the Northwind Traders customer form:

```
Maria Anders
Maria Anders
Maria Anders
```

To move the currency of the recordset variable position, you must use one of the four methods described in Table 28.2: `MoveFirst`, `MoveLast`, `MoveNext`, and `MovePrevious`. Remember that a recordset variable can represent a table (as in this code), a dynaset, or a snapshot, and these methods are available to each.

> **Note:** This section of the chapter is devoted to reading data from a table, not storing data in the table. To change table data, read later sections of this chapter.

The `BOF` property is true if the current position of the recordset variable is the first one in the recordset. The `EOF` property is true if the current position of the recordset variable is past the last record (at the end of the file). If both properties are true, there are no records in the recordset.

> **Tip:** The order of the records in a `Recordset` variable are random unless
> you use a primary key or index, as explained in the following sections. The
> data you retrieve has no correlation to the order that the data was entered
> into the underlying table.

Example

The following code properly uses `MoveNext` to move the recordset position ahead
one record after each assignment of the `Contact Name` field to variables.

```
Sub getContact ()
' Read three contact names from the Customers table into an array
  Dim myDB As Database, myTable As RecordSet
  Set myDB = DBEngine.Workspaces(0).Databases(0)   ' Assumes
  ➥Northwind'Traders is open
  Set myTable = myDB.OpenRecordset("Customers", DB_OPEN_TABLE)
  ' Declare three array variables to hold data from the table
  Static ContName(1 To 3) As Variant

  ' The next 3 lines store the first 3 contacts
  ContName(1) = myTable![Contact Name]
  myTable.MoveNext      ' Move the recordset position
  ContName(2) = myTable![Contact Name]
  myTable.MoveNext      ' Move the recordset position
  ContName(3) = myTable![Contact Name]

  Debug.Print ContName(1)    ' All three Prints
  Debug.Print ContName(2)    ' prints the SAME
  Debug.Print ContName(3)    ' names!
  myTable.Close            ' You cannot close a current database
End Sub
```

If you run this module on the Northwind Traders database, the immediate
execution window displays the first three contact names from the following
`Customers` table:

```
Maria Anders
Ana Trujillo
Antonio Morena
```

Example

Not every customer in the `Customers` table has a fax. The following code tests the `Fax`
field in the recordset for a `Null` value and prints the Customer ID of those customers

who do not have a fax and must be mailed letters. Although a dynaset `Recordset` variable is used rather than a table `Recordset` or snapshot `Recordset` variable, the difference in this program is not critical.

```
Sub noFax ()
' Print Customer IDs of all without fax numbers

  Dim myDB As Database
  Dim custDS As RecordSet
  Dim faxNum As Variant ' To hold incoming fax values from dynaset
  Set myDB = DBEngine.Workspaces(0).Databases(0)   ' Assumes
  ➥Northwind Traders
  Set custDS = myDB. OpenRecordSet("Customers", DB_OPEN_DYNASET)
  Do Until custDS.EOF      ' Loop until reach end-of-file

    If IsNull(custDS![Fax]) Then
       Debug.Print custDS![Customer ID]  ' Prints only if no fax
    End If
    custDS.MoveNext
  Loop
  custDS.Close
End Sub
```

This code uses several elements that you can now understand. A dynaset is created from the `Customers` table. The dynaset is not filtered in any way, so the dynaset looks just like the table. A `Do Until-Loop` is set up to walk through every record, from start to finish, of the `Customers` table. If any customer is found without a fax number, the customer ID is printed for reference.

> **Note:** With ReportWizards, you can generate a report that prints all cus-
> tomer IDs for those customers without fax numbers. You now are learning
> the database access methods; you should use and study these methods
> until you're comfortable with them.

Finding Table Records in a Different Order

Use the index defined for the table to retrieve table records in an order different from the arbitrary order that regular data retrieval provides. If no index files are defined for the table, you can use the primary key to retrieve the records.

The `Table` variable's `Index` property tells Access which index to use for the `Table` variable retrieval. Use `PrimaryKey`, `Index1`, `Index2`, `Index3`, `Index4`, `Index5`, or the name of the index field when assigning the `Index` property.

Tip: You can choose **V**iew **I**ndexes... from within the table's design view to see which indexes are defined. You also can use the Indexes collection described in Chapter 30. If you want to retrieve records in an order different from that of one of the indexes or primary key, you can create a dynaset RecordSet variable or use QueryDef.

Example

The following code prints the first three products in random order and then uses the primary key to print the first three products as defined by the key.

```
Function indexPrint ()
' Read three products from the Products table in their random
' order; then read the 1st three as determined by the key.
  Dim myDB As Database, prodTable As RecordSet
  Dim subsc As Integer    ' Loop subscript
  Set myDB = DBEngine.Workspaces(0).Databases(0)   ' Assumes
➡Northwind Traders
  Set prodTable = myDB.OpenRecordset("Products", DB_OPEN_TABLE)
  ' Print the first 3 lines
  Debug.Print "Without using the index:"
  For subsc = 1 To 3
    Debug.Print prodTable![Product Name]
    prodTable.MoveNext
  Next subsc
  prodTable.MoveFirst    ' Reset the position to the beginning
  ' Now, use the index
  prodTable.Index = " Category ID"  ' Use the Category ID key for
➡index
  Debug.Print "Using the index:"
  For subsc = 1 To 3
    Debug.Print prodTable![Product Name]
    prodTable.MoveNext
  Next subsc
  prodTable.Close           ' You cannot close a current database
End Function
```

Ordering *Dynaset* and *Snapshot* Records

The source
determines the
order.

If you want to reorder a Recordset variable, you must do so at the *source* of that variable. The order depends on whether you get the data from a table or another Recordset variable.

If you create a Recordset variable from a table, the order is in the underlying table's primary key order if the table has one (if not, the records are random in the Recordset variable).

If you create a Recordset variable from another Recordset variable, the Sort property of the matching Dynaset or Snapshot determines the order of the resulting records. You can set the Sort property to have more than one Recordset variable with different views of the same data.

Example

The following procedure creates a dynaset from the Customers table. The Customers table is ordered by its Customer ID primary key field and so is the resulting dynaset Recordset variable custDY. The first three customer IDs and names are printed in the immediate execution window, and the names appear in Customer ID order as shown in Figure 29.1.

```
Function dynaPrint ()
' Print 3 dynaset records ordered by the table's primary key
  Dim myDB As Database
  Dim custDY AsRecordSet
  Dim subsc As Integer    ' Loop subscript
  Set myDB = DBEngine.Workspaces(0).Databases(0)  ' Assumes
  ➥Northwind Traders
  Set custDY = myDB.OpenRecordset("Customers", DB_OPEN_DYNASET)
  ' Print the first 3 lines
  For subsc = 1 To 3
    Debug.Print custDY![Customer ID], custDY![Company Name]
    custDY.MoveNext
  Next subsc
  custDY.Close          ' You cannot close a current database
End Function
```

Example

The following example creates the same Recordset variable as in the preceding example. A second Recordset variable then is created after the Sort property is set to the Postal Code field. The resulting three records are printed in Postal Code order. You cannot order these Dynaset records in Postal Code order if they come directly from a table unless the table originally is ordered by Postal Code.

Figure 29.1

The first three
Dynaset variable
records ordered by
the primary key.

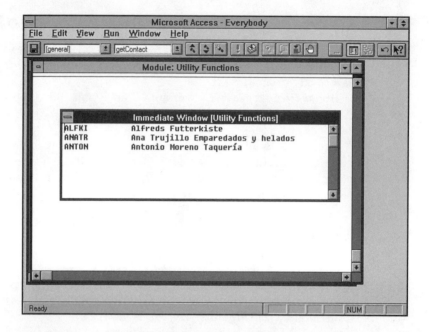

Note: If you use snapshot `Recordset` variables rather than dynaset
`Recordset` variables, the results are the same, except that a `Snapshot` of the
data is presented.

```
Function sortDY ()
' Print 3 dynaset records ordered by the Postal Code
  Dim myDB As Recordset
  Dim custDY As Recordset
  Dim postDY As Dynaset   ' The second dynaset variable
  Dim subsc As Integer    ' Loop subscript
  Set myDB = DBEngine.Workspaces(0).Databases(0)' Assumes
  ➡Northwind Traders
  Set custDY = myDB.OpenRecordset("Customers", DB_OPEN_DYNASET)

 custDY.Sort = "[Postal Code]"
  Set postDY = custDY. OpenRecordset(DB_OPEN_DYNASET)
  ' Print the first 3 lines
  For subsc = 1 To 3
    Debug.Print postDY![Customer ID], postDY![Company Name]
    postDY.MoveNext
  Next subsc
  postDY.Close
  custDY.Close            ' You cannot close a current database
End Function
```

Example

If you want to sort by more than one field, list each field in the Sort property separated from each other with commas. If you want any of the sorts to be descending rather than ascending (the default), add the DESC keyword after the field names.

The following example sorts by Postal Code in descending order and then alphabetically in ascending order by Company Name before creating the second Recordset variable named postCoDY.

```
Function postCoDyna ()
' Print 3 dynaset records ordered by the Postal Code
  Dim myDB As Database
  Dim custDY As Recordset
  Dim postCoDY As Recordset' The second dynaset variable
  Dim subsc As Integer      ' Loop subscript
  Set myDB = DBEngine.Workspaces(0).Databases(0)    ' Assumes
 ➥Northwind Traders
  Set custDY = myDB.OpenRecordset("Customers", DB_OPEN_DYNASET)
  custDY.Sort = "[Postal Code] DESC, [Company Name]"
  Set postCoDY = custDY.OpenRecordset(DB_OPEN_DYNASET)
  ' Print the first 3 lines
  For subsc = 1 To 3
    Debug.Print postCoDY![Customer ID], postCoDY![Company Name]
    postCoDY.MoveNext
  Next subsc
  postCoDY.Close
  custDY.Close             ' You cannot close a current database
End Function
```

Finding Specific Records

Tell Access exactly which record you want.

Whereas the Move... methods described in the previous section are useful for moving the recordset's position, the FindFirst, FindLast, FindNext, and FindPrevious methods are better at zeroing in on the records you want and only those records. Following is the general format of the Find... methods:

```
Find... criteria
```

The *criteria* expression must be a string expression. The sole purpose of the Find... methods is to move the recordset position to the record you want to work with next.

> **Caution:** The `Find...` methods work only on dynaset and snapshot
> `Recordset` variables. Use `Seek` (described later) to find data in a table
> `Recordset` variable.

If a `Find...` method cannot locate a record in the `Dynaset` or `Snapshot`, Access sets
the `NoMatch` property to `True`, and you have to assume that no valid record position
is set.

Example

The following code prints the IDs of customers in the `Customers` table who have no
fax numbers. Unlike the previous example, this one uses `FindNext` to position the
recordset position only to those records that have `Null` for the `Fax` field, therefore,
improving the efficiency from the example that printed the Customer IDs with `Null`
faxes.

```
Sub noFax ()
' Print Customer IDs of all without fax numbers
' Use the FindNext method to improve efficiency
  Dim myDB As Database
  Dim custDS As Recordset
  Dim faxNum As Variant ' To hold incoming fax values from dynaset
  Set myDB = DBEngine.Workspaces(0).Databases(0)  ' Assumes
  ➡Northwind Traders
  Set custDS = myDB.OpenRecordset("Customers", DB_OPEN_DYNASET)
  custDS.FindNext "[Fax] = Null"
  Do Until custDS.nomatch      ' Loop until reach no more matches
    Debug.Print custDS![Customer ID]  ' Prints only if no fax
    custDS.FindNext "[Fax] = Null"
  Loop
  custDS.Close
End Sub
```

Seek and You'll *Find* Table Data

Use the `Seek` method if you want to locate records in a `Table` variable rather than the
`Find...` methods that work with `Dynaset` and `Snapshot` variables. Following is the
format of `Seek`:

```
tableVariable.Seek comparison, key [, key] [...]
```

The *comparison* argument can be any of the string expressions from Table 29.1. The Seek method also accepts a variable number of arguments depending on the number of fields in the index you use for the table. The argument (or arguments) following *comparison* is the value you are comparing to a field in the index (or values being compared to more than one field in the index).

Table 29.1. The Seek comparison argument values.

String	Description
"="	Is equal to the key
">"	Is greater than the key
">="	Is greater than or equal to the key
"<"	Is less than the key
"<="	Is less than or equal to the key

> **Caution:** To change records with the Move..., Find..., or Seek methods, you must use the Edit and Update methods described later in this chapter.

Example

This example looks through the Customers table, storing in an array all company names that fall within the first half of the alphabet and storing the last half in another name.

```
Sub halfNames ()
 ' Store Customers whose ID is in upper and lower halves of
   ➥alphabet
 Dim custDB As Database
 Dim custTB As Recordset
 Dim subscr As Integer        ' Array subscript variable
 Set custDB = DBEngine.Workspaces(0).Databases(0)  ' Assumes
   ➥Northwind Traders
 Set custTB = custDB.OpenRecordset("Customers", DB_OPEN_TABLE)

 Static highCusts(1 To 100) As String  ' To hold A-N names
 Static lowCusts(1 To 100) As String   ' To hold O-Z names
 subscr = 1  ' First subscript
 ' Set the index to the right field
```

```
    custTB.index = "Company Name"
    custTB.Seek "<=", "N"        ' Seek out customers A-N
    Do Until custTB.nomatch Or (subscr > 100) ' Loop until reach
➡no more matches
      highCusts(subscr) = custTB![Company Name]
      subscr = subscr + 1
      custTB.Seek "<=", "N"    ' Seek again
    Loop
    custTB.MoveFirst              ' Reset position at beginning
    Do Until custTB.nomatch Or (subscr > 100)     ' Loop until
➡reach no more matches
      custTB.Seek ">", "N"         ' Seek out customers O-Z
      lowCusts(subscr) = custTB![Company Name]
      subscr = subscr + 1
      custTB.Seek "<=", "A"    ' Seek again
    Loop
    custTB.Close
End Sub
```

An Introduction to *QueryDefs*

QueryDef variables enable you to create queries in Access Basic.

After you create a QueryDef variable, you can use existing queries or create your own from within your Access Basic programs. Unlike the recordset variables, a QueryDef variable contains the query instructions but not any data.

> **Tip:** Queries are stored in the Queries section of your database, so that you can run your query from the database window after creating it from within Access Basic.

You must understand SQL statements to create queries from within Access Basic, but this book does not go into detail on that subject. However, the *QBE* (*Query By Example*) facility in Access is so convenient that you may as well use it to create your queries and then run them from your programs.

> **Caution:** QueryDefs contain no data, so you must create a dynaset or snapshot Recordset variable if you want to access data that the QueryDef generates. Do not create dynaset or snapshot Recordset variables from your QueryDef if the query is an action query because the action query is used to change or remove data and not produce a recordset, as the selection queries are. (You can run action queries using QueryDef variables, but you should not create recordset variables from such queries.)

As you do with other recordset variables, close your `QueryDef` variables with the `Close` method when your program is done with them.

> **Tip:** You are probably familiar with *parameterized queries* from your database work in Access. A parameterized query requires an argument in a manner similar to the way that some functions and sub procedures take arguments. Use the ! operator to assign parameters when you run queries that need parameters. You can, for example, assign a parameter named `Avg Age` to a parameterized query stored in the `QueryDef` named `myQU` as follows:
>
> ```
> myQU![Avg Age] = 18   ' Assign 18 to parameter named Avg Age
> ```
>
> After you assign values to all the parameters, you can create the `RecordSet` variables with OpenRecordset.

Example

Use the `QueryDef` keyword to declare `QueryDef` variables. The following statement declares a `QueryDef` variable named `QD`:

```
Dim QD As QueryDef
```

Example

The Northwind Traders database contains a query (`Daily Orders Total`) that selects all the daily orders from the Orders table. The following code creates a snapshot `Recordset` variable named `dOTotSN`, which contains the data from the query. Notice that the `OpenQueryDef` method is used to open and execute the query.

```
Function snapFromQ ()
' Create a snapshot from the Daily Orders Total query
  Dim myDB As Database
  Dim dOTotSN As Recordset
  Dim selQuery As QueryDef
  Set myDB = DBEngine.Workspaces(0).Databases(0)' Assumes
  ➥Northwind Traders

  ' Open the query to limit the snapshot

  Set selQuery = myDB.OpenQueryDef("Daily Order Totals")
  Set dOTotSN = selQuery.CreateSnapshot()
  ' Print the first 3 records in the snapshot
  Debug.Print dOTotSN![Order Date], dOTotSN![SumOfOrder Amount]
  dOTotSN.MoveNext
  Debug.Print dOTotSN![Order Date], dOTotSN![SumOfOrder Amount]
  dOTotSN.MoveNext
```

```
      Debug.Print dOTotSN![Order Date], dOTotSN![SumOfOrder Amount]
      dOTotSN.MoveNext
      selQuery.Close
      dOTotSN.Close             ' You cannot close a current database
End Function
```

Changing a Record

After you locate a record of interest, you may want to make changes to the data in that record. Update queries also can change table data, but the change you want to make may be too complex for a query to provide.

Access Basic ensures that you *want* to change a record before the change is made. You first must tell Access you want to change the record (with the Edit method), make the change, and then use the Update method to save those changes.

> **Caution:** If you leave out any step of the Edit, change, and Update procedure, Access Basic does not enable you to make changes. Also, you cannot change some fields, such as Counter fields.

Example

The following procedure creates a dynaset of the Customers table. Several records in the table have no fax numbers. This procedure displays the company name of each company without a fax number, one at a time, and prompts the user to fill in the number. After the user types a fax number, that number is written to the dynaset (and the underlying table) until all fax numbers are entered. The user can press Enter if a fax number is not yet available for a particular company.

```
Function changeFax ()
' Ask the user for fax numbers to replace those that are Null
' in the Customer table
  Dim myDB As Database
  Dim custDS As Recordset

  Dim faxNum As Variant      ' To hold incoming fax values from
  ➥dynaset
  Dim msg As String          ' For message box
  Set myDB = DBEngine.Workspaces(0).Databases(0)  ' Assumes
  ➥Northwind Traders
  Set custDS = myDB.OpenRecordset("Customers", DB_OPEN_DYNASET)
  custDS.FindNext "[Fax] = Null"
```

```
    Do Until custDS.nomatch      ' Loop until reach no more matches
      custDS.Edit      ' Prepare for edit
      msg = "Enter a fax number for " & custDS![Company Name]
      custDS![Fax] = InputBox(msg)
      custDS.Update    ' Make the actual change
      custDS.FindNext "[Fax] = Null"
    Loop
    custDS.Close
  End Function
```

Adding and Deleting Records

The AddNew method creates new records in a table or dynaset Recordset variable. AddNew creates a new blank record that your code can initialize. The Update method then saves the new record in the table or dynaset.

> **Note:** The position of the new record in a table Recordset variable de-pends on the active index you're using at the time. The record always is added to the end of a dynaset Recordset variable, but you can create a new sorted dynaset Recordset variable to hold the data in the correct position.

If you want to delete the record at the current position, use the Delete method. No Update method is needed or allowed after a Delete method, and you *must* use Move... to move the record position to the next record of interest.

Example

The Northwind Traders Orders table includes orders from three countries: USA, Canada, and the UK. Suppose that Northwind created a European sales office that handles all the orders in the UK. The following procedure deletes all the order records from the UK.

> **Note:** A delete query may be more appropriate for removing groups of records like these, but this procedure demonstrates the Delete method so that you can learn it quickly. Someday, you might need to use Access Basic to delete records that meet a certain sales quota and region formula that may be too complex for a delete query alone.

```
Sub RemoveUK ()
' Remove the UK orders so the newly formed
' European division can handle them.
  Dim DB As Database
  Dim ordTB As Recordset
  Set DB = DBEngine.Workspaces(0).Databases(0)
  Set ordTB = DB.OpenRecordset("Orders", DB_OPEN_TABLE)
  ordTB.MoveFirst
  Do Until ordTB.EOF
    If ordTB![Ship Country] = "UK" Then
      ordTB.Delete
    End If
    ordTB.MoveNext
  Loop
  ordTB.Close
End Sub
```

Note: For safety, this function cannot delete records that exist in the Order Details table. If such records were deleted, the Order Details table would contain record references that didn't exist in the Orders table.

Summary

This chapter gave you the preliminary tools so that you can begin using and modifying table data within Access Basic modules. The majority of the book has concentrated on the Access Basic tools needed to process the table data that this chapter told you how to store.

Although working with table, dynaset, and snapshot data is not difficult, you do need to study the examples and look at the various ways of doing things. For example, you can easily retrieve data from a table and store that data in a variable. If, however, you want to change the data or remove the record, you have to master additional methods such as Update and Edit, which you don't need for other kinds of data.

In the next chapter you learn how to find facts about a database, such as getting lists of tables, fields, and indexes in the database. Finding information *about* a database might be a first step in writing code that uses the data stored *in* the database. If you want to order table records based on an index, for example, but are unsure as to which index fields are specified in the table, you see how to produce a list of indexes.

Review Questions

Answers to review questions are in Appendix B.

1. What is the difference between the MoveFirst and FindFirst methods?

2. What does a QueryDef variable hold?

3. How can you determine if a record position is at the end of the table when you're accessing the records?

4. TRUE or FALSE: After you assign table data to a variable, the record position within that table is automatically updated.

5. Which work best on table Recordset variable data: the Find... methods or the Seek method?

6. TRUE or FALSE: When you add records to a file, Access Basic first inserts a blank record in the file.

7. What work does the Update method provide for you when you want to change table data?

8. Suppose that you are creating a dynaset Recordset variable from a table. How is the resulting dynaset Recordset variable ordered: randomly, by the table's primary key, or by the Sort method?

Review Exercises

1. Write a procedure that lists the Contact Name field for each customer in the Customer's table.

2. Write a procedure that creates a snapshot RecordSet variable for the customers in the Customers table who live in California. Order the Snapshot variable so that the customers appear in Postal Code order. (*Hint:* You may need to create two snapshot RecordSet variables—one for the table data and one for the requested data.)

3. Write a procedure that removes the Canadian records from the Orders table so that Northwind Trader's new Canadian division can take over those orders in its branch. The branch is working only on orders for the current decade and beyond, so don't remove those orders in which the Order Date field shows a date before January 1, 1990.

CHAPTER 30

What's in the Database?

This chapter wraps things up by explaining several administrative commands that you may need during your programming in Access Basic. Most of the routines described here are fact-finding routines that provide information about database tables, indexes, and the like.

Over time, a database's structure and contents might change dramatically from its original design. According to Microsoft, "You could write your code once, and it would automatically take these changes into account." Although, in theory, writing Access Basic procedures that always work no matter how the database structure changes is nice, being able to write such fluid code is not always advisable or even possible.

Many Access Basic programmers use the commands and methods described here to find information on the structure of the database. Even if you designed your database, you may forget certain design elements over time, and this chapter shows you how to go about finding information on your database makeup.

This chapter introduces the following topics:

♦ Listing table and query information

♦ Listing field information from recordset variables

♦ Listing indexes in a table

♦ Listing parameters for QueryDef variables

Several methods, generically called List... methods, provide the information you need. Each List... method provides a different kind of output, and each of the List... methods is described in the following sections.

> **Note:** Each of the `List...` methods returns a special `Snapshot` recordset. Each of these recordsets is described in the appropriate sections throughout this chapter.

The *ListTables* Method

The `ListTables` method works only for `Database` objects. This method makes sense when you realize that the database consists of tables and queries. Telling a different object, such as a `Dynaset` object, that you want to see all the tables and queries within that object makes no sense.

ListTables returns a *Snapshot* of tables and queries.

`ListTables` produces a `Snapshot` variable that contains a record for each table and each query in the database. Table 30.1 describes each of the fields returned in the resulting `Snapshot` variable. Most of the recordset methods you read about in the preceding chapter, such as the `Move...` methods, enable you to step through the recordset (such as the list of tables) returned from the `List...` methods.

> **Tip:** You can apply `ListTables` to any database, not just the current one.

Table 30.1. The *ListTables* record fields and their descriptions.

Field Name	Description
Name	Name of a table or query
DateCreated	Date that the table or query was created
LastUpdated	Date the table or query design was last changed
TableType	One of the following named constants:
	DB_TABLE for a native table DB_ATTACHEDTABLE for an attached table
	DB_ATTACHEDODBC for an attached ODBC table
	DB_QUERYDEF for a query
RecordCount	Number of records in the table or query

Field Name	Description
Attributes	Must be used with And and the named constant DB_SYSTEMOBJECT to determine if the table is an internal system table (not usable by you) or tested with one of the following named constants to determine the kind of query:
	DB_QACTION for an action query of some kind
	DB_QAPPEND for an append query DB_QCROSSTAB for a crosstab query
	DB_QDELETE for a delete query DB_QMAKETABLE for a make-table query
	DB_QUPDATE for an update query
	DB_SYSTEMOBJECT for a system query

Note: You don't need to test for the DB_ATTACHEDTABLE or DB_ATTACHEDODBC TableType values unless you interface Access with other database files.

Example

The following procedure calls the ListTables method and prints the results in an immediate execution window:

```
Function listThem ()
  Dim myDB As Database
' Must define a special Snapshot data type variable
  Dim tableList As Snapshot
  Set myDB = DBEngine.Workspaces(0).Databases(0)
  Set tableList = myDB.ListTables()  ' Does all the initial work
  ' Loop and print each of the resulting records
  Do Until tableList.EOF
    Debug.Print "Name: "; tableList.Name
    Debug.Print "Record Count: "; tableList!RecordCount
    Debug.Print "Type: ";
    If tableList.TableType = DB_TABLE Then
      Debug.Print "Table"
    ElseIf tableList.TableType = DB_ATTACHEDTABLE Then
```

```
        Debug.Print "Attached Table"
    ElseIf tableList.TableType = DB_ATTACHEDODBC Then
            Debug.Print "Attached ODBC"
    Else Debug.Print "Query"
    End If
    Debug.Print
    tableList.MoveNext
  Loop
  tableList.Close
End Function
```

The *ListFields* Method

The ListFields method works on both Table, Dynaset, and Snapshot objects, listing the fields in them. ListFields produces a Snapshot variable that contains a record for each field in the recordset. Table 30.2 describes each of the fields that ListFields returns in the resulting Snapshot variable.

Table 30.2. The *ListFields* fields and their descriptions.

Field Name	Description
Name	Name of the field
Type	The type of field with one of the following named constants:
	DB_BOOLEAN for Yes/No
	DB_BYTE for Byte
	DB_INTEGER for Integer
	DB_LONG for Long
	DB_CURRENCY for Currency
	DB_SINGLE for Single
	DB_DOUBLE for Double
	DB_DATE for Date/Time
	DB_BINARY not used through version 1.1
	DB_TEXT for Text

Field Name	Description
	DB_OLE for OLE object
	DB_MEMO for Memo
Attributes	Any combination (with And) of the following named constants:
	DB_AUTOINCRFIELD for a counter field
	DB_FIXEDFIELD for a fixed-length field
	DB_UPDATABLEFIELD for a changeable field
SourceTable	The name of the table that a Dynaset or Snapshot field list comes from or Null for a calculated field
SourceField	The name of the corresponding field that a Dynaset or Snapshot field list comes from or Null for a calculated field
CollatingOrder	Comparison code for language-sensitive string searches and compares in languages other than English

Example

The FieldInfo sub procedure (which follows) contains code that prints each field name and types in whatever table is passed to the sub procedure.

```
Sub FieldInfo (TableName, DatabaseName)
' Accepts: a table name, a database name
' Purpose: lists the field information for the specified table in
'          the Immediate window
' Returns: nothing
' Must define special Database, Snapshot, and Table data type
' variables to hold the incoming data
    Dim DB As Database, ssFields As Snapshot, dsTable As Table
    Set DB = OpenDatabase(DatabaseName)
    End If
    Set dsTable = DB.OpenTable(TableName)
    Set ssFields = dsTable.ListFields()
    Do Until ssFields.EOF
        Debug.Print ssFields.Name; " ";
            Select Case ssFields.Type
                Case DB_BOOLEAN
```

```
                        Debug.Print "Yes/No"
            Case DB_DATE
                        Debug.Print "Date/Time"
            Case DB_TEXT, DB_MEMO
                        Debug.Print "Text"
            Case DB_OLE
                        Debug.Print "OLE"
            Case Else
                        Debug.Print "Numeric"
        End Select
        ssFields.MoveNext
    Loop
    ssFields.Close
    dsTable.Close
    If DatabaseName <> "" Then
        DB.Close
    End If
End Sub
```

The *ListIndexes* Method

ListIndexes returns a *Snapshot* of all indexes in a table.

The ListIndexes method works only on tables and returns a record for each index in the table in a Snapshot variable. If the procedure has a primary key field, that field constitutes one of the index fields. Table 30.3 describes each of the fields that ListIndexes returns in the resulting Snapshot variable.

Table 30.3. The *ListIndexes* fields and their descriptions.

Field Name	Description
IndexName	Name of the index field
FieldCount	Number of fields that compose the index
IndexAttributes	Any combination (with And) of the following named constants:
	DB_NONULLS if Nulls aren't allowed DB_PRIMARY for the primary key field
	DB_UNIQUE if unique values in the index are required
FieldName	Name of the field

Field Name	Description
FieldOrder	This field's order in the index
FieldType	The type of index field with one of the following named constants:
	DB_BOOLEAN for Yes/No
	DB_BYTE for Byte
	DB_INTEGER for Integer
	DB_LONG for Long
	DB_CURRENCY for Currency
	DB_SINGLE for Single
	DB_DOUBLE for Double
	DB_DATE for Date/Time
	DB_BINARY not used through version 1.1
	DB_TEXT for Text
	DB_OLE for OLE object
	DB_MEMO for Memo
FieldAttributes	Can be equal to or not equal to the DB_DESCENDING constant to determine if the field is indexed in descending order
FieldCollatingOrder	Comparison code for language-sensitive string searches and compares in languages other than English

Example

The following sub procedure accepts a database and a table name and displays the index fields for that table:

```
Function listCustInd ()
' Prints all indexed fields in the Customers table
  Dim myDB As Database
  Dim custDet As Table
  Dim indexList As Snapshot
  Set myDB = DBEngine.Workspaces(0).Databases(0)
  Set custDet = myDB.OpenTable("Customers")
```

```
    Set indexList = custDet.ListIndexes()
    If indexList.RecordCount = 0 Then
      Debug.Print "There are no indexes currently defined."
    Else
      Do Until indexList.EOF
        Debug.Print indexList.FieldName;
        ' If primary key, say so
        If (indexList.IndexAttributes And DB_PRIMARY) = DB_PRIMARY
Then
          Debug.Print " (primary key)"
        Else
          Debug.Print ' Move cursor to next line without printing
        End If
        indexList.MoveNext
      Loop
    End If
End Function
```

This procedure produces the following output:

```
City
Company Name
Customer ID (primary key)
Region
```

The *ListParameters* Method

ListParameters returns a *snapshot* of a parameterized query.

The ListParameters method works only on QueryDef variables and returns a record for each parameter in a query. If the query object contains no parameters, no records are returned. Table 30.4 describes each of the fields that ListParameters returns in the resulting Snapshot variable.

Table 30.4. The *ListParameters* fields and their descriptions.

Field Name	Description
Name	Name of the parameter in the query
Type	Data type of the parameter that takes on one of the following named constants:
	DB_BOOLEAN for Yes/No
	DB_BYTE for Byte

Field Name	Description
	DB_INTEGER for Integer
	DB_LONG for Long
	DB_CURRENCY for Currency
	DB_SINGLE for Single
	DB_DOUBLE for Double
	DB_DATE for Date/Time
	DB_BINARY not used through version 1.1 DB_TEXT for Text
	DB_OLE for OLE object
	DB_MEMO for Memo

Example

The following example lists both parameters in the Sales By Date (Parameter) parameterized query:

```
Function listParams ()
' Prints all indexed fields in the Sales By Date query
  Dim myDB As Database
  Dim aQuer As QueryDef
  Dim queryList As Snapshot
  Set myDB = DBEngine.Workspaces(0).Databases(0)
  Set aQuer = myDB.OpenQueryDef("Sales By Date (Parameter)")
  ' Find the parameter information
  Set queryList = aQuer.ListParameters()
  If queryList.RecordCount = 0 Then
    Debug.Print "No parameters for the query"
  Else
    Do Until queryList.EOF
      Debug.Print "Parameter: "; queryList.Name
      queryList.MoveNext
    Loop
  End If
End Function
```

Summary

This chapter discussed four sets of methods that produce information about your database. It might be helpful to generalize some of the routines you saw here to accept any table, recordset, or query name so that you can pass to them the database element about which you want more information.

Using the List... methods, you can list virtually any database information such as field names, field types, and attributes.

Perhaps the only place that Access fails is its capability to produce reports about the database structure itself. Most competing database products provide the information automatically upon request; for the same information you have to write code using the List... methods in Access Basic. Perhaps future versions of Access will provide more automated reporting features of the database structure.

Review Questions

Answers to review questions are in Appendix B.

1. TRUE or FALSE: The List... methods report on the data in your database tables.

2. What is the data type of the return value from the List... methods?

3. Which operator—And or Or— do you use to test for attributes of the List... return values?

4. TRUE or FALSE: The ListQueries method lists all the queries in your database.

5. What is the difference between the Name and SourceField attributes in the ListFields method? Can they ever return the same results?

6. How can you determine if ListParameters evaluates a query that has no parameters?

Review Exercises

1. Write a procedure that prints the names and creation dates of every table in your database.

2. Rewrite the last example in this chapter as a sub procedure that accepts a query name as a Variant parameter and prints whatever parameters (or none at all) the argument requires.

The ANSI Table

ANSI Number	Character
0	Not used
1	Not used
2	Not used
3	Not used
4	Not used
5	Not used
6	Not used
7	Not used
8	Backspace
9	Tab
10	Line feed
11	Not used
12	Not used
13	Carriage return

continues

ANSI Number	Character
14	Not used
15	Not used
16	Not used
17	Not used
18	Not used
19	Not used
20	Not used
21	Not used
22	Not used
23	Not used
24	Not used
25	Not used
26	Not used
27	Not used
28	Not used
29	Not used
30	Not used
31	Not used
32	[Space]
33	!
34	"
35	#
36	$
37	%
38	&
39	'

ANSI Number	Character
40	(
41	)
42	*
43	+
44	,
45	–
46	.
47	/
48	0
49	1
50	2
51	3
52	4
53	5
54	6
55	7
56	8
57	9
58	:
59	;
60	<
61	=
62	>
63	?
64	@
65	A

continues

ANSI Number	Character
66	B
67	C
68	D
69	E
70	F
71	G
72	H
73	I
74	J
75	K
76	L
77	M
78	N
79	O
80	P
81	Q
82	R
83	S
84	T
85	U
86	V
87	W
88	X
89	Y
90	Z
91	[

ANSI Number	Character
92	\
93	]
94	^
95	_
96	`
97	a
98	b
99	c
100	d
101	e
102	f
103	g
104	h
105	i
106	j
107	k
108	l
109	m
110	n
111	o
112	p
113	q
114	r
115	s
116	t
117	u

continues

ANSI Number	Character
118	v
119	w
120	x
121	y
122	z
123	{
124	|
125	}
126	~
127	Not used
128	Not used
129	Not used
130	TrueType-dependent
131	TrueType-dependent
132	TrueType-dependent
133	TrueType-dependent
134	TrueType-dependent
135	TrueType-dependent
136	TrueType-dependent
137	TrueType-dependent
138	TrueType-dependent
139	TrueType-dependent
140	TrueType-dependent
141	Not used
142	Not used
143	Not used

ANSI Number	Character
144	Not used
145	'
146	'
147	TrueType-dependent
148	TrueType-dependent
149	TrueType-dependent
150	TrueType-dependent
151	TrueType-dependent
152	TrueType-dependent
153	TrueType-dependent
154	TrueType-dependent
155	TrueType-dependent
156	TrueType-dependent
157	Not used
158	Not used
159	TrueType-dependent
160	[Space]
161	¡
162	¢
163	£
164	¤
165	¥
166	¦
167	§
168	¨
169	©

continues

ANSI Number	Character
170	ª
171	«
172	¬
173	–
174	®
175	—
176	°
177	±
178	²
179	³
180	´
181	µ
182	¶
183	·
184	¸
185	¹
186	º
187	»
188	¼
189	½
190	¾
191	¿
192	À
193	Á
194	Â
195	Ã

ANSI Number	Character
196	Ä
197	Å
198	Æ
199	Ç
200	È
201	É
202	Ê
203	Ë
204	Ì
205	Í
206	Î
207	Ï
208	Ð
209	Ñ
210	Ò
211	Ó
212	Ô
213	Õ
214	Ö
215	×
216	Ø
217	Ù
218	Ú
219	Û
220	Ü
221	Ý

continues

ANSI Number	Character
222	Ð
223	ß
224	à
225	á
226	â
227	ã
228	ä
229	å
230	æ
231	ç
232	è
233	é
234	ê
235	ë
236	ì
237	í
238	î
239	ï
240	ð
241	ñ
242	ò
243	ó
244	ô
245	õ
246	ö
247	÷

ANSI Number	Character
248	ø
249	ù
250	ú
251	û
252	ü
253	ý
254	þ
255	ÿ

Answers to the Review Questions

Chapter 1 Answers

1. A program is a list of instructions.

2. False

3. Access Basic fully interacts with your database files, forms, and other database elements and also offers some object-oriented features as well.

4. All of an Access database is stored in a single file.

5. Your computer cannot understand spoken language yet, so you must learn the computer's language.

6. Back up the Northwind Traders database now, so that you can restore it after trying the examples and changes described in this book during your learning of Access Basic.

7. Event-driven programming is composed of programs that respond to certain events such as a keystroke or mouse click.

8. False; Access does not contain all the elements necessary for true object orientation, but Access Basic includes many object-oriented-like features.

9. Macros, sub procedures, and function procedures

10. Windows does not enable you to copy files that are open.

Chapter 2 Answers

1. A macro is an automated routine consisting of one or more instructions called actions.

2. An action is an individual instruction within a macro.

3. True

4. Macros save time and prevent errors.

5. Comment macros so that you and your users can understand them later.

6. Arguments

7. Single-stepping

8. Type their names or use the drag and drop method.

Chapter 3 Answers

1. A conditional macro is a macro that executes when certain actions occur.

2. A macro group is a group of separate but related macros stored under a single name.

3. A function can return a maximum of one value.

4. A function argument is a value you send to a function to work on. The string and number of characters to retrieve from that string are examples of `Right$()` arguments.

5. Use a macro group if several macros logically go together because you've categorized them similarly.

6. You can trigger a report by opening the report to print, formatting the report to print, printing a section of the report, and closing the report after printing it.

7. A period separates an individual macro from the macro group. The exclamation point indicates that the macro is an action macro and also can be used to separate parts of a condition.

8. The macro must be triggered by an event in the command button's property window.

9. `Where` ensures that matching records from related forms print together.

10. False; `StopMacro` is unneeded at the end of macros because Access knows when a macro is at the end.

Chapter 4 Answers

1. Choose Module from the Database window and then choose **Design**.

2. False; you can add new procedures to an existing module.

3. With the menus (F2 is the shortcut key) or clicking the mouse over the procedure name in the selection window

4. False

5. The Split Bar enables you to resize two module windows.

6. Press F6 or click with the mouse in the other window.

Chapter 5 Answers

1. The Access help system provides context-sensitive help, indexed help topics, cut-and-paste help operations, and cross-referenced help.

2. Press F1, click the question mark in the upper-right corner of the screen, or use the pull-down menus.

3. Cross-referenced help topics are underlined on the help screens.

4. An underlined cross-reference has its own help screen. A dotted underlined cross-referenced help topic has a related pop-up box for further explanation or a term's definition.

5. Syntax is the spelling and linguistics of a language.

6. True

Chapter 6 Answers

1. Module

2. You must type Access Basic statements correctly so that Access understands them.

3. The correction and modification of a program

4. A function procedure is a procedure that you write.

5. Programs should be broken into separate tasks called *procedures* in Access Basic.

6. The world that uses computers and programs, so the programs must change to reflect the changing world

Chapter 7 Answers

1. A variable is a data set that is stored in memory.

2. True

3. The contents of variables can change.

4. `94actPay!  act Pay94!`

5. False; there is no such data type as `Double Integer`.

6. True

7. One

8. False; use only as large a variable as your data requires.

Chapter 8 Answers

1. A string is data made up of zero or more characters.

2. Use `Dim` and the `String` keyword or append the dollar sign to the end of the variable name.

3. Any of the data type keywords such as `Integer, Double,` or `Variant`

4. A pound sign

5. False

6. `money` is a `String` data type, and `carAllowance` is `Variant` unless it is declared as a different data type elsewhere in the procedure.

7. Assign `Null, 0, " "`, or leave the variable empty without assigning it a value. A true `Null` value, however, requires the word `Null` or an assignment from a form's control that contains no value.

8. `Variant` variables can hold any data type.

9. You cannot mix together constants with different data types. Remove the quotation marks from `56` to make the expression correct.

Chapter 9 Answers

1. The `Print` command is one way to output to the screen.

2. True

3. A print zone appears every 14 columns and enables you to print data in uniform columns.

4. Separate the values with a semicolon or comma.

5. The comma forces output over to the next print zone, whereas a semicolon forces output to appear to the immediate right of the previously printed value.

6. 14

7. `Tab` sends data to a specific column, whereas `Spc` spaces the output to the right a specific number of spaces.

8. So the user knows what the data is for

9. 20

10. 31

Chapter 10 Answers

1. ! (exclamation point)

2. . (period)

3. `Database`, `Table`, and `Query`

4. Object names, such as those with spaces in them, do not always conform to the Access Basic naming rules.

5. False; there is no `DefTable` keyword.

6. When you designate an object's name, such as a database name, with a string expression

7. True

8. True

Chapter 11 Answers

1. Remark

2. The computer ignores the rest of the line.

3. False; you cannot name a variable `Rem`.

4. Remarks should explain what the code does, not duplicate the code.

5. Function names must have an equal sign before them.

6. In the parentheses

7. The apostrophe

Chapter 12 Answers

1. A. 5

   B. 6

   C. 5

2. A. 5

   B.   7

3. `Print 3.14159 * (4.0 * 4.0)`

4. A. `a! = (3 + 3) / (4 + 4)`

   B. `x! = (a! - b!) * ((a! - c!) * (a! - c!))` or $x! = (a! - b!)*(9! - c!)^2$

   C. `f! = (a! ^ 1/2) / (b! ^ 1/3)`

   D. `d! = ((8 - x!^2) / (x! - 9)) - (4 * 2 - 1) / (x! ^ 3)`

5. $1.5E + 01$ $-4.3E-05$ $-5.4543E+04$ $5.9312349E+05$

Chapter 13 Answers

1. The declarations section is used for declaring global variables and setting database options.

2. True, although not every declarations section has code

3. True

4. So that you can have more freedom with the editor while coding your programs. You might want to enter an outline of a procedure before specifying the specifics.

5. `Option Compare Database`

6. Global

7. Global

Chapter 14 Answers

1. Name clashes occur when two or more variables with the same scope have the same name.

2. False

3. One

4. None

5. `DoCmd` runs a macro action, whereas `RunCmd` runs a macro.

6. So that more than one function can share data that is visible within only one of them

7. The local `sales` is changed.

8. By reference

9. By value and by reference

10. A wrapper procedure calls another procedure and passes some arguments for you so that you don't have to do as much work when calling the second procedure.

Chapter 15 Answers

1. `MsgBox` is a statement, and `MsgBox()` is a function.

2. `InputBox()` returns a `Variant` data type, whereas `InputBox$()` returns a string.

3. **B.** The `MsgBox()` function can test for button presses.

4. `InputBox()`

5. False; all three tables explain combinations of the same `MsgBox` argument.

6. 1/1440th of an inch and 1/567th of a centimeter

7. You have to be able to tell the user what you are asking.

8. `MsgBox` uses `Microsoft Access` as the title.

9. `InputBox` uses `Microsoft Access` as the title.

10. In the center of the screen

Chapter 16 Answers

1. **A.** False

   B. True

   C. True

2. False

3. **A.** False

   B. True

   C. False

4. True

5. The expression returns False.

6. You must use `ElseIf` rather than `Else If`.

Chapter 17 Answers

1. `IIf()`

2. True

3. False. You can test for strings with the `VarType()` function.

4. The `VarType()` function returns a value that indicates the data type of its argument.

5. An empty value has not been initialized, a `Null` value contains a reserved `Null` value, `0` is a number in numeric variables (that tests as `Null` only for numeric variables), and a zero-length string contains no characters.

6. False

7. `Choose()` returns `Null`.

Chapter 18 Answers

1. A loop is a series of one or more statements that execute more than once.

2. The differences in the `Do` loops lie in their placements of the condition and the `While` and `Until` keywords.

3. Adds 1 to the `Counter` variable

4. An endless loop appears when you don't allow a termination condition to become true in a loop.

5. By pressing Ctrl+Break

6. Five times

7. Access does not save the editing buffer to the table if you don't.

8. Zero times

9. Three times

10. The loop is endless; n never changes inside the loop.

Chapter 19 Answers

1. Five times

2. True

3. Zero

4. `Forms`, `Form`, and `Reports`

5. `Exit For` always terminates the current loop. An `Exit For` statement without an `If` preceding it is too strong a statement and would invalidate using the `For-Next` in the first place.

6. 30 times

7. False

8. Access Basic assumes a `Step` value of 1 if you do not specify a value.

9. True

10. The order of the `Next` statements is backward.

11. `Do...Loop`

12. Determines the number of controls on a form or report

Chapter 20 Answers

1. `Select Case` statements are easier to code and read.

2. There are three `Select Case` formats.

3. False; the colon is optional.

4. The `Case Else` usually appears at the end of a `Select Case` statement and determines the action if no other `Case` matches.

5. True

6. `To`

7. True; `Is` never appears with `To`.

Chapter 21 Answers

1. A set of records in a table or query

2. True

3. The *criteria* argument

4. If the population contains fewer than two arguments

5. To count fields with `null` values

6. `DFirst()` and `DLast()` find the first and last values in a domain. `DMin()` and `DMax()` find the lowest and highest values in a domain.

7. One works with a population, and one works with a population sample.

8. By using an expression with operators as the domain function's first argument

Chapter 22 Answers

1. `Int()` and `Fix()`

2. You get an error message.

3. `Null`

4. `Int()` returns an integer value equal to or less than the argument, and `Fix()` returns the truncated argument.

5. So that `Rnd` produces a different value when the procedure runs

6. True

7. `Int` returns -10 because it returns the integer less the argument. `Fix` returns -9 because it truncates the .5. `CInt` returns -10 because it rounds .5 for even integers only. If the argument was -8.5, `CInt` would return -8.

8. True

Chapter 23 Answers

1. False

2. `CStr()`

3. `Variant`

4. `String`

5. The `Mis$()` function is on the right of the equal sign and the statement is on the left.

6. `Len()` cannot have a dollar sign after its name.

7. `LSet` and `RSet` justify strings within a fixed length. `LTrim()` and `RTrim()` remove spaces.

8. 192

Chapter 24 Answers

1. False

2. `Time()` returns the current time.

3. True

4. `Date()` returns a `Variant`, and `Date$()` returns a `String`.

5. The data type of arguments each requires

6. `@`

7. `74135-`

8. The hour number and a lowercase *am* or *pm*

9. `012345.67`

10. `  12345.67` (Notice the space before the number.)

Chapter 25 Answers

1. The process of tax-deducting an investment over time

2. Straight-line, double-declining balance, and sum-of-years'-digits

3. Money increases over time due to interest it earns.

4. Companies can write off an asset faster in the early years.

5. Present value is today's evaluation of a dollar amount, and future value is the value of that dollar amount at a future date.

6. You have to specify the time period of the payment you want.

7. The answer depends on the interest rate you can get on your money, so not enough information is given in the problem.

8. $5,000

9. $0 (you pay it off)

Chapter 26 Answers

1. True

2. By a subscript

3. Yes. Variant arrays can hold data of different types.

4. 79 elements

5. Use the To keyword.

6. Net present value works with cash comparisons, and internal rate of returns compares interest rates.

7. 23 elements

8. Modified internal rate of return assumes that the interest you pay on a loan is different from the rate you can invest in.

Chapter 27 Answers

1. The first subscript represents rows, second columns.

2. 28 elements

3. Matrix or table

4. 28 elements

5. Nested For-Next loops

6. **A.** 2

   B. 12

   C. 91

7. **A.** 5

   B. 8

   C. 2

Chapter 28 Answers

1. A recordset is a collection of records.

2. False; a variable is declared, but no database is associated with it.

3. From tables, dynasets, queries, and snapshots

4. `DBEngine.Workspaces(0).Databases(0)`

5. Closing the variables releases resources for other programs.

6. True

7. False

Chapter 29 Answers

1. `MoveFirst` locates the first record in the recordset, and `FindFirst` locates the first record that meets a criteria.

2. A `QueryDef` variable holds a query definition, not data.

3. Use the `EOF` method.

4. False

5. The `Seek` method

6. True

7. `Update` writes your changes to the file itself.

8. By the table's primary key

Chapter 30 Answers

1. True

2. A `Snapshot` variable

3. `And`

4. False; there is no `ListQueries` method.

5. The `Name` is the name in the query, and `SourceField` is the name of the field from which the query's field came. You can return the same result.

6. No records are returned.

Glossary

actions—The individual commands in macros.

arguments—The values you pass to macros, functions, and subroutines.

array—A list of data with the same name differentiated by subscripts.

array element—A value from an array.

assignment statement—An Access Basic statement that stores a value into a variable.

binary states—The on and off states of electricity inside the computer.

by reference—The process of passing variables that allows the receiving procedure to change the calling procedure's variables.

by value—The process of passing variables that does not allow the receiving procedure to change the calling procedure's variables.

calling procedure—A procedure that triggers another procedure's execution.

code—Another name for programming statements.

comparison operator—An operator that compares one data value to another and reports the true or false result of the comparison. Also called *conditional operator*.

compiler—The system program that takes your source code and translates it into machine-understandable instructions.

concatenation—The process of merging two strings into one.

conditional macros—Macros that run only if a certain condition is true.

conditional operator—See *comparison operator*.

constant—A value that does not change.

criteria—The conditions that must be met before an action or command is carried out.

data types—The different kinds of data such as integers and strings inside Access.

database engine—The code inside Access that sends data to and from tables of files.

data-inspection functions—Functions that return a result based on the contents of variables and expressions.

debugging—Eliminating errors from a program.

declarations section—The location at the top of all modules where module options and global variables are declared.

declare—To tell Access Basic about a variable's name and data type before you use the variable. Also called *define*.

delete mode—The text editor's mode in which characters you type replace those under them.

depreciation—The process of writing off a financial asset over time. Access Basic supports three kinds: straight-line, double-declining balance, and sum-of-years' digits.

dimension—Declares variables of all data types.

domain—A set of records in a table or query.

domain functions—Functions that work on domains of data, also called *domain aggregate functions*.

empty variable—In Access Basic, a variable that is declared but has no values stored in it.

event-driven—When a program responds to events such as mouse clicks, menu selections, and key presses.

free-form—The lack of restrictions placed on program spacing and indention in Access Basic.

function procedures—Sections of code inside Access Basic programs that return values.

functions—General term for function procedures.

future value—The value of a specified dollar amount of money at a later date.

global variables—Variables known across modules.

GUI—Stands for *Graphical User Interface* and names Windows-like products.

hierarchy of operators—See *order of operators*.

immediate execution window—See *immediate window*.

immediate window—A window you can use to see values of variables and Access Basic output. Also called an *immediate execution window.*

insert mode—The text editor's mode in which characters you type go before other characters without overwriting them.

integers—Whole numbers without decimal points.

local variables—Variables known only within their procedures.

logic error—A syntactically correct statement that incorrectly instructs the computer to do something.

macro—A database object that carries out actions you supply.

macro group—A collection of related macros.

matrix—An array with more than one dimension.

members—Objects embedded within other objects such as sub-forms.

module—An Access Basic program.

module variables—Variables known within all the procedures in a module.

modulus—Integer division that discards the remainder.

named constant—See *symbolic constant*.

nested—A loop or conditional statement embedded within another.

null strings—See *zero-length strings*.

object-oriented—A modern-day programming philosophy that lends itself well to event-driven programs.

object variables—Variables with data types that mirror database objects such as tables, queries, and dynasets.

OOP—Acronym for object-oriented programming.

operator—A word or symbol that performs an operation on data, usually mathematical, such as addition.

order of operators—The default ordering that Access Basic uses to evaluate expressions. Also called a *hierarchy of operators* and *precedence of operators*.

passing arguments—Sending a local variable from one procedure to another.

precedence of operators—See *order of operators*.

present value—The value of a specified dollar amount of money today.

print zones—A column set aside every 14 positions within the immediate window.

procedural—A type of programming style that leads the user through a series of actions instead of the user controlling the events within the program.

procedure—The Access Basic general terminology for a sub procedure or a function procedure that contains code.

program—A list of instructions that tells the computer what to do.

program maintenance—The act of changing programs to reflect changing business conditions the program works within.

RAM—An acronym for random-access memory inside your computer.

real numbers—Numbers with decimal points that show precision.

receiving procedure—A procedure that receives arguments from a calling procedure.

recordset—A collection of records.

remark—A statement in the program for the programmer, not for the computer.

running—Executing a program's instructions.

scientific notation—A shortcut method for evaluating real numbers with precision.

single-step mode—A mode that enables you to walk through the execution of Access Basic programs a line at a time.

source code—The program you write using the text editor.

strings—One or more characters such as a name or Social Security Number taken together.

sub procedures—Sections of code that cannot return values inside Access Basic programs.

subroutines—Generic term given to sub procedures.

subscript—A numeric index value that differentiates one array element from another.

symbolic constant—A constant that has been named, also called a *named constant*.

syntax—The spelling and ordering of commands and options.

text editor—The word processor-like system in Access that helps you enter and edit Access Basic programs.

truncating—Removing a portion of data.

twip—A screen position that is 1/1440th of an inch and 1/567th of a centimeter.

unary operator—An operator that works on a single data value or expression.

variable—A storage place inside memory for data.

visible—The term applied to variables that are usable within a procedure, module, or database.

whitespace—Blank lines and extra spacing in programs.

zero-length strings—An empty string.

Your Next Step with Access Basic

Now that you've tackled the first step towards mastering Access Basic, you are ready to learn the other possibilities that await you in Access Basic. This book now has accomplished its intended goal: to teach, by example, programming fundamentals with Access Basic. If you never programmed before opening this book, you now understand variables, loops, data types, Function and Sub modules, and the other facets of the Access Basic programming language.

This appendix describes a little of what is in store for you as you learn more about Access and Access Basic. Unlike the chapters throughout this book, this appendix is more descriptive than instructive. For example, there is no way that you can learn the ins and outs of OLE programming in a single appendix; in fact, entire books have been written on OLE! Instead, this appendix simply describes a few additional features that might interest you as an Access Basic programmer.

At the end of this appendix, you'll see a list of other books that will interest you as an intermediate to advanced Access Basic programmer. You'll find that between the book you now hold and the other books offered by Prentice Hall Computer Publishing, you eventually can master every aspect of Access programming without enrolling in a college course!

OLE 2—Integrated Power

There is a subtle difference between *linking* and *embedding*.

OLE stands for *Object Linking and Embedding*. Starting with Access 2.0, Microsoft added OLE 2.0 support. Before OLE, an application such as Access worked with its own data. Although some forms of data sharing (such as importing and exporting table data from and to other database products like Paradox) exists in most applications, nothing offers seamless sharing of an application's data like OLE. With OLE, one application's data becomes a packet called an *object* that you can integrate directly into other applications such as Microsoft Excel. Once you embed one object inside another application's object (the other application's data), you can manipulate that object inside the other application.

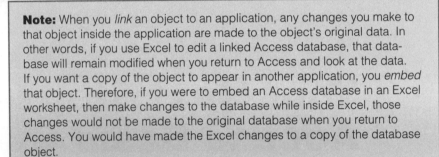

> **Note:** When you *link* an object to an application, any changes you make to that object inside the application are made to the object's original data. In other words, if you use Excel to edit a linked Access database, that database will remain modified when you return to Access and look at the data. If you want a copy of the object to appear in another application, you *embed* that object. Therefore, if you were to embed an Access database in an Excel worksheet, then make changes to the database while inside Excel, those changes would not be made to the original database when you return to Access. You would have made the Excel changes to a copy of the database object.

OLE has been around in several forms for a few years. OLE is a Windows technique and not an Access-specific feature. Any application that fully supports OLE (as Access does) can link and embed other OLE objects.

When you viewed the sample Northwind Traders database Employees table, you saw an example of an OLE object embedded in the form. Figure D.1 shows the first record from the Employees table. The employee's bitmapped picture is an example of an OLE object.

Figure D.1

This record's picture is an embedded OLE object.

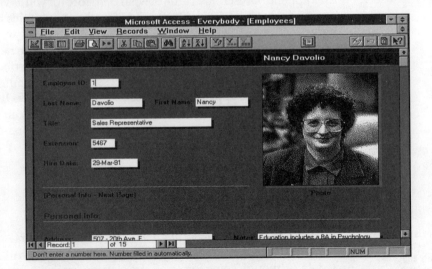

Access supplies no tools that enable you to edit and manage pictures. Yet, as you can see from the Northwind Traders database, you can include pictures inside your tables. Access does not need to support any drawing or picture tools as long as Access supports OLE. As you know, if you want to change any Access data on a form, you can move the cursor to the field and change the data. The picture, however, requires slightly more work. Double-click the picture, wait a few moments, and your screen will display the Windows Paintbrush program, with the employee's picture displayed, right on top of the Access application as shown in Figure D.2.

Figure D.2

After clicking the picture, you can edit it through OLE.

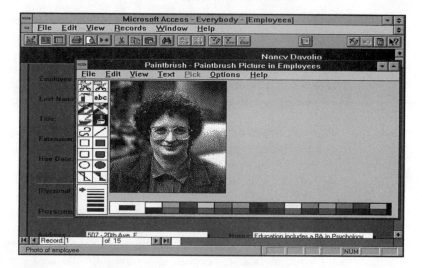

The Windows Paintbrush program does supply the tools needed to edit pictures. Rather than duplicating those tools, Access gives you a direct path to the graphics editing tools from within Access. As you can see, all of the Access menus and toolbar buttons are available. You still can work with Access while keeping the Paintbrush program loaded in its own window. (Choose File Exit to leave Paintbrush and return to Access.)

> **Note:** Before OLE's newest version 2.0, you could not do anything with Access until you completely exited Paintbrush. OLE 2 brings the embedded object's menus and commands directly into your application. Paintbrush does not really support OLE 2; if it did, there would be even more seamless integration of the two programs' menus.

Following are some additional OLE objects that your Access application can manage:

♦ A Microsoft Word document

♦ A Microsoft Word Basic program

♦ A Microsoft Excel worksheet

♦ A Microsoft Excel chart

♦ A Microsoft Graph chart

With Windows, your applications need to work together more than ever and OLE supplies the tools needed to enable one application to modify another's objects.

Access Basic supplies lots of support for OLE-aware applications. Through Access Basic, your application can trigger OLE methods that do the work for you and set OLE properties so that the OLE object looks and responds the way you need it to.

OLE Automation enables your Access Basic programs to control OLE objects.

The previous description of embedded OLE objects is nothing new to Access or to many Windows programs. The new OLE support resides in the Access Basic control functions available in Access 2.0.

Although this discussion scratches only the surface of OLE from within Access Basic, you should know that the techniques described here are called *OA*, or *OLE Automation* techniques. OA enables your Access Basic program to manipulate external OLE objects without the user ever knowing that your program accessed another program's data. OA enables you to update reports, spreadsheets, and graphs automatically, depending on the data the user enters into your Access application. Conversely, within each of those applications that supports OA, you can write applications (from within Excel, for example) that update an Access table. This "behind-the-scenes" data manipulation means that your user has to do less work; rather than opening and closing several different applications, the user can work behind a single Access application and still update data elsewhere.

Access supplies a new object data type to support OLE. To define a new OLE object, for example, you could define an object variable such as the following:

```
Dim myObject As Object
```

You now can associate the myObject variable to an OLE object. Suppose that you wanted to manipulate a Word for Windows document from within an Access Basic application. The following statement would associate the object variable to a Word document:

```
Set myObject = CreateObject("Word.Document")
```

The CreateObject function does not create the document. Instead, CreateObject creates an OLE object whose properties match that of a Word document. To specify which document myObject represents, use Fileopen in the following way:

```
myObject.Fileopen "C:\WINWORD\SALES.DOC"
```

As you work with OLE, you'll find lots of shortcuts. The following statement both associates the myObject variable to the Word document named SALES.DOC in a single step:

```
Set myObject = GetObject("C:\WINWORD\SALES.DOC", "Word.Document")
```

After you attach the specific object to your object variable, there are all kinds of functions, methods, and properties you can manipulate. You can, for example, insert text, change the document's font, add bookmarks, check spelling, insert Access data, and insert text within an Access field. Each type of OLE object contains its own list of methods and properties you can use from Access Basic, so be sure to check your application's OLE section for a list of things your Access application can do.

> **Note:** Although they weren't yet available at the time of this pre-release writing, Access 2.0 is supplying OLE hooks that enable you to use Visual Basic custom controls (often called *VBX* controls) for use with your Access forms. Visual Basic developers have created numerous 3-D, scrolling, rolling, and colorful controls for data manipulation, such as a control button or message box, that go far beyond those standard controls found in Access. Microsoft will make these custom controls available to your Access Basic applications with the official release of Access 2.0.

Additional Microsoft Access Tools

The Developer's Toolkit provides professional Access application development assistance.

Microsoft offers a few additional Access add-on programs you can use to extend the power of your Access Basic applications. Starting with Access 2.0, Microsoft offers an Access 2.0 Developer's Toolkit software pack that provides an Access Wizard that walks you through the creation of a complete Access application for others to use. The Developer's Toolkit includes many disks and booklets that provide additional programming information beyond that of your Access Basic manuals.

The Developer's Toolkit also includes runtime support to enable you to provide stand-alone Access applications in environments that don't currently include the Access program. Users can manipulate an Access database with your application without having Access on their system.

In addition, the Developer's Toolkit also provides the Microsoft Help Compiler that enables you to add custom help screens to your applications easily. You also will find that the supplied setup Wizard enables you to create an installation program for your users so that they can install your Access applications as painlessly as possible.

The Access Solutions Pack provides lots of examples.

As you already know, Access supplies the Northwind Traders and Orders sample database applications you can study and use for your tutorial sessions with Access. If you want additional samples to try, you might want to obtain Microsoft's Access Solutions Pack that contains the following sample databases:

Access Asset Management System: Enables companies to track their asset inventories, depreciation schedules, and maintenance cost schedules. Companies often own a tremendous number of assets from employee coffee pots to 3-story cranes. Tracking such company-owned assets could be a nightmare without the help of the Access Asset Management System.

Access Computer Help Desk: Tracks a company's computer support calls from both in-company personnel who need computer assistance and customers outside the company who call in for trouble-shooting hardware and software advice.

Access Registration Desk: Have you ever attended a large seminar or trade show and wondered how the show keeps track of speakers, vendors, attendees, support people, time schedules, and all the other people details that go into making a trade show a success? The Access Registration Desk makes it easy to sign-up, track, and register on-site the people involved with conferences. In addition, the Access Registration Desk enables you to send letters to attendees and provide after-event surveys so that you'll know if your show was deemed a success by the attendees.

Access Sales Contact Manager: Salespeople have a tremendous burden on their hands. Not only must they stay up-to-date on their products, they also must keep track of countless facts about their customers and potential customers. The Access Sales Contact Manager enables you to track customer lists. The Access Sales Contact Manager provides *tickler* information that reminds you to call or send a card to clients on a certain day (such as a birthday), as well as client schedule histories, mailing lists, and all the other record-keeping that goes into making a good salesperson an excellent salesperson. The Access Sales Contact Manager ensures that a salesperson doesn't forget important details about clients.

The Access Basic developer can benefit greatly from these professional sample databases.

Each of these sample databases is a powerful, full-functioning Access application that takes advantage of all Access features. As a budding Access Basic developer, you might wonder how these additional sample databases will benefit you. Nothing offers a better Access learning tool than seeing professional databases in action and the code behind those databases. Some of these additional sample databases require lots of Access Basic code working behind the scenes to provide a professional and powerful integrated database application. By studying these professional sample database applications, you'll learn more about when and how to use Access Basic. You also will find ways to improve your own applications that you may never have thought of without seeing the samples.

> **Note:** Both the Access Developer's Toolkit and the Access Solutions Pack are available from Microsoft.

Where Do I Go from Here?

You now have mastered the fundamentals of programming and of Access Basic. If anything, your appetite now is only slightly whetted and you're ready to dig deeper into the Access Basic internals and find out what else Access Basic is capable of.

No book of this size could reach all readers of all levels. When you first began this book, you were probably an Access user but not an Access Basic developer. Now, you understand what it takes to be a programmer, you've mastered the fundamentals of Access Basic, and you're ready to take your skills to their next higher level to develop advanced Access applications that take full advantage of the extended power of Access such as OLE support.

The following book list was selected specifically with you, the reader of *Access 2 Programming By Example*, in mind. With these books, you can tackle the tough areas of Access and improve your programming skills so you gain the title of *Master Access Programmer*!

Access Power Programming, Que Corporation. This book is the perfect companion for readers who have mastered *Access 2 Programming By Example*. You'll learn how to create bullet-proof end-user applications.

Using Access, Que Corporation. Even master Access Basic programmers need help with some of the more obscure features of Microsoft Access. The Access manuals scatter information throughout several books and the on-line help, while supportive, cannot offer you as much detail as you often need when developing advanced Access applications. *Using Access* provides you with a complete reference to all areas of Access in one volume.

Access Developer's Guide, Sams. This book provides the material you need that can't be included in a reference manual. You'll learn all sorts of tips, shortcuts, and cautions that separate a professional-looking Access application from an amateur application. Throughout this book, you'll learn how to create eye-catching forms, efficient tables, and tight Access Basic code that create stunning database applications.

Index

Index

Index

Index

Q-R